BACKBOARDS & BLACKBOARDS

BACKBOARDS & BLACKBOARDS

College Athletes and Role Engulfment

PATRICIA A. ADLER
PETER ADLER

COLUMBIA UNIVERSITY PRESS   NEW YORK

COLUMBIA UNIVERSITY PRESS

NEW YORK   OXFORD

Copyright © 1991 Columbia University Press

All rights reserved

LIBRARY OF CONGRESS CATALOGING-IN-PUBLICATION DATA

Adler, Patricia A.

Backboards & blackboards : college atheletes and role engulfment /
Patricia A. Adler, Peter Adler.

p. cm.

Includes bibliographical references and index.

ISBN 0-231-07306-2 (alk. paper)

1. Basketball—Social aspects—United States—Case studies.

2. College athletes—United States—Case studies.

3. Self—Case studies.

4. Social role—United States—Case studies.

5. Social psychology—United States—Case studies.

I. Adler, Peter. II. Title.

III. Title: Backboards and blackboards.

GV889.26.A33   1990

796'.071'173—dc20

90-40396

CIP

*Casebound editions of Columbia University Press books are Smyth-sewn
and printed on permanent and durable acid-free paper*

Printed in the United States of America

c 10 9 8 7 6 5 4 3 2 1

To Coach,
a man of integrity, leadership, and generosity,
who always knew which battles were the important ones,

and

To Louis A. Zurcher,
a man who lost his battle,
but whose inspiration, energy, caring, and fight live on.

Contents

Acknowledgments

BEGUN IN 1980 and finally finished in the latter portion of 1989, this work reflects the socio-historical times of the decade in which it was researched and written. The team we studied was located in the oil and sun belts of the southwestern United States that first boomed in the early 1980s and then went bust in mid-decade as oil prices plummeted. At the same time, college basketball experienced its greatest rise in popularity, becoming transformed into one of the most commercially successful spectator sports in America. With this rise came an era of scandal, rocking the college athletic landscape with recruiting violations, spurious admittance practices, and controversial treatment of student athletes. Sweeping changes in educational reforms also occurred during this period, spurred by William Bennett's (then Secretary of Education) and Allan Bloom's *(The Closing of the American Mind)* attacks on American higher education. This created an atmosphere where the place of athletics on college campuses, for the first time in decades, was called into question. This environment was exacerbated by severe cutbacks in funding for higher education, reflective of President Reagan's curious set of fiscal priorities, which provided additional pressures, as the arena of college athletics became seen as one of the few bastions of profitability that could lead institutions out of these financial doldrums. It was within this context of expansion and scrutiny, allegations of improprieties, and paranoia and secrecy, that we conducted our research.

Given this milieu of distrust, it is even more remarkable that the head coach, his staff, and all of the players with whom we shared intimate times and space during this period actually allowed us the unexpurgated glimpse into the everyday world of college athletics to which we were privy. To them we owe a debt of gratitude that can never fully be repaid. We hope that the trust and friendship they accorded us, as we present both the joyous moments and seamy side-shows of their world, are proven worthy. We have attempted to por-tray a sympathetic, albeit realistic portrait of this social scene that reflects the pressures and strains they so commonly experienced. The risk that they took in allowing us total, unbridled access has never gone unappreciated.

Throughout the decade, numerous scholars lent their critical eye and provided us with constructive comments and criticisms that we hope have made this final product better. Jean Blocker, who nursed us through every stage of the research process, offered the benefits of her keen sociological eye, from her position as both an insider and out-sider. Confusing times in the field were always bolstered by her buoy-ant personality and penetrating mind. Louis Zurcher, our intellectual father throughout the research process, to whom this book is dedi-cated, and who sadly and unexpectedly passed away before he could see this work come to fruition, lent unswerving support for the theo-retical notions we were trying to advance. His own contributions to role theory and symbolic interactionism have served as the inspiration by which this book was written. Peter Manning, whose strength and trust in our relationship allowed him to react to portions of the manu-script harshly, negatively, and critically, without fear of retribution or reprisal, forced us to examine our thinking and was a rare and expe-cially appreciated friend. The indefatigable John Van Maanen, who brilliantly and patiently commented on both earlier articles and the manuscript in draft, called our attention to the writing process, and helped us bring order, clarity, and perspective to the book when we got too close to provide these ourselves. Our friend Chuck Gallmeier, whose love for us and encouraging comments that kept us going when we were exhausted, reminded us that the human condition must be balanced with levity, humor, and a sense of purpose that includes seriousness, but not obsession. Our colleague Paul Colomy served as role model of a brilliant and committed scholar, a synthetic and ecu-menical thinker, and never wavered about his enthusiasm for the proj-ect. Tom Staley helped and taught us in many ways, by creating an opportunity to do this reseach, by fostering an atmosphere to do the analysis, and by imbuing us with his passion for excellence in the aligned enterprises of teaching, research, and administration. Still others, such as Mitch Allen, David Altheide, Gordon Clanton, Marv Cummins, Doug Eckberg, Chuck Edgley, Rob Faulkner, Gary Alan Fine, Andy Fontana, John Johnson, Barry Kinsey, Alan Klein, Joe Kotarba, Stanford Lyman, Doug Mitchell, Tom Murton, David Pittman, Burke Rochford, David Snow, Malcolm Spector, Ralph Turner, Carol Warren, and Ray Yasser, were supportive, responsive, and honest in their appraisals and criticisms of the burgeoning ideas we were developing at various points during the decade.

We were also supported by a group of friends who didn't care about the vagaries of the academic arguments in which we were debating. Their support came simply from the uncritical understanding and perpetual faith they showed in us. To Jim Morgan, Gina Kuecks-Morgan, Tanice Foltz, Dana Larsen, Diane Duffy, Steven Rotter, Heidi Glow, Bruce Herman, and that irrepressible group of "brodskis," we thank you for standing by us throughout our periodical fits of obsession, compulsion, and paranoia. Our parents understood that the intellectual process required periods of rejuvenation, which they unselfishly and happily provided for us.

Given that this research took place not only across ten years, but in three different cities, covering five separate universities, a myriad of support personnel were responsible for helping with the typographical, administrative, mechanical, and editorial assistance they provided. We thank Reba Lee, Shar Weber, Adele Tuchler, Andrea Silverstein, and the irreplaceable Dorene Miller, without whom our sanity would no doubt have been long abated. Similarly, Louise Waller, our editor at Columbia, dogged us for years, made us feel that the project was worthwhile, and provided all the possible incentives to keep us going during the times of turmoil and tumult. Ann Miller and Leslie Bialler saw the manuscript through to completion with diligence and care.

Finally, our children, Jori and Brye, have managed to survive yet another book, with its incumbent deadlines, frantic searches, and intense, nervous fears. Rarely did they complain or fail to understand our mutual agendas, both professional and personal, so that we could, all together, collectively conduct our (and their) ethnography of everyday life. As parents, we are constantly in awe of their astute minds, creativity, and empathic treatment of other individuals. As much as we hope we are for them, they have been role models for us.

If it is permissible, we would like to thank each other, for creating a relationship and mutual respect that has allowed the type of collaborative work we do to occur. Our total dedication to one another, in all phases of our life, unusual to say the least, would not be traded for a single minute. This book, as all our previous work, is the product of both of our passions and desires.

For you, our readers, we hope that the following pages provide a portrait of a people that many of you might know from a distance, but have never seen this intimately. For any student at an American university, it is not uncommon to see these gladiators walking around campus, but their story is a different one than you might expect. This book attempts to relate their tale. Although it is, by definition, filtered through our lenses, we expect that the vision is a clear, true, and vivid depiction that sheds light on this often misunderstood group. Scholarly custom now tells us to take the blame for any errors or inaccuracies that might appear; while we do, the story herein is that of the players and coaches, told as much as possible through their words and deeds.

Portions of earlier versions of the Prologue and chapters 5, 6, and 9 appeared as, respectively: Peter Adler, "The Sociologist as Celebrity: The Role of the Media in Field Research," *Qualitative Sociology*, vol. 7, no. 4, copyright 1984 Human Sciences Press; Patricia A. Adler and Peter Adler, "From Idealism to Pragmatic Detachment: The Academic Performance of College Athletes," *Sociology of Education*, vol. 58, no. 4, copyright 1985 the American Sociological Association; "The Gloried Self: The Aggrandizement and constriction of Self," *Social Psychology Quarterly*, vol. 52, no. 4, copyright 1989 the American Sociological Association; and "The Reconstruction of Role Identity Salience: College Athletes and the Academic Role, *Social Science Journal*, vol. 24, no. 4, copyright 1987 JAI Press. We are grateful to the publishers and copyright holders for permission to reprint this material.

BACKBOARDS & BLACKBOARDS

PROLOGUE
Studying College Athletes

OUTSIDE, IT was a cold, dark, wintry evening. Inside, the air bristled with excitement as the ten thousand fans who filled the stadium prepared for another evening of college basketball. The band had played the theme songs, the two teams had taken their turns warming up and shooting baskets, and the radio and television announcers were at their microphones. People central to the program had already been at the stadium for hours, talking with the coaches and players before the team retreated into the locker room to change for the game, gathering the latest tidbits of information from their friends and media people about the team and various individuals associated with it, and catching up on acquaintances made and sustained through interaction before and during the games. Five minutes before game time, most of the fans had settled down with their preliminary round of hot dogs, popcorn, soda, and candy. They were in their seats, standing near other people's seats, or still milling around the refreshment stands when the familiar refrain broke out that signaled the home team's departure from the locker room. A giant cheer broke out from the stands, as the fans leapt to their feet and applauded rhythmically. Some cheerleaders tumbled, jumped, and ran, while others lined the walkway from the locker room to the playing floor, waving team flags and chanting into megaphones. Then, the first of the players broke into view. Excitement gripped everyone in the stands, as they prepared themselves for another game.

This team, with a new coach and several new starting players, was a team of emotion; theirs was not a slow-down, methodical style, but rather a running, dazzling play that capitalized on speed, conditioning, tough, man-to-man defense, and quick reacting to the ball. Everyone in town seemed to know that something different was happening, that after years of frustrating losses and dreary play, these players represented new life for the University and the entire city. That is why they turned out in such numbers. Packed from the gym floor to the rafters, everyone who could get a ticket to the game was in attendance.

The team had gotten off to a good start this season, playing well in the preseason and winning all but one of the non-conference games scheduled during the early weeks in December. They had beaten their crosstown rivals the week before at a tournament hosted at their opponents' arena, attracting the attention of the national news media. This team, with its charismatic new coach and up-tempo playing style, seemed to reflect the optimism and wealth that characterized the community. The coach was capturing the attention of the people through his flashy brand of basketball and string of victories. With the team's song, "Ain't No Stopping Us Now" booming in the background, it seemed like an anthem, not only for this young team, but for the city as a whole. This was not lost on anyone, as all those in the stands sensed the electricity. Something extraordinary was beginning.

Tonight would be an especially big game for the team; they were playing one of the enduring dynasties in basketball. If they could win this game it would be a major upset and prove to both the home crowd and the national audience that they were legitimate. And so, as the crowd hunkered down to await the start of the game, the anticipation they felt was greater than usual. They rose for the playing of the national anthem and cheered as the starting players, whose names were only now beginning to be indelibly etched in their minds, were announced. On these players their hopes and dreams of victory, vicariously experienced, rested. As the opposing team was announced, the spectators felt the power of their tradition. This was a program that had won the national championship the previous year, that had sent many players to the pros, that had their pick of elite high school athletes, and that had a coach with a pedigree. The individuals they would watch tonight were college athletic stars, people who would undoubtedly go on to the professional ranks. The anticipation was intense.

Once the game began, it was everything they had hoped for: fast-paced, dramatic, full of thrills and despair. Individual moments stood out in a melange of images that then blended together again. It was close all the way. Breathless, the fans totally immersed themselves in the action on the court.

Up in the highest row of the stadium, about as far away from the floor of the arena as they could be, sat two spectators who were also new to this town, having only months before arrived to teach at the University: a man and a woman in their late twenties. Joining them were a group of rabid, loyal fans, other members of the sociology department who had suffered through the previous regime of poor players and endless losses. These seemed like distant memories now, with all thoughts focused on the present, on the nascent season and what it could hold. They strained, from their balcony perch, to see the faces and movement down on the floor. The man, a passionate sports fan since childhood, was concentrating on one particular player, a student in a class he was teaching that semester. They had hit it off well, and had spent some out-of-class time talking about schoolwork and the basketball program at the University. When the crosstown tournament began, this player had given them complimentary tickets. It was there that they first heard him referred to by the nickname "Apollo."

With four minutes left in the game, there was Apollo standing at the foul line. His nearly seven-foot frame leaned forward, with bent legs, as he inhaled and exhaled slowly. After getting his breath he raised himself up with deliberation, wiping the inside of his moist palms on his socks as he uncurled his spine. These socks were distinctive, as they extended just above his kneecaps. Straightening himself, he turned and made a deliberate glance to the side. He looked up into the stands, right to the place where the two were sitting, and stared directly at them. He then took two deep breaths as he carefully bounced the ball in front of him. This glance was not lost on the couple, nor on any of their friends. They relished having been singled out in that way, feeling special and involved. It was intoxicating.

The moment passed, the game was won in the closing seconds, and the team went on to have a fantastic year, going to the finals and winning their postseason tournament championship. A "Cinderella" team, they came out of nowhere to exceed everyone's expectations. The town went wild with jubilation after the final game of the tournament, meeting them at the airport with 500 people in the middle of the night, and holding a downtown pep rally the next day attended by the mayor, the governor, and 10,000 others. At the celebration, the man and woman were there with their young daughter. As the players beckoned him onto the stage, he ascended, with his child, and triumphantly shared with the team in its glory. This was only the beginning of several wild and exciting years for the University, the town, and the couple, as they lived with the roller coaster ride of this team's successes and failures, and the wax and wane of seasons. For these sociologists, however, those years were more than just exciting experiences; they were research. Their involvement and differential roles will unfold.

Peter's Role

By the start of the next year, I was sitting on the floor of the sports stadium, in the front row of the team bench, beside all the other coaches. I had acquired a nickname, "Doc," earned a spot on the team, and was on my way to becoming a key figure associated with it.

Initially, I drifted into the research; I had no prior intention of making this setting a focus of study. Shortly after my arrival on campus in September 1980, I met Apollo in one of my classes and gave him a reprint of an article Patti and I had co-authored on momentum in sport (Adler and Adler 1978). He read "the pamphlet" and passed it along to the coaching staff, who liked it and invited me to their offices to get acquainted. As a result of our meetings, they asked me to come down to the gym to address the team about momentum. I arrived during practice and watched, from that close vantage point, the team run through complex drills. Afterward I gave my talk to this tired, sweaty, assembly. The coaches seemed to like it, as they invited me back to speak at several basketball clinics they put on throughout the 1980–81 year. These were a series of day-long seminars for junior high schoolers about basketball fundamentals, where students could meet team stars and be coached by basketball experts at the college level. My role was to address groups of students about the social psychological aspects of the game. Along with my talk, I showed video footage of the team playing important games and did momentum analyses of the play. The kids liked this because they got to see their heroes playing. The coaches liked it because I spoke right after lunch and it gave the kids a break and a chance to digest their food. By developing a regular slot on the clinic "schedule," I unwittingly achieved a designated role within the basketball program. This enabled me to hang around the coaching offices when I had free time two or three days a week. I felt comfortable with the players and coaches. They shared with me news about recent team developments, while I offered my opinions, which were accepted with interest and respect. After a while, Coach concluded that I could benefit the team in several ways. First, I could speak at his clinics and summer camps and keep the paying students busy for an hour. Second, he thought that to have my name and title associated with his program would lend it legitimacy (as one administrator told him, "It looks good to have someone with a Ph.D. on the team"). Third, he liked me and respected my knowledge of sport. My base of knowledge was rather different from his own, complementing it nicely; he knew the playing end, while I had broad knowledge of a host of trivia I had amassed from studying the various sport magazines, tabloids, and newspapers: statistics on various players; who were the hot high school prospects; and what other collegiate programs were doing. I thus began my involvement with the team in this role as a regular, paid speaker and "friend of the program."

From this vantage point, I saw a variety of complex, often conflicting forces pressuring players and coaches. Some of these seemed structural and others situational. The more I saw, the more I wanted to get closer to the scene, learn who the significant individuals and groups were, and learn what motivated their thoughts, actions, and relationships. I thus tried to cast aside my preconceptions about college athletes and athletics by "defocusing" (Douglas 1976) as I began the research.

The informal nature of my interaction with team members also helped to reduce the "distance" between us, in spite of our racial, socioeconomic, and educational differences. Building on the legitimacy they afforded me for my degree, my published works, and my range of sports knowledge, I was able to gain some acceptance as a knowledgeable outsider. I soon observed, though, that this role was limited. I had overcome some of the barriers of secrecy that characterize most sports settings (see Jonassohn, Turowetz, and Gruneau 1981), which keep out most fans and boosters, but other barriers remained. Unlike the fans, I had not tried to enter. Rather, I was recruited. Like the ubiquitous journalists, I could ask questions, but the answers did not satisfy me as a sociologist. I realized that I could get more intimate knowledge only if I used my speaker role as a springboard, finding other means of observing and conversing informally with players and coaches so that I could build trust and rapport.

I continued my work as a speaker at Coach's basketball camps

during the summer of 1981. During this off-season my relationship with
the team grew closer as the number of outsiders dwindled and my
casual conversations with players and coaches grew lengthier and more
intimate. Although I was not accepted as an insider or member, I had
become more than a fan. I became comfortable enough to begin
offering my advice to players and coaches on topics I considered within
my areas of sociological and sport expertise: interpersonal relations,
team dynamics, delegation of authority, leadership, academic affairs,
athletic careers, post-athletic career planning, and a host of other topics. After a while Coach and other team members began to call on me
for informal social psychological, academic, and practical advice, and
actively sought me out for confidential talks whenever they had problems they believed other team members could not solve. My role thus
gradually shifted into one of an informal consultant to the team itself.
This change was acknowledged in a conversation I had with Coach
during the early fall of 1981, when I officially asked his permission to
study the team. He already knew about my sociological interest in
college athletics, but now I asked him if I could have "access" to the
dressing room, locker room, and practice facility (to observe the scene
more closely). Not realizing that I had made the critical gaffe of
couching my request in the language of social science rather than the
members' jargon, I was stunned when he replied, "Sure, Doc, we have
an extra locker. You can use it to hang your clothes in when you go
swimming or stuff." I smiled as I mentally kicked myself in the rear
and started again. Despite this *faux pas,* we were able to establish a
reciprocity in our relationship (see Wax 1952) where they made use of
my title and expertise in the fields of sport and social psychology (much
like what Schein, 1987, has called a "clinical" ethnographer), and I used
my acceptance by the team as an opportunistic research strategy (see
Riemer 1977).

As the 1981–82 season began I was given team equipment to wear:
the game sneakers, team warmups, and a shirt with the University's
coaching insignia. This symbolic "wearing of the armor" indicated to
other members that I had become an insider. From that point on, I
attended all the practices, the community functions to which the team
was invited, made local televised appearances with the team, accompanied coaches on recruiting trips, wrote letters to prospective recruits,
and spent countless hours in the coaching suites and the athletic dorm.
I often ate and traveled with the team, was privy to conversations and

meetings in which no other outsider was permitted, and was given a position on the bench during games next to the rest of the coaching staff. Patti and our three-year-old daughter sat right behind me, in the row reserved for Coach's special guests. Throughout this time, others in the community came to know me by my new-found moniker, Doc, but they had only a faint notion of what it was that I did for the team.

In January 1982, my consulting role was revealed to the public the day I appeared on Coach's weekly television show, when he introduced me as an assistant coach, and described how I helped the team. During this season, the team rose meteorically into the national rankings and drew a great deal of media attention, of which I was often a part. Reporters looking for a different angle on their features made me both a regular source of information about the team and a story in my own right. I was "spotlighted" by a close-up camera shot during a time-out of a nationally televised game while the commentators discussed my unique role with the program ("the only team in the country with its own sociologist").

Over the next several months I was "media blitzed:" I was featured on another nationally televised game, on three regional telecasts, on three local sports shows, on the local TV news countless times, in several national sport magazines and newspapers, in articles that appeared in local and regional newspapers, and in approximately 15 to 20 radio interviews. This media attention transformed my role from that of a behind-the-scenes researcher and resource person for the team into a celebrity in my own right. Celebrity status did not lessen the insecurity I felt about team members' and coaches' acceptance of my role. Remarks by outsiders questioning my position on the team or my right to sit on the bench stung me, and I constantly sought reaffirmation from Coach that I was not intruding. Near the end of this 1981–82 season I therefore initiated a third shift in my role, as I created, and cleared through the University's athletic and academic administrations, a new position as Academic Adviser to the entire intercollegiate athletic program. Through this formalized role I spent the 1982–83 season working with all of the athletic programs in an official capacity, advising student-athletes academically, discussing players' academic problems with coaches, being a liaison between the athletic and academic realms, and all the while observing the college athletic world. Throughout these subsequent playing seasons, media attention remained a part of my research (and then administrative) experience, waxing and waning with the team's success and the availability of other stories to cover.

THE SOCIOLOGIST AS ACTIVE FORCE

In addition to the roles I created for myself, several roles were cast upon me by others. During the first consulting year, my discussions with players and coaches involved their feelings, relationships, and other social and psychological dynamics. Thus it was not altogether surprising that I was referred to by Coach in front of reporters as the team "shrink." In addition, Coach told an academic administrator who questioned my presence on the bench, "Doc's here because he solves the problems I can't solve." Yet the media stories tended to impute some relationship between my work with the team and their on-the-court performance. This included such newspaper statements as: *"He might also be one of the reasons it [the team] is 12–2"* (emphasis in original).

Although I had never directly asserted that my analyses or advice could help the team play better, especially in the beginning when I was unsure and feeling out my role, media portrayals of me as an active force changed the way insiders treated me. Increasingly, players and coaches sought me out for confidential advice when they had conflicts, uncertainties, frustrations, felt like they were in a rut, or had other problems. Problems they brought to me included: relations with women; relations with teammates; relations with coaches; relations with boosters; playing time during games; handling injuries; handling academic matters; dealing with University administrators, and delegating responsibility among the coaching staff. While I had previously discussed many of these topics with the few players and coaches with whom I felt close, my media involvement brought other players to me as they read or heard that I could help them.

Their expectations generated doubts in my mind about my role. Was my advice really helpful? Did I actually have any impact on their performance during games? An excerpt from my field notes during the fall of 1981 illustrates their expectations and my uncertainty:

This has certainly been one of the most hectic, busy weeks ever. The team returned from the loss at North Carolina full of anger, confusion, and self-doubt. There was factionalization among players and hostility between the coaches and players. And for some reason they all want to talk to me. I've been hit for individual "talks" in the locker room and the coaching suite. I guess they think they've got a sociological problem. I don't know what I'm doing or if it's any good, but I'm working awfully hard at it.

Despite my uncertainty, when people came to me and asked for my analyses and advice, I gave my opinions, both to help them and to strengthen my acceptance. My ideas were usually well received, for I often heard them passed among setting members or repeated back to me. This tended to confirm my impression that my ideas were accurate and reinforced my desire to continue this informal consulting.

THE SOCIOLOGIST AS INSIDER: "BEARER OF THE TRUTH"

A second role into which I was thrust was that of insider, someone who knew all the participants well, who attended team functions, and who had access to information available only to insiders. This inside information could be divided into two categories: non-secret and secret. Non-secret inside information consisted of details about the everyday life of players, coaches, or administrators that differed from what was public knowledge only in detail, recency, or triviality. Secret information consisted of knowledge about team conflicts, misbehavior, or negative feelings. Such occurrences were carefully guarded from the public eye, although avidly discussed among insiders.

Secret knowledge gave me both status and power. At times outsiders reacted with envy to my inside position and the trust in which I was held by the team. Simmel (1950) has discussed the fascination of secrecy, noting that the exclusion of outsiders from secret knowledge enhances its possession. The content of the knowledge becomes secondary to its exclusive character. My access to team secrets strengthened my intimate relations with players, coaches, and media personnel, while giving me prestige with fans, boosters, colleagues, and friends.

Ranging from good friends to people who barely knew me, outsiders expected that I would gossip with them about the team. I was perceived as more approachable than other team members because I was close to the players yet still a "civilian" (I had never renounced my non-athletic role). I was considered fair target at any time, for any interested party. For example, one day in February 1982, I went to the doctor for a physical examination and cardiogram. I sat down in his office so that we could discuss the tests, and the first question he asked me was, "Tell me, do those basketball players really go to class?"

When asked, I tried to act like a coach and provide people with at least some information because, as a public figure, this was expected. When people afforded me the opportunity to speak positively about the team I offered non-secret information, while reserving secret information that I thought players or coaches would consider too private to reveal. When I did not know the answer to an inquiry, I produced some related information or offered knowledge that I had acquired from the newspaper, trying to make it sound firsthand.

Being an insider and having knowledge of team secrets was not always pleasant. Having information I could not reveal made me aware of the burden of inside secrets. I first felt this dimension of my insider role after a particularly controversial team meeting I attended in December 1981. Coach had given the players a severe "chewing out" for excessive curfew breaking, partying, poor work habits, and other infractions of his behavioral code. Both the tone of his voice and the content of his accusations made me realize that I was not going to be able to just go up to anyone I met and say, "Coach thinks these negative things about the team." Right then I knew I had to filter what I was seeing and hearing when talking with others in order to protect the team's image: I realized I had to be careful.

THE SOCIOLOGIST AS MEMBER:
"DEFENDER OF THE FAITH"

During the first two years of my association with the team I took a very informal role, letting my relationship develop as the members saw fit. I had negotiated no formal entree with gatekeepers other than the head coach, and my presence was unsanctioned by the University's administration. This ultimately began to bother me for two reasons. First, a team draws clear boundaries around its space. Who may or may not be there is defined. Outsiders knew this and commented on my possible violation of this norm. Thus I felt uncomfortable and insecure each time an outsider (acquaintance, fan, booster, University administrator, or other professor) questioned my role on the team and my right to be present in the locker room or on the bench. Second, I wanted to learn more about the administrative structure surrounding the team, and its influence on team dynamics. This necessitated some direct contact with administrators. I therefore created the official university position of Academic Adviser, obtained a temporarily reduced teaching load, and became formally legitimated as a team member.

The sports information department's media announcement of my appointment triggered a series of reactions toward me from outsiders as they read the articles discussing my new role. Handshakes and congratulations came from athletic and academic administrators who barely knew my name beforehand. In addition, I began to deal with these people in my new official capacity. My position involved setting up special programs for athletes, linking the athletic and academic realms, and working with the Athletic Director and other coaches to recruit players and do public relations. Through these experiences I began to understand the concerns and motivations of the administrators, and to see things from their perspective. This helped me understand their effect on the coaches and players.

The boosters also made themselves accessible. Major team supporters who had previously not taken much notice warmed considerably in their attitude toward me. I became a regular on their pregame conversational rounds. They invited me out to restaurants and into their homes. They called me when they became aware of players who had particular problems.

Third, my transition from informal member also affected a few insiders who had been guarded toward me. This included the assistant coaches, secretaries, booster club officials, and lower-echelon administrators who acted as informal gatekeepers around the team.

My formal appointment also increased the amount of public recognition I received as a coach. This was a direct outcome of media coverage. Increasingly, fans, boosters, colleagues, and even friends began to treat me as a "conduit." I had seen this done to the other coaches, but I had never had to deal with it myself. Suddenly, people were coming up to me, telling me what was wrong with the team, what should be done about it, and expecting that since I had the coach's ear I would pass their suggestions along to him. They also asked me what was wrong with the team or why things were being done in certain ways. No longer was I being asked for my personal opinion; I was now being asked as a representative of the team. I often had to fend off outsiders, defer to their theories, or cool them out by listening politely to their string of complaints. By being polite and seeming interested in their remarks, I usually relieved some of their irritation or overenthusiasm. I began to "work the public" for the team. Perhaps the most trying type of response for me was the one that involved "defending the faith." I watched the other coaches to see how they fielded criticisms, did facework, and managed the party line. I found myself speaking in a new language, "sportuguese." This was especially necessary when media reporters tried to pry information from me that they had been unsuccessful in obtaining from others. Defending the faith became a frustrating obligation of my new role as member. As the following example illustrates, it required holding back my actual feelings, offering carefully measured "party lines," and speaking nicely to people who were rude.

One January, after a month-long absence due to a debilitating knee injury, Apollo made an attempt to resume playing for the season. The team was nervous, as he was a key starter. He was put into the game during the second half and looked okay at first. After a short time, however, he collapsed and had to be carried off the court. The mood in the locker room while the doctors administered to him was somber. We all believed this meant the end of his hopes for a professional career. At the point of his fall the whole team had deflated, and barely managed to escape with a two-point victory after being ahead by a large margin. I was at an all-night pharmacy, obtaining a prescription for painkillers that the doctor had given Apollo, when the druggist realized who I was and offered the following remarks: "What's wrong with those guys? Aren't they trying to win? They should have blown those guys out. The problem with them is they don't have no heart." Even though I was enraged by the insensitivity of his comments, I somehow managed to smile and reply that "The competition is tough," that, "Yes sir, we are trying our hardest," and that "We appreciate your pulling for us." As a member, I was forced to withhold my private feeling in favor of the prescribed manner of representing the team to the public.

THE SOCIOLOGIST AS EXPERT: "PLAYING SHRINK"

Another role I was cast into by the media was that of an expert regarding intangible dimensions of the team's collective psyche. Media people attributed mystical powers to me. This image affected the types of interaction I had with people interested in the team, particularly boosters and fans. The first dimension of my role as an expert involved peoples' *expectations of my healing powers*. From my beginnings as a friendly and helpful observer who occasionally offered some opinions, I had been presented by Coach to the media, and by the media to the public, as someone who could fix the team's social ills and produce victories. My conversations with people took the tone of, "What's wrong with the team?—Fix it!." These comments became frequent during one season when the team was perceived to have a problem playing on the road and lost to schools that they clearly outranked in talent. People turned to me for explanations for the team's poor road performance. They also wanted me to tell them how this deficiency could be overcome. It was as if they saw me as having a magic wand that I could wave over an individual or the team to fix their problems.

The second dimension of my expert role involved peoples' *expectations of my omniscience*: I was looked upon and treated as a soothsayer. In this guise I was called upon to predict future performances. Everywhere I went, but particularly within the context of a sporting event, someone would inevitably walk up to me and say, "Well, Doc, who's going to win?"; "How're they going to do?"; or "Are they psyched?" I treated this media-induced aggrandizement of my role in much the same way I reacted to being treated as an active force. Sometimes, out of a sense of modesty, I tried to fend off these expectations by saying, "I'm not doing anything." But as the season wore on I found it simpler to acquiesce and say, "Oh yeah, they're ready, they'll produce."

During the second half of the 1981–82 season the increased frequency of basketball games and the intensity of the championship race escalated my expert role to godlike status. The entire community's identification with the team caused people to approach me with near-desperation. The expectations of what I could accomplish increased to the point where I began to hear, "I hope they can play better in this area. I know you've fixed that area, but do you have them ready here?."

THE SOCIOLOGIST AS CELEBRITY

The final, all-encompassing role that my other roles and my barrage of media publicity combined to create was that of local celebrity. This had profound effects on both my sense of self and on the research.

Becoming a celebrity during the course of doing this project was the result of three factors: the celebrity of my research subjects, my consulting role as the team sociologist, and the media's perception of me as "good copy." The media coverage I received filled me with the conflicting emotions of pleasure and guilt, satisfaction and irritation. On the one hand, being a celebrity was dazzling and exciting. It felt great to be placed on the level of the famous sports stars I was studying, to see my name in the paper along with theirs, to watch myself on TV, and to be recognized by strangers in public. As I met publicly known media people I could chat casually with them as one of the in-crowd. It made me feel important to think I was considered worthy of so much media attention.

The end of that intoxicating season brought a second rude shock: the loss of my celebrity status, at least until the next season began. Coming down to earth was something for which I had not been prepared. I had been spending all my energy rushing between too many commitments. Suddenly I was no longer a part of an intense public spectacle; it had vanished. No longer was I routinely surrounded by fanfare, glamour, and people. I experienced a multi-dimensional emptiness: (a) a vacuum in my time, going from three games and several practices weekly to "nothing;" (b) a vacuum in my social life, going from frequent, close contact with members of the team and their coterie of associates to dispersement and subsequent isolation, and (c) a vacuum in my sense of self, as my media-induced identity ceased to be supported by periodic appearances on the sports pages and evening television news.

Overnight, with the end of the season, I had to don my Clark Kent garb and return to the mundane world of everyday life. I felt a sense of sadness and loss, missing the fast life into which I had risen. I thought about how difficult coming out of the limelight must be for people who had lived in it much longer than I, and who had earned their own celebrity rather than deriving it from someone else's "coattails." But I felt a sense of relief as well: an escape from the pressure, a chance to be with my family, and a chance to be myself once again. Since the cycle was over, I could reflect on my media self, through which I had been relating to my other self as well as to others.

With the start of the 1982–83 season, I was met by national magazine reporters on opening day. Yet even though the media coverage continued regularly throughout the season, it did not affect me the same way it had the first year. I had already lived through the high-powered college basketball "world" and the media celebrity. I had experienced both the glamour and the mundane aspects of the team's day-to-day routines. I ceased to be as awed by my celebrity role and my media self, and simply added them to my repertoire of roles. This produced a change in my core self, the one that evolves in response to the ongoing stream of personal experience. I felt more confident, more adroit, more tested, and more seasoned.

DISENGAGEMENT

Sociologists often make their decision to leave the setting when they feel they become saturated with data. Leaving for this reason may cause their subjects to resent them (see Snow 1980), since it is perceived as a voluntary abandonment on the researcher's part. I never had the opportunity to make that decision, as it was made for me.

During my fourth year, I began to hear rumbles around the University that people were unhappy about my research. At first I paid no attention to these, as I was used to encountering the jealousy of my colleagues, many of whom wished they could get as close to the team as I. Secretly, many of them wondered whether I was really doing research, or just "sniffing jocks" (getting my thrills as a fan). The other reason I discounted these was that I was used to faculty members taking a derisive attitude toward sport research in general, relegating this subfield to minor status, at best. Yet I did not worry about people holding either of these two attitudes because I thought that the serious and scholarly aspects of my work would become apparent, and I focused on the evaluation of the national, rather than local, audience. Still, the rumors and grumblings continued, and even started to swell.

Toward the end of that basketball season, the chairperson of my department spoke to me about the dangers he perceived associated with continuing in my ongoing research. Through his connections to the University's president, he assured me that these dangers were real, indeed, and that my tenure could be "in serious jeopardy" if I did not withdraw. At this point I began to take the whisperings seriously, and consulted several knowledgeable and influential people around the University who knew the nature and inner workings of the administration. They assured me that I should heed these warnings carefully. I was confused, upset, and resentful. I did not relish being forced out of the research setting I had worked so hard to penetrate because of some unfathomable University politics. Nevertheless, I began to disengage.

After the season, I discussed my situation with the players and coaches. Coach had also heard some of these murmurings, and concurred with the advice that I should take these warnings seriously. We decided together that the best thing to do would be to make my role with the team less visible. Consequently, by the next year, I had moved from the front (coaches' and players') bench to the second row (with Patti), and was trying to take a low profile. Apparently this was not enough of a disengagement, as the warnings continued. At the end of that season, then, I terminated all formal and visible contact with the team. I proclaimed my research project over, and I stopped going to games. I still continued my informal associations with those team members (players and coaches) with whom I was close, going down to the coaching offices occasionally, and socializing with the individuals I had befriended as key informants. From this position I could observe what was going on with the team and the players I had been following and I could continue to talk informally as well as do taped interviews with them.

Being forced out of the setting made my leaving more palatable to my subjects, although they still felt somewhat abandoned. I was angry that outsiders had interfered in the decision, but I was also somewhat relieved, as I had felt I was getting close to the point of data saturation, and had not known how to terminate my research. It looked like I might just stay in the research setting for as long as I remained at that school (which I thought would be forever). Also, despite the intense and self-involving character of the research, once I left I did not miss it as much as I had anticipated. Other things arose to fill its place, and by this time I was busy with other projects.

Patti's Role

Peter's burgeoning involvement with the basketball team was initially very exciting for me. Getting a behind-the-scenes peek into the private, inner arena of the program was thrilling, and some of the people I began to meet were different and wondrous. Apollo, in particular, was sharp-witted, exciting, and bright. I also became close with Buck, who, when he was not around the other players (and having to act macho), was sensitive and funny in a quiet sort of way. I loved having players over for dinner, feeding these hungry guys huge platters full of food and listening to their emotional exclamations and colorful expressions ("handling the rock," "shooting a J"). As Peter began to immerse himself in the team and bring players into our home and office, I met a new crowd of people that brightened up the otherwise dull routines of our dreary social lives. The members of the basketball program were not like the other staid individuals who filled the town, ensconced in their religious communities, complacent in their conservative material- ism and upward mobility. The basketball players felt as alien in this scene as we did, albeit for different reasons. They brought with them their rural and small-town backgrounds, their experiences in inner-city ghettos. Just as they felt alienated as blacks in a lily-white town, so, too, did we feel isolated as Jews in this center of Christian fundamen- talism and born-again revivalism. Our mutual marginality served as a bonding force for us, forging us together through the knowledge that reality was not limited to the way the locals presented it.

GENDER

Getting to know the players and becoming friendly with them was harder for me than for Peter. I had not spent my youth and weekends watching sports, and did not have the extensive knowledge that he shared with them. Even more importantly, I was a woman. In their world, women did not go out with the "boys," but rather, sat at home alone while their men went out and socialized. Their women waited on them subserviently, bringing them dinner and cans of coke or beer, or tending the kids (which a few of the college players had) in the background. They were neither outspoken nor independent. I was both. I was a professional woman from a progressive background who spoke my mind. They found me shocking but interesting. They also found that I was present a lot around them when they left the athletic and dormitory areas, as Peter and I spent most of our time together.

Initially, they did not know how to treat me, or how to talk to me. They fumbled over how to address me. Since I was a professor and a person approximately ten years their senior, they felt as if they should show me respect. They therefore could not call me a nickname like they did Peter. They tried to call me "Mizz Adler," but I pleaded with them to drop that formality as it made me feel too old. They then tried to call me "Mizz Patti" (somewhat more informal), but I told them it made me feel like a Southern plantation belle. After about six months of my hanging around, they were finally able to comfortably address me by my first name. Some got used to my ways more than others, and these people became some of the closest friends I made in six years of living in that town.

As the research escalated and Peter's role in the setting became more established, I found myself spending more time around the other participants: the coaches, their wives, the boosters, and the media people. I loved listening to the coaches "chew the fat" and tell stories about life on the road. I also liked to hang out with the media people, who spoke warmly and freely with me because of their friendship with Peter. But at the times before and after games, when the players and coaches retreated into the locker room, I found myself spending more time with the girlfriends and wives of the team members. Eventually I became closer with them, and caught some inside glimpses into their lives and feelings. My relationships with the players' girlfriends were more successful than with the coaches' wives, although my status was more consonant with the latter. I became friendly with several of the players' girlfriends and played on city-league athletic teams (basketball, softball) with them. I also spent time observing the boosters' social scene, and was occasionally invited to sit in their choice game seats, to accompany them out to dinner after important victories, and to eat in their homes. I thus experienced, first-hand, many of the social settings and interactions with a range of participants, that the players and coaches encountered. While I would not consider my position an active membership role, such as Peter assumed, I became a peripheral member (see Adler and Adler 1987). I was an accepted participant in the social scene, knew most of the key figures, and had direct, and sometimes intimate, contact with them from an inside position. Clearly, however, the gendered nature of this setting prevented me from getting as close to some of the members and much of the action as I would have liked.

Throughout the course of this research, we carefully wrote field notes at the end of each day based on our observations. We recorded the events of the day, the reactions and comments of each participant and ourselves as close to verbatim as possible, and discussed the emergence of possible patterns. Often, we tape recorded these sessions to preserve our exact memories as freshly as possible.

INTERVIEWING

After two years of gaining entree and learning the scene, we decided it was time to begin our depth interviewing. We conducted a repeated series of intensive, taped interviews with members of the coaching staff and with all 39 members of the basketball team who were associated with the program during these five years. Usually we did this by inviting people over to our house, feeding them dinner, and sitting around the table afterward for a focused, tape-recorded conversation. Many of the players were interviewed alone, others (especially the less articulate team members) were interviewed in groups. (Some of the coaches' interviews were conducted in their offices, often on the weekends in between the morning and afternoon practices.) Here, too, I took a different role from Peter.

It was my job to do most of the questioning. I began the interview by asking them to give a life history account of their experiences with sport. I guided them to focus on their backgrounds, and then led them up to and through their college experiences. I then asked them to describe their view of the significant aspects of college athletics. As we discussed these years, I asked questions about both their concrete experiences and their conceptual interpretations, about specific events and about the scene in general. All this while Peter sat silently at the table, or moved around the room. It was easier for me to ask questions that they thought Peter should know the answers to, since I was not the active member. They felt compelled to articulate more comprehensive answers to me, since I could take the ignorant stance more easily (see Douglas 1985). When someone began to give us frontwork, though, or to feign ignorance, Peter would step into the interview and call them on it. "What do you mean?" he would ask, "What about the time when you did this?" or, "How can you say that when I distinctly heard you say something else to someone?" His vast knowledge of their conversations, relationships, and behaviors was invaluable here.

My differentiated role also helped me in dealing with Peter. His contribution lay in his entree into and immersion in the membership experience. Mine lay in my ability to see it, but to detach from it. There were times during the research when he went "native" in the setting. He would come back from a practice, booster function, or strategy meeting of the coaches totally enmeshed in the practical problems of their world. Their world had become his world, and at times his athletic identity was his most salient one. My job, in cases like this, was to pull him out of it, to pull him back to the sociological perspective. I would focus our thoughts and attention on developing conceptualizations as we combed through his thoughts and experiences together. As we brainstormed, I tried to combine my perspective with his, to get a detachment that complemented his immersion.

Using Glaser and Strauss' grounded theory (1967), we let significant patterns and concerns emerge from the data. We triangulated (Denzin 1970) the perceptions and generalizations of various members by cross-checking them against other accounts, our own observations and experiences, and hard data wherever possible (team records, transcripts, media accounts, scouting reports) (Douglas 1976).

We then analyzed the data according to Glaser and Strauss' grounded theory model. We began by generating *categories* and their properties through clumping respondents' observations around particular themes. Examples of these included the stripping down of the self, the role of the peer culture, the loyalty contract, and learning loyalty. Each of these categories were composed of subgroups that described how they operated, including both structural components and processes. We then searched our field notes and the transcribed interview tapes for instances that represented these categories and their properties, examining them to further check on the validity of our conceptualizations.

Once patterns emerged we began to ask about them more routinely in our interviews, searching for the limits and variations of their applications and parameters. We also looked for relations between different patterns and concepts, seeking to understand how they arose and influenced each other. As some of them yielded more fruitful data we delved into them further, and centered our thinking around them as analytical concepts. At this point we abandoned some of the earlier concepts that seemed routine or theoretically uninteresting. The result of these searches were what Wiseman (1970) has called total patterns, or collective belief systems held by the group, and data clusters, or combinations of events and occurrences that coalesced in the group we studied. These included such broader concepts as self-engulfment and glory, as well as more routine but mundane occurrences such as "puffing" and "snapping." These careful and rigorous means of data collection and analysis were designed to maximize both the reliability and validity of our findings.

ADVANTAGES AND DISADVANTAGES

This was the first time we had used differentiated roles in our research, and it brought with it both pros and cons. On the positive side, we used our differentiated roles in the setting to befriend different people. Peter was more friendly with the coaches and administrators, I with the women. He cracked some of the tough cases, while I attracted the softer ones. He also got the insiders' perspective, while I saw how outsiders were regarding both the team and him. And by being in different places, talking to different people, we were able to cross-check the various accounts people gave us (Douglas 1976).

We were also able to overcome some of the narrowing associated with becoming totally involved in the members' perspectives. We could understand how difficult it was for members to struggle to build a winning program, to recruit players and keep them eligible, and to try to keep up with academics while thrust into the maelstrom of games and celebrity. At the same time, however, we saw the effect of this single-focusedness on the long-term prospects of the players and coaches, saw the goals and dilemmas of the academic administrators and the NCAA, and saw the way members were caught up in the thrill of their fame, losing sight of other concerns. We thus were able to attain a more multi-perspectival view of the scene and utilize our potential as a field research team (Douglas 1976).

On the negative side, taking differentiated roles put a strain on our personal relationship. Under the influence of different perspectives, we felt different allegiances, held different goals, and had divergent schedules. Peter was often off with the team somewhere. During several of the research years, by the time the season had run into mid-February, I felt like I hardly ever saw him. He was off being a celebrity, and he enjoyed it too much to let it go. He did not want to think about data saturation, about conceptualization, about losing his tenure. All he knew was that this arena was so compelling, he had to be there. While it helped us understand the choices and decisions made by athletes when caught in the grip of this powerful and alluring scene, it was tough on us. He, in turn, felt like I was standing between him and something he had always wanted to do, like I was pulling him home with a ball and chain around his leg. I became fearful that the season would never end and that I would never see him again. I chafed at my secondary role and secondary status. We took these things out on each other. Yet the seasons ended, we resumed normal lives, and the research benefited from our differentiated roles.

Conclusions

In this research we have made use of several different methodological techniques. Data gathering does not occur only through the detached observational role, but through the subjectively immersed role as well. We therefore abandoned the sterility of the completely objectivist stance to take membership roles. We delved deeply and unabashedly into the subjective realm, seeking answers to the common social psychological question (drawn from Dilthey), "How is meaningful experience possible?" We thus immersed ourselves in this sphere of life as fully as we were able. We did this for two reasons. First, we desired to facilitate our entree and rapport so that we could become as close to the members as possible. When researchers take membership roles they are recognized and treated by others as members. They become privy to members' innermost thoughts, activities, and emotions. This is particularly important in settings characterized by secrecy and/or exclusiveness (which, to some degree, most settings are). Second, we did this to put ourselves in the position of members. When researchers participate in the routine practices of members as one of them, they experience the members' world. By doing membership work we were forced to assume the obligations and liabilities of members. We thus organized our behavior and formed constructs about the setting's everyday reality like the members and felt the same pulls and emotions about the setting as members. In some ways we were similarly transformed by the setting as members. This was a critical part of our experience in the scene, without which our *verstehen,* or meaningful understanding, would not have been as profound. We thus used ourselves as instruments of our analyses (Reinharz 1979) and drew "self-observations" (Johnson 1975) on our acquired memberships.

That fieldwork is a subjectivist methodology, however, does not preclude its being a rigorous methodology. At the same time we employed differentiated research roles to triangulate specific knowledge (Denzin 1970) and obtain a multi-perspectival understanding of the setting. Although Patti's being blocked from certain aspects of the setting was unwanted, her resultant entry into different (although overlapping) circles and a different type of involvement in the scene ultimately benefited us. While she clearly became a member (was accepted as a member, felt the feelings of members), her degree of self-immersion in and identification with the arena and its activities remained secondary to her other concerns. Peter got involved more deeply and hence made the kinds of emotional commitments and involvements more common to the other participants. At times, this became his primary sphere of involvement, pushing others aside. This dualism helped us understand the existential thrust of how and why members became drawn into the dynamics of the setting and how they thought and felt about their experiences at the same time as we could see the larger picture of what factors caused this and what effects it was having.

Our research in this setting also illustrates our commitment to another epistemological approach: researching in the "yard." Researchers' definitions of what constitutes the field, or the appropriate location for gathering data, has varied among disciplines and among practitioners of various methodological approaches. Anthropologists have traditionally felt that they had to leave their own country and culture to acquire meaningful knowledge (Clifford 1989). Psychologists, especially of the experimental persuasion, have regarded the laboratory as the field. Others have felt the field was somewhere one was theoretically driven in search of answers to an objective research question. We, in contrast, have always believed strongly in the conception of the yard as the field.[1] It is not necessary to venture far away to find diversity and realize meaningful knowledge. Rather, the pastiche of contemporary life close at hand displays enormous variation in people's beliefs, values, behavior, and culture. American society is an especially pluralist arena, filled with myriad diverse groups from different subcultures, classes, religions, ethnicities, regions, occupations, and leisure pursuits.

Remaining close to home is not just a technique of convenience, however. It represents the field researcher's commitment to "exploiting their biography" as a research technique. In exploiting their biography by staying within the figurative yard, researchers have the best opportunity to get close to their subjects. Only by living with them on a daily basis can researchers meaningfully penetrate subjects' worlds. In this research, we lived and worked with our subjects over the course of five seasons, year in and year out. We worked with them, we played with them; we argued with them, we rejoiced with them; we met their families and they met ours; we were there when exciting things were happening, we were there when nothing was happening. Living this closely in the setting enabled us to penetrate behind its glamour and see it as a mundane work-a-day world, the way members saw it. In studying a setting where we not only worked every day, but also brought to it a long-term interest and familiarity (as collegiate athletic fans), we risked the danger of overinvolvement: adopting the perspective of members so thoroughly that we lost our analytical distance. Yet researchers have recently come to realize that ignorance, distance, and misunderstanding are far more difficult to overcome than the hazards of propinquity and involvement.[2] The advantages gained by researching close or familiar settings, thus, where the researcher can get as intimate with members as possible, far outweigh the potential disadvantages.

1
Overview

IT WAS a world of dreams. They expected to find fame and glory, spotlights and television cameras. There was excitement and celebrity, but also hard work and discouragement, a daily grind characterized by aches, pains, and injuries, and an abundance of rules, regulations, and criticism. Their lives alternated between contacts with earnest reporters, adoring fans, and fawning women, and with intimidating professors, demanding boosters, and unrelenting coaches. There was secrecy and intrigue, drama and adulation, but also isolation and alienation, loss of freedom and personal autonomy, and overwhelming demands. These conflicts and dualisms are the focus of this book. This is a study of the socialization of college athletes.

For five years we lived in and studied the world of elite NCAA (National Collegiate Athletic Association) college basketball. Participant-observers, we fit ourselves into the setting by carving out evolving roles that integrated a combination of team members' expectations with our interests and abilities. Individually and together, we occupied a range of different positions including friend, professor, adviser, confidant, and coach. We observed and interacted with all members of the team, gaining an intimate understanding of the day-to-day and year-to-year character of this social world. From behind the scenes of this secretive and celebrated arena, we document the experiences of college athletes, focusing on changes to their selves and identities over the course of their college years.

The team we researched had many features of the average liberal arts college or state university, yet athletically it lay in the upper echelon of competitors. Although not an established dynasty, it had a newly hired coach who rapidly built a strong team through his winning reputation and energetic recruiting practices. The result was a team with an outstanding record that quickly captivated the interest and enthusiasm of the community. In this book we offer a detailed description and analysis of the players, coaches, supporters, news media, and other key personnel comprising the inner circle of the team. We depict the problems, pressures, and rewards characteristic of the intense, high-visibility, swiftly moving world of college athletics.

This world is the intricate result of complex, interdependent factors and people, all of whom operate to fulfill their own needs and ends. The way these come together creates the composite that is big-time college athletics. While we will reveal facts that will surprise both casual observers and those knowledgeable about college athletics, many of our findings are consistent with the image generally portrayed by investigative media accounts. What our long-lens perspective offers is a close, detailed, and sympathetic portrayal of the virtues and vices inherent in this social world, hidden to most people. We illuminate the processes that operate within the "black box" of college athletics, showing how and why the transformations and outcomes occur.

Existing knowledge about the world of college athletics comes from two basic sources: academic research and journalistic accounts. While the former literature has addressed important concerns and offered significant findings,[1] its methodological character has limited its scope to some extent: it is composed entirely of survey research, the analysis of secondary data, and armchair theorizing. These methods can tell us something about *what* is going on in college athletics, but they can do no more than speculate about the profound and often complex motivations, causes, and other factors underlying the social conditions they document. To date, there have been no systematic academic participant-observation studies of college athletics.[2] Through our five-year in-depth investigation, we go beyond previous correlational studies to shed light on the social dynamics and process of socialization in the world of college athletics.

Journalistic accounts, the second source of knowledge about college athletics, fall into two distinct types. Some are simply the standard institutional propaganda touting the benefits of athletic participation and community cohesion. More commonly, however, journalists interested in college athletics have leaned toward investigative reporting,

producing exposés that are meant to highlight the exploitative characteristics of athletics in American higher education. Some of the best
investigative reports have used unstructured interviewing and depth
involvement to produce insightful and complex portrayals.[3] Many of
these accounts are rich in data, but limited in other ways: reporters
typically gather information over a relatively short-term period; they
do not apply the canons of data-gathering required for scholarly research, and they fail to provide deeper theoretical explanations linking
the specific behavior they describe to a greater understanding of human
nature, human behavior, social structure, and social change.[4] In this
book we use a longitudinal approach, carefully follow ethnographic
verification and validation procedures, and make conceptual links by
providing a theoretically informed analysis based on the social psychological theory of symbolic interactionism. We use the experiences of
college athletes to offer insights into the relation between the individual, society, and social trends.

Theoretical Approach

This is not only a study of college athletes, then, but also a study in the
social psychology of the self.[5] Our observations reveal a significant
pattern of transformation experienced by all our subjects: *role-engulf-
ment*. Many of the individuals we followed entered college hoping to
gain wealth and fame through their involvement with sport. They did
not anticipate, however, the cost of dedicating themselves to this realm.
While nearly all conceived of themselves as athletes first, they possessed
other self-images that were important to them as well. Yet over the
course of playing college basketball, these individuals found the demands and rewards of the athletic role overwhelming and became
engulfed by it. However in yielding to it, they had to sacrifice other
interests, activities, and, ultimately, dimensions of their selves. They
immersed themselves completely in the athletic role and neglected or
abandoned their identities lodged in these other roles. They thus became extremely narrow in their focus. In this work we examine *role
domination,* the process by which athletes became engulfed in their
athletic role as it ascended to a position of prominence. We also
examine the concomitant process of *role abandonment,* where they
progressively detached themselves from their investment in other areas

and let go of alternative goals or priorities. We analyze the changes this dual process of self-engulfment had on their self-concepts and on the structure of their selves.

The self has been approached from a variety of social psychological perspectives. In examining the experiences of college athletes, we focus on the structure and dynamic processes of their selves within the context of the surrounding culture and social structure. As athletes struggle to adapt to a confusing and conflicting social world, striving to integrate their previous expectations with their individual and joint definitions of the situation, they experience profound changes in their selves. These arise due to the interplay between improvised behavior (agency) and imposed structure, as these meet in the domain of collectively forged interaction. Our approach integrates elements from related, but divergent, models of social psychology. We draw on the structural elements of role theory to enhance a basic foundation of symbolic interactionism.[6] The structural social psychological perspective examines the composition of the self and its relation to social norms and structures. We employ several key concepts from this approach in this analysis.

Role theory focuses on the systems, or institutions, into which interaction fits. According to its tenets, _statuses_ are positions in organized groups or systems that are related to other positions by a set of normative expectations. Statuses are not defined by the people that occupy them, but rather they are permanent parts of those systems. Each status carries with it a set of role expectations specifying how persons occupying that status should behave. _Roles_ consist of the activities people of a given status are likely to pursue when following the normative expectations for their positions. _Identities_ (or what McCall and Simmons 1978, call role-identities), are the self-conceptions people develop from occupying a particular status or enacting a role. The _self_ is the more global, multirole, core conception of the real person.

Because in modern society we are likely to be members of more than one group, we may have several statuses and sets of role-related behavioral expectations. Each individual's total constellation of roles forms what may be termed a _role-set,_ characterized by a series of relationships with role-related others, or role-set members (Merton 1957). Certain roles or role-identities may be called to the fore, replacing others, as people interact with individuals through them. Individuals do not invest their core feelings of identity or self in all roles equally, however. While some roles are more likely to be called forth by the expectations of others, other roles are more salient to the individual's core, or "real self,"[7] than others. They are arranged along a *hierarchy of salience* from peripheral roles to those that "merge with the self" (Turner 1978), and their ranking may be determined by a variety of factors. Role theory enhances an understanding of both the internal structure of the self and the relation between self and society; it sees this relation as mediated by the concept of role and its culturally and structurally derived expectations.

The interpretive branch of symbolic interactionism focuses on examining agency, process, and change. One of the concepts most critical to symbolic interactionism is the self. Rather than merely looking at roles and their relation to society, symbolic interactionism looks at the individuals filling those roles and the way they engage not only in role-taking, but also in active, creative role-making (Turner 1962). The self is the thinking and feeling being connecting the various roles and identities individuals put forth in different situations (Cooley 1962; Mead 1934). Symbolic interactionism takes a dynamic view of individuals in society, believing that they go beyond merely reproducing existing roles and structures to collectively defining and interpreting the meaning of their surroundings. These subjective, symbolic assessments form the basis for the creation of new social meanings, that then lead to new, shared patterns of adaptation (Blumer 1969). In this way individuals negotiate their social order as they experience it (Strauss 1978). They are thus capable of changing both themselves and the social structures within which they exist. Symbolic interactionism enhances understandings of the dynamic processes characterizing human group life and the reciprocal relation between those processes and changes in the self.

In integrating these two perspectives we show how the experiences of college athletes are both bounded and creative, how athletes integrate structural, cultural, and interactional factors, and how they change and adapt through a dynamic process of action and reaction, forging collective adaptations that both affirm and modify existing structures.

The Setting

We conducted this research at a medium-size (6000 students), private university (hereafter referred to as "the University") in the southwestern portion of the United States. Originally founded on the premise of a religious affiliation, the University had severed its association with the church several decades before, and was striving to make a name for itself as one of the finer private, secular universities in the region. For many years it had served the community chiefly as a commuter school, but had embarked on an aggressive program of national recruiting over the past five to ten years that considerably broadened the base of its enrollment. Most of the students were white, middle class, and drawn from the suburbs of the South, Midwest, and Southwest. Academically, the University was experimenting with several innovative educational programs designed to enhance its emerging national reputation. Sponsored by reforms funded by the National Endowment for the Humanities, it was changing the curriculum, introducing a more interdisciplinary focus, instituting a funded honors program, increasing the general education requirements, and, overall, raising academic standards to a fairly rigorous level.

Within the University, the athletic program overall had considerable success during the course of our research: the University's women's golf team was ranked in the top three nationally, the football team won their conference each season, and the basketball program was ranked in the top forty of Division I NCAA schools, and in the top twenty for most of two seasons. The basketball team played in post-season tournaments every year, and in the five complete seasons we studied them, they won approximately four times as many games as they lost. In general, the basketball program was fairly representative of what Coakley (1986) and Frey (1982a) have termed "big-time" college athletics. Although it could not compare to the upper echelon of established basketball dynasties or to the really large athletic programs that wielded enormous recruiting and operating budgets,[8] its success during the period we studied it compensated for its size and lack of historical tradition. The University's basketball program could thus best be described as "up and coming."[9] Because the basketball team (along with the athletic department more generally) was ranked nationally and sent graduating members into the professional leagues, the entire athletic milieu was imbued with a sense of seriousness and purpose.

The team's professionalism was also enhanced by the attention focused on it by members of the community. Located in a city of approximately 500,000 with no professional sports teams, the University's programs served as the primary source of athletic entertainment and identification for the local population. When the basketball program meteorically rose to prominence, members of the city embraced it with fanatical support. Concomitant with the team's rise in fortunes, the region—part of the booming oil and sun belts—was experiencing increased economic prosperity. This surging local pride and financial windfall cast its glow over the basketball team, as it was the most charismatic and victorious program in the city's history, and the symbol of the community's newfound identity. Interest and support were therefore lavished on the team members.

The People

Over the course of our research, we observed 39 players and seven coaches. Much like Becker et al. (1961), we followed the players through their recruitment and entry into the University, keeping track of them as they progressed through school. We also watched the coaches move up their career ladders and deal with the institutional structures and demands.

Players, like students, were recruited primarily from the surrounding region. Unlike the greater student population, though, they generally did not hail from suburban areas. Rather, they predominantly came from the farming and rural towns of the prairies or southlands, and from the ghetto and working class areas of the mid-sized cities.

DEMOGRAPHICS

Over the course of our involvement with the team, two-thirds of the players we studied were black and one-third white. White middle class players accounted for approximately 23 percent of the team members.[10] They came from intact families where fathers worked in such occupations as wholesale merchandising, education, and sales. Although several were from suburban areas, they were more likely to come from mid- to larger-sized cities or exurbs. The remaining white players (10 percent) were from working-class backgrounds. They came from small factory towns or cities and also from predominantly (although not exclusively) intact families. Some of their parents worked in steel mills or retail jobs.

The black players were from middle, working, and lower class backgrounds. Those from the middle class (15 percent) came from the cities and small towns of the Midwest and South. They had intact families with fathers who worked as police chiefs, ministers, high school principals, or in the telecommunications industry. A few came from families in which the mothers also worked. Several of these families placed a high premium on education; one player was the youngest of five siblings who had all graduated from college and gone on for professional degrees, while another's grandparents had received college educations and established professional careers. The largest group of players (33 percent) were blacks from working class backgrounds. These individuals came from some small Southern towns, but more often from the mid- to larger-sized cities of the South, Midwest, and Southwest. Only about half came from intact families; the rest were raised by their mothers or extended families. Many of them lived in the ghetto areas of these larger cities, but their parents held fairly steady jobs in factories, civil service, or other blue-collar or less skilled occupations. The final group (18 percent) was composed of lower class blacks. Nearly all of these players came from broken homes. While the majority lived with their mothers, one came from a foster family, another lived with his father and sister, and a third was basically reared by his older brothers. These individuals came from the larger cities in the Southwest, South, and Midwest. They grew up in ghetto areas and were street smart and tough. Many of their families subsisted on welfare; others lived off menial jobs such as domestic service. They were poor, and had the most desperate dreams of escaping.

CLIQUES

Moving beyond demographics, the players fell into four main coalitions that served as informal social groups. Not every single member of the team neatly fit into one of these categories or belonged to one of these groups, but nearly all players who stayed on the team for at least a year eventually drifted into a camp. At the very least, individuals associated with the various cliques displayed many behavioral characteristics we will describe. Players often forged friendship networks within these divisions, because of common attitudes, values, and activities. Once in a clique, no one that we observed left it or shifted into another one. In presenting these cliques, we trace a continuum from those with the most "heart" (bravery, dedication, willingness to give everything they had to the team or their teammates), a quality highly valued by team members, to those perceived as having the least.

Drawing on the vernacular shared by players and coaches,[11] the first group of players were the *"bad niggas."*[12] All of these individuals were black, from the working or lower classes, and shared a ghetto upbringing. Members of what Edwards (1985) has called the underclass (contemporary urban gladiators), they possessed many of the characteristics cited by Miller (1958) in his study of delinquent gangs' lower class culture: trouble, toughness, smartness, excitement, fate, and autonomy.[13] They were street smart and displayed an attitude that bespoke their defiance of authority. In fact, their admiration for independence made it hard for them to adjust to domination by the coach (although he targeted those with reform potential as pet "projects"). Fighters, they would not hesitate to physically defend their honor or to jump into the fray when a teammate was in trouble. They worked hard to eke the most out of their athletic potential, for which they earned the respect of their teammates; they had little desire to do anything else.[14] These were the players with the most heart. They may not have been "choir boys," but when the competition was fierce on the court, these were the kind of players the coach wanted out there, the kind he knew he could count on. Their on-court displays of physical prowess contributed to their assertions of masculinity, along with sexual conquests and drug use. They were sexually promiscuous and often boasted about their various "babes." With drugs, they primarily used marijuana, alcohol (beer), and cocaine. Their frequency of use varied from daily to occasional, although who got high and how often was a significant behavioral difference dividing the cliques. This type of social split, and the actual amounts of drugs team members used, is no different from the general use characteristic of a typical college population (see Moffatt 1989).

Tyrone was one of the bad niggas. He came from the ghetto of a mid-sized city in the Southwest, from an environment of outdoor street life, illicit opportunity, and weak (or absent) parental guidance. He was basically self-raised: he saw little of his mother, who worked long hours as a maid, and he had never known his father. Exceptionally tall and thin, he walked with a swagger (to show his "badness"). His speech was rich with ghetto expressions and he felt more comfortable hanging around with "brothers" than with whites. He often promoted himself boastfully, especially in speaking about his playing ability, future professional chances, and success with women. His adjustment to life at the University was difficult, although after a year or so he figured out how to "get by"; he became acclimated to dorm life, classes, and the media and boosters. When it came to common sense street-smarts, he was one of the brightest people on the team. He neither liked nor was favored by many boosters, but he did develop a solid group of friends within the ranks of the other bad niggas.

Apollo was another bad nigga. His family upbringing was more stable than Tyrone's, as his parents were together and his father was a career government worker (first in the military, then in the postal service). They had never had much money though, and scraped by as best they could. He was the youngest of six children, the only boy, and was favored by his father because of this. Tall and handsome, he sported an earring (which the coach made him remove during the season) and a gold tooth. One of the most colorful players, Apollo had a charismatic personality and a way with words. He was a magnetic force on the team, a leader who related emotionally to his teammates to help charge and arouse them for big games. He spoke in the common street vernacular of a ghetto "brother," although he could converse in excellent "White English" when it was appropriate. He was appealing to women, and enjoyed their attention, even though he had a steady girlfriend on the women's basketball team. Like Tyrone, Apollo was intelligent and articulate; he was able to express his perspective on life in a way that was insightful, entertaining, and outrageous. He was eager to explore and experience the zest of life, traveling the world, partying heavily, and seizing immediate gratification. He disdained the boring life of the team's straighter members, and generally did not form close relations with them. Yet he managed to enjoy his partying and playing and still graduate in four years. He would never have thought about college except for basketball, and had to overcome several debilitating knee injuries, but he ended up playing profession-ally on four continents and learning a foreign language.

A second group of players were the "*candy-asses.*" These individuals were also black, but from the middle and working classes. Where the bad niggas chafed under the authority of the coach, the candy asses craved his attention and approval; they tended to form the closest personal ties with both him and his family. In fact, their strong ties to the coach made them the prime suspects as "snitches," those who would tell the coaches when others misbehaved. They "browned up" to the coaches and to the boosters and professors as well. The candy-asses were "good boys," the kind who projected the public image of conscientious, religious, polite, and quiet individuals. Several of them belonged to the Fellowship of Christian Athletes. They could be counted on to stay out of trouble. Yet although they projected a pristine image, they did not live like monks. They had girlfriends, enjoyed going to discos, and occasionally drank a few beers for recreation. They enjoyed parties, but, responsibly, moderated their behavior. The candy-asses enjoyed a respected position on the team because, like the bad niggas, they were good athletes and had heart. As much as they sought to be well rounded and attend to the student role, they did not let this interfere with their commitment to the team. They cared about the team first, and would sacrifice whatever was necessary—playing in pain, coming back too soon from an injury, relinquishing personal statistics to help the team win, diving to get the ball—for its benefit. Above all, they could be counted on for their loyalty to the coach, the team, and the game.

Rob was one such player from a large, extended working class family in a sizable Southern city. He was friendly and easy-going, with a positive attitude that came out in most of his activities. Although he was black and most of his close friends on the team were as well, Rob interacted much more easily with white boosters and students than did Tyrone. Rob transferred to the University to play for the coach because he had competed against him and liked both his reputation and style of play. Once there, he devoted himself to the coach, and was adored by the coach's wife and children. He often did favors for the family; one summer he painted the house in his spare time, and ate many of his meals there during the off-season. Rob's family was very close-knit, and both his mother and brother moved to town to be near him while he was at the University. They grew close with the coach's family, and often did things together. They also became regulars at the games, and were courted by many boosters who wanted to feel as if they knew Rob. Rob kept his academic and social life on an even keel during his college years; he worked hard in class (and was often the favorite of the media when they wanted to hype the image of the good student-athlete), and had a steady girlfriend. She was also very visible, with her young child from a previous boyfriend, in the basketball stadium. Like one or two of the others on the team, Rob spent one summer traveling with a Christian group on an around-the-world basketball tour.

Another typical candy-ass was Darian. He lived next door to Rob for two of the years they overlapped at the University, and the two were very close. Darian came from a middle class family in a nearby state and his family came to town for most of the home games. He was much more serious about life than Rob, and worked hard in everything he did. He was recruited by the team at the last minute (he had health problems that many thought would keep him from playing), yet he devoted himself to improvement. By his senior year he was one of the outstanding stars and had dreams of going pro. He wanted to make the most of his college education as well, and spent long hours in his room trying to study. Most people on the team looked up to him because he did what they all intended to do—work hard, sacrifice, and make the most of their college opportunity. His closest friends, then, were others with values like his, who were fairly serious, respectful, and who deferred their gratification in hopes of achieving a future career.

The *"whiners"* constituted a third category of players. Drawn from the middle and working classes and from both races, this group was not as socially cohesive as the previous two, yet it contained friendship cliques of mixed class and race. These individuals had neither the athletic prowess of the candy asses nor the toughness of the bad niggas, yet they wanted respect. In fact the overriding trait they shared was their outspoken belief that they deserved more than they were getting: more playing time, more deference, more publicity. In many ways they envied and aspired to the characteristics of the two other groups. They admired the bad niggas' subculture, their independence, toughness, and disrespect for authority, but they were not as "bad." They wanted the attention (and perceived favoritism) the candy-asses received, but they could not keep themselves out of trouble. Like the bad niggas, they enjoyed getting high. While their athletic talent varied, they did not live up to their potential; they were not willing to devote them- selves to basketball. They were generally not the kind of individuals who would get into fights, either on the court or on the street, and they lacked the heart of the previous two groups. Therefore, despite their potential and their intermittent complaining, they never enjoyed the same kind of respect among their teammates as the bad niggas, nor did they achieve the same positions of responsibility on the team as the candy-asses.

Buck fell into this category. A young black from a rural, Southern town, Buck came from a broken home. He did not remember his father, and his mother, who worked in a factory, did not have the money to either visit him at the University or attend his games. Yet he maintained a close relationship with her over the phone. Buck had gone to a primarily white school back home and felt more comfortable around white people than most of the black players; in fact, several of his best friends on the team were white and he frequently dated several white girls. He had a solid academic background and performed well in his classes, although he was not as devoted to the books as some of the candy-asses. He liked to party, and occasionally got in trouble with the coach for breaking team rules. He spent most of his time hanging around with other whiners and with some of the bad niggas, sharing the latter's critical attitude toward the coach's authoritarian behavior. He felt that the coach did not recognize his athletic potential, and that he did not get the playing time he deserved. He had been warned by the coach about associating too much with some of the bad niggas who liked to party and not study hard. Yet for all their partying, the bad niggas were fiercer on the court than Buck, and could sometimes get away with their lassitude through outstanding play. He could not, and always had the suspicion that he was on the coach's "shit list." Like the candy-asses, he wanted to defer his gratification, do well in school, and get a good job afterward, yet he was not as diligent as they were and ended up going out more. He redeemed himself in the eyes of his peers during his senior year by playing the whole season with a debilitating chronic back injury that gave him constant pain.

James was another player in this clique, who also fell somewhere in between the bad niggas and the candy-asses. Like Buck, he socialized primarily with whiners and with some of the bad niggas, although he was white. He came from a middle class family in a small town near the school, and was recruited to play along with his brother (who was a year younger). James came to the University enthusiastic about college life and college basketball. He threw himself into the social whirl and quickly got into trouble with the coach for both his grades and comportment. He readily adapted to the predominantly black ambience of the players' peer subculture, befriending blacks and picking up their jargon. He occasionally dated black women (although this was the cause of one major fight between him and some of the football players, since black women were scarce on this campus). He had heart, and was willing to commit his body to a fight. The most famous incident erupted during a game where he wrestled with an opponent over territorial advantage on the court. Yet he had neither the speed nor the size of some other players, and only occasionally displayed flashes of the potential the coaches had seen in him.

The final group was known to their teammates as the "*L-7s*" (a "square," an epithet derived from holding the thumbs and forefingers together to form the "square" sign). Members of this mixed group were all middle class, more often white than black. They were the most socially isolated from other team members, as they were rejected for their squareness by all three other groups, and even among themselves seldom made friends across racial lines (the white and black L-7s constituted separate social groups). They came from rural, suburban, or exurban backgrounds and stable families. They were fairly moralistic, eschewing drinking, smoking, and partying. They attempted to project a studious image, taking their books with them on road trips and speaking respectfully to their professors. Compared with other players, they had a stronger orientation to the student population and booster community. They were, at heart, upwardly mobile, more likely to consider basketball a means to an end than an end in itself. Because of this orientation, several of the white players landed coveted jobs, often working at boosters' companies, at the end of their playing careers. They tended to be good technical players bred on the polished courts of their rural and exurban high schools rather than on the street courts of the cities; they knew how to play the game, but it did not occupy their full attention. They had varying (usually lesser) degrees of athletic ability, but they were even less likely than the whiners to live up to their potential. In contrast to the other groups, they had decidedly the least commitment, least loyalty, and least heart.

Mark was a dirty-blond-haired white boy from the West Coast with a strong upper body, built up from surfing. He was clean cut, respectful, and a favorite of the boosters. His sorority girlfriend was always on his arm, and helped create his desired image of a future businessman. He consciously worked to nurture this image, ostentatiously carrying books to places where he would never use them, and dressing in a jacket and tie whenever he went out in public. It was very important to him to make it financially, because he came from a working class family without much money. He had arrived at the University highly touted, but his talent never materialized to the degree the coaches expected. He was somewhat bitter about this assessment, because he felt he could have "made it" if given more of a chance. Like Buck, part of his problem may have lain in the difference between his slow-down style and the fast-paced style favored Coach. He roomed and associated with other L-7s on the road and at home, but he also spent a lot of his time with regular students. After graduation he got a job from a booster working for a life insurance company.

CONSTELLATION OF ROLE-SET MEMBERS

Basketball players generally interacted within a circle that was largely determined by their athletic environment. Due to the obligations of their position, these other role-set members fell into three main categories: athletic, academic, and social. Within the athletic realm, in addition to their teammates, athletes related primarily to the coaching staff, secretaries, and athletic administrators. The coaching staff consisted of the head coach, his first assistant (recruiting, playing strategy), the second assistant (recruiting, academics, some scouting), a part-time assistant (scouting, tape exchange with other teams, statistics during games), a graduate assistant (running menial aspects of practices, monitoring study halls, tape analysis), the trainer (injuries, paramedical activities), and the team manager (laundry, equipment). Let us portray each of them briefly.

The coaching staff was led by the head coach, a black man of enormous musculature. Resembling a football player more than a basketball player, he had the ability to bellow forcefully, like a bull, when he was angry. More often, however, he was stern but compassionate. He had high standards, he gave tough advice, and he firmly commanded respect, but he was sensitive and cared deeply about his players; once he recruited them, he felt responsible for them. Gentle by nature, he could address even the smallest child with sincerity and interest. Yet within his inner circle he was given to raucous practical jokes, magic tricks, and unrestrained guffawing, and the pranks he had gotten into with his long-time friend and first assistant coach were notorious. Extremely intelligent and insightful, he had achieved his current position, in large part, through his ability to figure things out logically, and by applying his keen intuition about people and human nature. From a poor background, he had worked his way up through the coaching ranks, starting at the high school level. Like most coaches, he was passionate about his job, and identified himself completely by it (even his wife referred to him as "Coach").

During our five-year tenure with the team, the position of first assistant coach was held by two different people. When we first came to the University, we met Stubbs, Coach's closest friend and longtime compatriot. One could not help but like this jovial and outgoing black man instantly. Warm, caring, and with a huge belly that shook whenever he laughed, Stubbs would engage anybody in conversation about basketball at any time and any place. His demeanor conveyed the flavor of his down-home Southern upbringing, with his lack of pretension and colorful expressions. He worked hard on developing rapport with prospective players and their families, and was an outstanding recruiter not only because he had a flair for recognizing talent (he had spotted many diamonds-in-the-rough), but because of his natural gregariousness. He was a good foil for Coach because he could play "good cop" to some of Coach's "bad cop" routines, and because he knew him well enough to break him out of his brooding when the heat of the season got too intense. After three seasons at the University he left the team to assume a head coaching job at another university. His post was filled by Stanger, a black man distinct from Stubbs in both character and style. Quiet and unassuming, Stanger struck people as somewhat cold and distant. Tall, thin, and dapper, he was not a typical recruiter. He was less successful attracting players to the team because he had difficulty getting prospects to warm up to him. In fact, due largely to his withdrawn and formal demeanor, no one on the team really got to know him very well, even after two years.

The second assistant, a young man named Mickey, was the highest ranking white coach on the team. Originally brought to the University as a graduate assistant, he was promoted before the start of his (and Coach's) first season. He had the primary responsibility for players' academic schedules and performance, in addition to his recruiting duties, which increased as he gained experience. Handsome, well-dressed, muscular, and macho, he conveyed the feeling of solid Mid-western beliefs and values. He was friendly but somewhat reserved, trying to fill the role of coach despite his youth. Due partly to his inexperience, he lacked confidence for the first few years and had difficulty treading between the players, to whom he was closer in age, and the coaches, whose status he shared. His job, however, required that he make decisions and command respect. He eventually grew into the role, and became fairly authoritarian and rule-oriented. Grateful to Coach for his opportunity, and wanting to learn everything he could, he displayed unquestioning loyalty to the program.

Two different individuals also held the job of part-time assistant over the course of our five years. Fielding was tall, thin, white, bespec-kled, and balding, and looked like a former basketball player. Not youthful like Mickey, he had tried for several years to leave basketball, but found himself continually drawn back to the game. He therefore got a high school coaching job and kept applying for slots on college teams, anything to get his foot in the door. Fielding was a gym rat and a real student of the game. He liked both the politics of the game and talking strategy for hour upon hour. He traveled throughout the region, while he worked at the University, to talk with legendary retired coaches about their experiences, the history of basketball, and his theories of offense and defense. These people eventually advised and helped him, writing letters that assisted him in landing a coaching job at a nearby junior college. When he left, Coach hired Gordon in his place. Shorter, heavier, and more swarthy, Gordon shared Fielding's intense commitment and involvement in the sport. He had formerly been a full-time assistant coach on an unsuccessful program, but left it to work part-time for the University, because it had a successful program from which he thought he could more readily springboard into a coaching career. Beyond riding Coach's coattails, he (like Fielding) would often write to other coaches for jobs and to gain experience and sponsorship. Through his position at the University he had the opportunity to network on the road, meeting members of the coaching fraternity. At home, he had pet projects, players he had singled out to take under his wing. This came at some risk because, like Fielding, Gordon was an "X's and O's" man (that is, they both approached the game through methodical, set offenses and defenses), and this did not fit into Coach's run-and-gun style of playing (bringing the ball rapidly up court, finding an opening in the defense, and taking a quick shot or making a quick pass to the "open man").

Several graduate assistants worked with the team over five years. Todd was a fairly representative example. Fresh out of college, he was there to get his start in coaching any way he could. He would probably end up coaching high school, but might make it to the college level if he "caught a break." He was therefore working on his Master's degree, a requisite for most college jobs and some of the better high school ones. Like all of the lower ranking team personnel, Todd was white, with a background more akin to the community and students than the upper ranking coaches and players. He was a go-fer, doing all the dirty work for the coaches, but still trying to maintain some degree of status over the players. At times he appeared hyperactive, as he rushed around, trying to make himself indispensible to the coaches. And like all the coaches except the head coach, he "dipped" (chewed tobacco). At times, the row of them on the bench during games appeared almost comical, as they tried to dip discretely, spitting their brown tobacco-spit into styrofoam cups which they kept under their folding chairs.

At the bottom of the hierarchy was the team manager. This was a position that turned over every year or two, being filled by an under-graduate student who was on a "work-study" job. Most of these indi-viduals were scrawny little acned white kids who were both efficient and officious. The players clearly regarded and treated them as punks, as they ran around collecting the towels, shirts, underwear, and jock straps, and filling the water cooler for each game. These kids were not interested in the program as a stepping stone to a professional career, like all the others, but were there for the hourly wage and the oppor-tunity to bask in the team's reflected glory.

The final member of the coaching staff was the trainer. This individ-ual filled a paramedical position, applying treatments, taping ankles/knees/wrists, and obtaining and dispensing medicines from the team's doctors. A thorough knowledge of anatomy, the effects of drugs, and the treatment of injuries was required, and younger trainers were the most professionalized. The team's trainer was an integral part of the program, making every road trip and developing a relationship with all the players. As with several other slots, we had a chance to observe two people in this job. The first was Harrington, a dark, handsome, well-dressed athletic man in his early thirties who fancied himself a ladies' man. Some of the players mistrusted him because they thought he looked out for the team doctors' interests over theirs; he did eventually leave to accept a position with the doctors when they opened a sports injury rehabilitation clinic. Flannigan took his place and was welcomed by the team members. Fair-haired and small-boned, he was not as flashy or assertive as Harrington, but did his job quietly and compe-tently. He was a conservative Midwesterner with solid roots, a wife and a young child. Although these men differed in appearance and demeanor, they were both referred to as "Doc."

Mothering the whole group was Coach's secretary, Thelma. A plump, older woman with local roots, she often brought her granddaughter around the coaching offices. She was not the brightest or best educated of women, but she was kind and caring. She typed the players' papers, administered Coach's summer camps, and handled both his personal and professional finances. She knew more about him than any other person, and could be absolutely trusted to keep his confidences. While she was slow and old-fashioned, she brought a homey atmosphere to the office and was very personable in answering the phone and receiving visitors.

Secondary members of the athletic role-set included boosters, fans, athletic administrators (the Athletic Director, Sports Information Director, and their staffs), and members of the media. The boosters could be divided into three main groups: the elite, the inner core, and the outer ring. The elite consisted of a small circle of the big money men and their wives, numbering about two to five couples. These people contributed around $30,000 to $50,000 a year to the program, in addition to buying large blocks of prime stadium seats and hosting parties and banquets. For this kind of money they expected to have open access to the practice court at any time they wanted. The top two supporters, one a Jew and the other an old line WASP, both around 60, also had access to the locker room in the basketball stadium before and after games and during halftime. This gave them the most intense feeling of being a part of the team's inner circle. The elite boosters also liked to socialize with Coach and his wife (although Coach always kept some distance between himself and them). This meant that they could invite Coach over to dinner and expect him to make time for them in his schedule, or they could invite him to their country club for lunch or a round of golf and he would accept. Members of this top echelon of boosters maintain a steady connection to the program, despite the replacement of one coach after another. Some may feel a personal liking or comfort with one coach more than another and vary their friendship patterns accordingly, but they remain steadfast supporters of the school's athletic effort, concentrating their attention on one sport specifically. With this level of booster, the onus is on the coach to get along with them, no matter how he feels about them.

The next group of boosters, members of the University's "Double Dribblers" club, comprised the inner core of the team's supporters. About 60 to 70 people, either alone or in couples, belonged to this organization, for which they had to pay an annual fee ($1000 per year). This entitled them to purchase season tickets in the stadium, to buy elite "slam dunk" jackets, to attend official pregame or halftime fundraising functions (such as cocktail parties or dinners) either at the stadium or in a private club or restaurant. They also attended many of the weekly banquets held during the season. Some of these people were very rich, but many of them were not. They were usually businessmen or professionals from the upper or upper-middle classes. More than money, they gave significant amounts of their time to the team. Double Dribbler members were also invited to perform favors for the coach, either at home or on the road. Some of the most devoted members went to most of the away games. Boosters who drove large recreational vehicles to these games often were asked to transport players' family members or even coaches, the team manager, or trainer. Once there, they provided transportation for the team from the hotel to restaurants or the stadiums. They enjoyed the excitement and having the extra social life during basketball season provided by membership in this group. Attending team functions enabled them to visit more frequently with the coaches and players, and to single out particular players and get to know them. They could then invite specific individuals with whom they had developed a relationship over to their house for dinners or special occasions. Many of these people were older, in their fifties and sixties, and had either grown children or no children. Their contact with the players served almost as a substitute parental relationship. Some boosters took players on fishing trips in the summer, ran over to the dorms to help if one of their favorite players was sick or injured, or cared about them sincerely and treated them like close friends or family. Others saw the relationship more in terms of status, where they could boost their role among their friends and with other members of this club by belonging and giving to the team and players.

The final group, the "Cheetah" club (named after the University's mascot), represented the outer ring of boosters. These people joined a less expensive supporter club ($250 per year) and were entitled to buy season tickets in the stadium. While they did not have a regular round of social occasions to attend, they were occasionally invited to rallies and fundraising events. These people were essentially devoted fans.

Within the academic arena, athletes' role-set members consisted of professors, tutors, and students in their classes, and, to a lesser extent, academic counselors and administrators. The players also tended to regard their families as falling primarily into this realm, although family members clearly cared about their social lives and athletic performance as well.

Socially, athletes related to girlfriends, local friends, and other students (non-athletes), but most especially to other college athletes: the teammates and dormmates (football players) who were members of their peer subculture.

Overview

The main body of the book portrays the socialization experiences of college basketball players, following a chronology from their early experiences with sport through the end of their college playing careers. This begins in chapter 2 with a discussion of their athletic backgrounds and their various recruitment experiences. Next, we present an overview of the expectations they brought with them to college. While many of these athletes' ideas about their social lives were shared, we examine differences in their academic aspirations and show how these influenced their selection (with, through, or by the coaches) of a major. We then discuss their arrival on campus and their early experiences leading up to the official start of basketball season.

During their first year or two on campus they learned the various dimensions of the college athlete status: the athletic, social, and academic roles. We discuss each of these in chapters 3, 4, and 5. Chapter 3 addresses the athletic role: players' introduction to college level basketball, the professionalization and commercialism of this arena, their molding by Coach into University ballplayers, and their interactions with fans, boosters, and the media. In chapter 4 we contrast their social expectations with the reality of the social life they encountered: its isolation from other students, insulation within the athletic dorm and athletic peer subculture, and some of the characteristics of the various cliques. In chapter 5 we present the players' experiences within the academic realm, their handling by coaches, their feelings of detachment from academic responsibility, their classroom disappointments, and their relations with professors and other students. Chapters 4 and 5 also introduce their gradual awakening to the conflict inherent between their athletic, social, and academic roles.

The effect of their intense and often conflicting college experiences on their inner selves was multifaceted. While parts of their selves became expanded and aggrandized, other parts were constricted and diminished. In chapter 6 we discuss the development and character of these social psychological dynamics as all athletes, from the stars to the bench warmers, experienced fame and celebrity, developing the "gloried" self.

Continued involvement in the athletic subculture meant coming to grips with this role conflict and figuring out some way to manage it.

In chapter 7 we discuss the changes athletes made to their expectations of self in each role, their resultant changes in behavior, and the influence of these modifications on their commitment to each role.

As they came to their final year and approached the end of their playing careers, athletes had to deal with how to terminate their athletic participation and identity. In chapter 8 we examine how their treatment by members of the athletic setting changed, leading them to reformulate their conceptions of their experience. We outline the plans they made (or did not make) for the future, and the difficulties they had grappling with the problems of disengagement from their former roles.

We conclude in chapter 9 with an overview of the changes we observed in athletes' selves and the implications of these changes. We discuss players' engulfment in the athletic role to analyze the structure and dynamic character of the self, and the relationship between engulfment and social trends.

2
Role Expectations

HIGH SCHOOL athletes who came to the University left behind the secure and comfortable arena of interscholastic athletics and entered a new realm. They left behind their families, their friends, their coaches, and the athletic worlds they knew. For all the players we observed, it was their first move away from home. They arrived with certain preconceptions and expectations about the nature of college life and Division I college basketball. We now examine the backgrounds of basketball players who came to play at the University, and the expectations and impressions they both brought with them and formed during the early period of their college careers.

Recruitment Histories

The athletes who passed through the University's basketball program were diverse not only racially, geographically, and socioeconomically, but also athletically. Some were highly touted and recruited players, while others had received relatively little attention. We examine and contrast three categories of players according to the different amounts and types of recruitment they experienced: those who were *inundated*, *sought*, and *overlooked*. We also consider these players' athletic experiences, identities, and aspirations.

INUNDATED

About 27 percent of the players we studied had been inundated by recruiters from Division I schools. Typically, these players were characterized by a range of common experiences beginning in their elementary school and continuing throughout their junior high and high school years.

Their first exposure to organized sport usually came early, for some as early as seven or eight (cf. Fine, 1987). Slick, one of the most talented of the whiners, described his first basketball experiences:

> I started playing in grade school, really organized games. You don't find too many grade schools that play organized basketball, like uniforms, officials. We had leagues, trophies given out, most valuable player, and all that way back then.

Inundated players showed an early ability to excel in basketball. As Messner (1990) also found in interviewing elite athletes, sport came very naturally to most of them. Several factors motivated them to continue their involvement with basketball. First, it felt good. It was something they could readily master that gave them a sense of accomplishment and superiority. It pleased them to perform well in this area. Second, it benefited them socially, as they were always among the first selected by their peers to play on teams when it came time to choose up sides. Third, they were encouraged to play by others. Most individuals had a brother, a cousin, a mother, or a father telling them that they were good at basketball and that they should continue to develop their ability.[1] Another player said:

> My brother was always the one who took an interest in my basketball. He'd come and watch me play. He'd take me to summer clinics and all that. He took a lot of pride in how I could play, and so it was sort of a bond between us.

Fourth, they were motivated to play by the extrinsic rewards of sport. At the younger ages this took the form of certificates and trophies. Slick described how he felt about these:

> The trophies they gave out back then were real trophies, not no plastic. Good trophies. And when you was a kid, that's all you

wanted, as many trophies as you could get. That really inspired me a lot.

While some future inundated players were drawn exclusively to playing basketball, others were interested in a variety of sports. They had good all-around athletic ability, and did not specialize at an early age. Their natural athletic aptitude led them to be recognized and rewarded by their peers, family, and community for their sports accomplishments. Depending on their talent in other areas, they began to construct self-identities in which athletics played an important role (see also Messner 1989, 1990; Sabo 1985). Because of the high degree of societal interest in sport, especially at the professional or serious amateur levels, these youngsters developed vivid dreams of careers as professional athletes from very early in their childhoods. The role model of athletics as a path to success was an especially prevalent one in communities where other routes of upward mobility were less available (Edwards 1984; Rudman 1986).

As these individuals passed from elementary into junior high and high school their exposure to organized athletics increased. The league structure outside of school became more competitive (see Fine 1987). In school they entered varsity level competition and found their coaches more serious about playing. Their trophies were replaced with varsity letters and letter jackets, and the casual respect of their peers became more formalized. Some inundated players participated in tournament play during their early years in high school; they went to championship rounds at the local, state, and regional level. Most of them were at least on the varsity team by their freshman year. They usually had significantly more interest in basketball than any other sport, displaying a driving passion to play it. James recounted his feelings about sport at a young age:

> I loved basketball more. I thought about it all the time. I could always play it all year round, in my room and outside, and it's something I could play by myself.

Several inundated players had a very close relationship with their high school coach. They spent time at his house, knew his wife and family, and relied on him in a paternalistic manner. Ben, James' younger brother, who was a highly recruited player and who also played for the

University's basketball team, described how he and James were sought out by the coach as soon as their family moved to town:

> We had just moved in, and our U-Haul van was still in the driveway. Everything was kind of crazy. We were trying to unload the furniture, and Mom and Dad were trying to figure out where to put things. We didn't even hardly know anybody in town, when this car pulled up in the driveway, and out came the basketball coach from the local high school. He had heard a family with two big six foot guys was moving into town, 'cause we were tall, even back then. And before we knew it, we hadn't even been in town three hours, we were down at the high school getting a tour around and playing pick up with the other guys in the gym.

These players developed a bond with their coach and his family that lasted throughout high school. Tyrone, who did not come from as stable a community or family, also felt an intimacy and special closeness to his high school coach. He described this relationship:

> My coach was always looking out for me because I showed some kind of leadership. I had street sense. He always stressed my positive side—he said I was great around people. I confided in him and discussed my personal problems with him. We was really tight.

Those who achieved this degree of intimacy were usually more likely to be of the same race and class as their coach.

As these athletes advanced into the later years of high school, their play became more serious and the competition more intense. They grew in height and bulk, developing their basketball abilities significantly. By this time they were filling the role of the star player and leading scorer on their team. Their talent often took the team into statewide tournament play and gave them the experience of winning major competitions. These victories led them to dream even more strongly of one day advancing to the National Basketball Association (NBA). In this, they were primarily encouraged by their friends and like-aged relatives. Their coaches and older relatives, in contrast, were more apt to regard and speak of their athletic abilities as an avenue toward college. They realized, however, that the route to the NBA was through college, and that in order to make it in the pros they were going to have to put in some time at college. One player described his expectations:

> When I was 15–16 I had some wild NBA dreams that I would just stay in college one year and go right on to the pros. I was six foot eight at the time.

As a result of their outstanding play these individuals received regular coverage in their local media and enjoyed identities among their high school peers as recognized and popular athletes (cf. Coleman 1961; Cusick 1973; Eitzen 1975; Rehberg and Schafer 1968; Sabo 1985; Spady 1970). They saw their names in the paper often, and created scrapbooks filled with newspaper stories and clippings about their exploits. Their level of local fame caused them pride. As Tyrone casually remarked:

> My friends in the park would say to me—"Did you see what you said in the paper the other day?" And I'd say, "Yeah, wait 'till you see tomorrow!"

Their recognition continued to grow. When they went to pep rallies, meetings, or banquets they were always the ones standing up receiving awards. Some even received national media or other athletic attention. Slick described his experiences and how it made him feel:

> My senior year I was elected to the National High School Hall of Fame. They picked the five most outstanding high school basketball players in the country graduating that year and they brought us and our families all down to this place. There was a big ceremony with all these media people and a lot of hoopla. They had made life-sized posters out of us that were backed onto some sort of cardboard so they stood up, and there they all were, just standing there, ready to be inaugurated into that Hall of Fame. And they had Adrian Dantley, Antoine Carr, and Ralph Sampson there with me. I was in pretty good company [the three have had NBA careers]. And so I thought, for sure, I'm a shoo-in to the NBA. It's just a matter of time.

All this stardom and coverage brought them to the attention of the national scouts, who came to watch them play. They could also be seen by scouts if they played in summer basketball camps such as "Five Star," where the scouts regularly watched the participants. Those who were good were written about in the nationally distributed scouting

sheets, subscribed to by almost every major college coach. These athletes performed well and became the targets of recruiting efforts.

Numerous college coaches and their assistants came to watch inundated players. They spoke with them before and after their high school
games, wrote them letters, called them, visited them at home, and
invited them to visit their campuses. This recognition was exciting and
flattering, but it eventually became overwhelming. Damon Evans was
a member of the candy-asses group. He spoke politely, showed others
his respect, and strove to be a good person. While not especially
religious, he believed in God and hung around with some of the more
"Christian" players. He liked to have a good time, but he tempered it
with moderation. Damon came from a rural area where there were not
many white people. During his senior year he was an outstanding
national player and was inundated with media and college coaches'
attention. He recalled his reaction:

> Really, I got tired, 'cause every night they'd call, and you can
> only visit five schools, and it start getting to your head. You get
> tired and you've got to worry about playing, them calling you,
> schoolwork. I had to go over to my girl's house to get my
> homework done.

When college coaches came to visit they would sit in the stands
where they would be easily noticed, showing players they were seriously interested in them. Sitting with them in their living rooms, later,
coaches discussed how the player's style would fit in at the college they
represented. Some coaches made relatively reasonable remarks; others
made more grandiose claims. Slick recalled:

> Coaches would come up to me offering me the moon and stars.
> They would flatter me and flatter their program. Coaches would
> come up and tell you, "I can see the NBA written on your
> forehead," and stuff like that.

Another player described how a head coach emphasized the importance of attending his university:

> People told me I had the talent. Dean Smith [coach at the
> University of North Carolina], he told me so. He said I sure had
> the ability to play pro basketball, I probably would'a had the
> chance, that's what he said. He said that I would make the pros,

definitely, if I would'a came there. And played four years, or however many years, because of his program.

In evaluating prospective colleges, inundated players had various criteria. Their primary concern was basketball—the coach and his program. They selected the University for several reasons: Coach's reputation (he was known as a winner and as a disciplinarian with "good values"); the style of game he played (running, fast break); how much playing time they thought they would get ("He plays everybody —he don't have no starting five"); how much television exposure the team received ("I wanted to go somewhere people could see me on TV"), and the chances they thought they would have of making it in the pros. They were also interested in selecting a college where they could have a good social life. Many players wanted a campus in an urban community (especially those from small towns), not too far from home (so their parents could come up for games), and a moderately large school (6000 looked big to them) with an active campus life where they could make friends but not get lost. A few players also had academic concerns. Like the majority of college students (Moffatt 1989), they wanted a school with a pre-law program, an undergraduate architecture degree, or some other specialty that would prepare them for their intended future careers. Others cared about the quality of their education but were not as clear about their future intentions. They sought merely "a school where academic-wise, you get a scholarship, you come here and get your degree, you can really get a job." A third and larger group did not give academics much thought at all.

Their recruiting visit to the University's campus was fairly uninspirational. Coach's policy was to let them hang around with his players so that they could get a feel for the type of life they would lead. In contrast to other programs, where several players had been taken out for expensive meals, fixed up with dates, offered cash, cars, jobs for their parents, or home remodeling, and been presented with personalized jerseys and/or videotapes hyping them as star players for the program, the University's coach did not attempt to dazzle them on their visit. Tyrone described his recruiting visit:

It was the worst visit of all the schools I went to. Coach never had anything to do with me the whole weekend. Whatever the players were doing that weekend, that was my visit. I saw one booster, and he didn't say too much about the school. Other

visits were more as I expected—pinch me, I'm alive. So many
people coming up and telling me they wanted to be with me,
what they could do for me. Pretty much what a young black
expects when he thinks about going to play college ball —they're
going to give him some money, he's going to sign.

Yet they still came. They came for various reasons, some social (the
school's size, its closeness to home, its urban location, its campus social
life), some academic (its courses of study, its academic reputation, that
it was private), and the majority athletic (the success of the basketball
program, its exposure, the recommendation of their high school coach,
and ultimately the University's coach and what they thought he could
do for them—his reputation, his style of play, that he played freshmen,
and that he routinely gave around ten players considerable playing time
rather than having a first string of five to six players and a second string
who rode the bench).

SOUGHT

A second group of players received some recruiting attention from
Division I major college programs, but they were not overwhelmed.
These players constituted the largest bulk (46 percent) of the University's recruits. Their playing and recruitment histories contrasted with
the inundated players.

Most sought players did not have the same early aptitude for athletics as the inundated players. They impressed their peers, families, and
older friends as being good athletes, but did not stand out as great. As
a result, they were not as successful and did not get as involved with
the game, the trophies, or the winning in their elementary school years.
They thus did not develop self-images as athletes from as young an
age, and had the opportunity to entertain other dreams before getting
locked onto visions of an NBA future.

As they moved into junior high and high school their ability to play
basketball developed. Most sought players did not grow unusually tall
early in high school but, because they enjoyed playing, they went out
for the varsity basketball team. Several played other varsity sports as
well. By around sophomore year, many of them began to abandon
their involvement in these other sports to specialize exclusively in
basketball. Some players formed this decision themselves, while others
acted on the advice of friends and advisers:

My ninth grade coaches got me out of football and said that they think my career should be in basketball. So I started thinking about it. They said I was good in academics, and I might want to go to college. So since there's more good football players you have a better chance in basketball.

Several players did not immerse themselves completely in basketball, remaining involved with other extra-curricular activities such as the band. Because they were talented, this diffusion of interest usually met with the coach's disapproval.

Sought players' high school experiences were diverse. A few played on teams as freshmen or sophomores that had older stars who led their schools into championship play. These individuals had the advantage of being seen by college coaches in their early years and developed a good reputation at those colleges. They also received some media exposure, although it was not directed primarily at them. Playing on a winning team brought them attention from peers as well as coaches and the media, and they achieved high social status. This reinforced their athletic identity and their desire to feed that identity.

Players who did not have older superstars on their teams moved more gradually into the limelight. They advanced through the junior varsity, making the varsity squad by their sophomore or junior years. There was a lot of variability within this group; some individuals were highly talented but not earnestly directed toward basketball, others were steady and dedicated but lacked outstanding ability. Yet despite these differences in talent, for one of several reasons they all received a moderate level of recruiting attention.

Good players who wanted to make it in basketball but who came from little known high schools could fall into this category, as well as players who were second best on their teams behind dynamic super-stars who led their squad to major victories. Ray, an L-7 from the nearby area, was a good example of the latter; playing behind a pow-erful center, he helped take his team to the state finals in his senior year. While the outstanding center was inundated with attention, many schools also talked to Ray. It was hard to separate the accomplishments of the two players, and several schools were willing to take a chance that the championship was not attributable solely to Ray's teammate. Other sought players were good athletes who had academic problems that discouraged many schools from pursuing them. Frank was one of these; a bad nigga from a ghetto background in the Southwest, he had a learning disability that compounded his poor high school education, putting his grades and test scores in the lowest quadrant. Throughout his years at the University, he was a major burden for the academic advisers, who had to find him special tutors and constantly negotiate permission with his professors for him to take oral exams. Still others were simply moderately skilled ballplayers who could fill a role on a particular team, and a coach became interested in them because he had room for another scholarship, or he needed another guard, or another power forward, or whatever.

Future sought players did not develop the clear goal of making it in the NBA as early as the inundated players. As children, they had fantasized about being professional athletes when they watched games on television and played with their friends, but as they aged they learned how to put these fantasies into perspective. For them, the first reconsideration of a life at least temporarily centered around basketball began to occur in their early high school years. In contrast to the inundated players, they worked their way into the idea gradually. Two candy-asses, Marcus and Darian, recalled the change in their attitudes as they slowly let themselves approach the idea of getting a college scholarship:

> I just played because I enjoyed it. But sophomore year I saw a player on my team getting heavily recruited by college coaches who were coming to watch him play. That's when I got the idea that maybe I could go to college, too, on a scholarship.

> I knew my parents could probably send me to a school, but it would have been a much smaller school which wouldn't have been much different from high school. My parents thought it was great for me to go off to a major college. So around the beginning of junior year I started to set my sights on getting good enough in basketball to get a scholarship.

What these players were thinking about was the possibility of using their athletic ability to go to college. They did not seriously think about future careers in the NBA; rather, this idea lay inside them as a suppressed dream, something they regarded as nothing more than a childhood fantasy. As Darian said:

> You always think about that type of thing when you're in any type of sport. From when you're young. But I didn't think about it serious to where I knew I had a shot.

During their senior year their aspirations of getting recruited into a major college program began to look more possible. To varying degrees, they received letters, feelers, or some amount of watching from college scouts or coaches. Their high school coaches were also contacted about them, and had an impact on their future placement. Most of the time coaches gave their players positive references. Buck, however, recalled the opposite:

> He didn't like me because I wouldn't give up band and play on basketball only. He thought I had a bad attitude. So he gave out bad reports on me and made it hard for me to get a scholarship.

These players, who wanted scholarships but knew it was not guaranteed, did whatever they could to help their chances of getting noticed. Summer attendance at the basketball camps and clinics could help lift players from unknown schools or areas to recognition and thus "boost their stock."

Players who were not nationally recognized as being of "blue chip" caliber were rarely recruited by schools outside their local area. Most colleges had limited recruiting budgets, and ventured far away only for clearly superior athletes (cf. Rooney 1980). They left the good players to schools in those players' regions who could woo them more frequently and inexpensively, appeal to players' regional allegiance, and offer them the advantage of being close to home. Sought players, then, were contacted by schools within or near their home state. These schools were generally the less elite members of Division I.

A few sought players signed early, guaranteeing their chances of getting a scholarship. Most were not given this opportunity, however, as coaches waited to see which of their top choices they got before making a commitment to their lesser favorites. Most sought players did not go on the full five visits the NCAA permitted; thus, the interest they received was limited and came later in the season.

In some instances a player of higher calibre would fall into the sought category because his apparent preference for one school dissuaded others from recruiting him heavily. Yet the vicissitudes of the recruiting game occasionally caused these players to become unexpectedly available late in the year. As Rob described:

> I thought for sure I would be going to State University, the way they were pursuing me. They had their coaches down to see me all the time, they had me up for a visit, and told me they liked

the way I played. So no other schools came after me too hard. I guess they knew I was going to State. But then I guess they got some players they hadn't expected to, and at the last minute they had no more scholarships left for me. So I was back on the market with not too much interest, and I was kind of lucky to get picked up by the University.

OVERLOOKED

The third category of players, comprising 27 percent of the group we studied, were fundamentally overlooked by college coaches. A Division I athletic scholarship was usually offered them through some last minute stroke of luck.

These individuals were not extraordinary athletes as children. They were not recognized and rewarded for their athletic prowess at a young age, and they never developed any strong athletic self-identity. Most of these individuals played basketball on their high school teams, but they did not play varsity or become starters until late in their careers, if at all. Apollo recalled:

I went out for the team in high school, but I sat on the bench. I didn't hit it off too well with the coach. He said I had a attitude problem. I thought I might 'a been major college material, if he'd 'a given me the playing time and experience. But instead, I played about eight minutes my whole senior year. I'd be sitting on the bench knowing I wasn't going to play, but dreaming that everybody fouled out and they put me in and I won the game.

These individuals enjoyed playing basketball, but their chances of getting recruited were uncertain. Some had been looked at by major college teams as possible back-ups to more highly favored players. Others were considered by nearby colleges who thought it would benefit community relations to draft some of the "local talent." A few were noticed by coaches who were watching one of their teammates or leaguemates. Several were contacted by schools from other divisions, such as the NAIA, Division III of the NCAA, or junior colleges, and gave serious thought to going to one of these. Most were not recruited at all. Any hopes they had of playing major college ball started to slip away by the end of their senior year when they received little or no Division I attention.

Like the sought players, individuals in this category comprised a varied collection of assorted types. Some were simply players of lesser talent than the sought individuals. There is a hierarchy of talent, and many of these players were at the bottom rung of the Division I pool. Others could be characterized as "diamonds-in-the-rough," players who had not been stars in high school, but who struck a particular coach as having potential. Perhaps it was the chemistry of their team that alerted a scout's attention, or perhaps when a particular coach watched them play he saw something in them no one else did. Some overlooked players were given scholarships because their high school coach had a good reputation. Others were taken on the chance that they might be late bloomers or because their bone structure suggested possible future growth. Many of these players were the gambles, the ones coaches took a chance on; by the time coaches got to them the season was usually over and they had not watched them play in competition.

While most overlooked players were found through these normal channels, coaches found others in unusual ways. They got tips from high school coaches they knew, they heard about them from old friends in communities where they used to live, or they received information from rural scouts or local people who knew them. In short, they found players through the informal grapevine of networks that all coaches work hard to cultivate. Apollo described how he was found through such serendipity:

> One day I was playing street ball in the park near my house and [assistant] Coach Stubbs was picnicking there with his family. He told me he might know somebody who needed a college player, and he told Coach about me.

These players had even lower athletic aspirations than their sought counterparts. They derived considerably less social status from their peers for their athletic ability and consequently had limited self-identification as athletes. Some of them had family members who believed in them and their ability to play, but carving out a future in athletics was a more remote dream for them than for the established high school stars (the inundated and sought players). Not only was the NBA beyond their reasonable fantasy, many of them had to stretch to imagine themselves getting a college scholarship. Few had any plans for the future; if they did, these rarely included either basketball or college.

Lamont, a working class bad nigga from a mid-sized Southwestern city recalled:

> When I graduated from high school I didn't really think I was going to college, not at all. I was thinking about the army, or something—some armed forces, 'cause that's what most of my boys did.

When offered the chance to go to college, overlooked individuals felt extremely fortunate. Apollo described his recruiting experience:

> Coach called me up, said "Son, I heard you can play a little ball." It was July fourth, and he said, "Come on down to the gym by the church." He had his players there, they come down to see if I could play. Ten—eleven guys. I just played that day—about five pick up games. He was watching every second. After we played he asked me, "did I want to go to school?" I said, "Hell yes!"

While some of these overlooked players were signed by Division I colleges at the end of the season, others went to junior colleges or other schools. From a junior college, if they played well and developed their ability, they could move to a major college program after the end of their second year (without having to sit out the NCAA required one year penalty for transferring).

Athletes who entered the University to play basketball thus had discernible patterns in their backgrounds with regard to their athletic experiences, athletic identities, recruitment experiences, and athletic aspirations. While talent was the single most significant characteristic influencing individuals' past athletic experiences and future athletic orientations, there were other, more sociological, factors that affected them as well. Most prominent was the amount and kind of recruiting attention they received, which, while affected by athletes' talent, was also a function of several other elements: their geographical location (some states were stronger basketball centers than others, and remote rural areas did not receive the notice of urban areas); their team's win/loss record; the prestige of their team or league; their high school coach's fame and connections; early signing or other indication of strong early interest (discouraging other teams from pursuing them); their height and physical development; and being the older brother or best friend of an outstanding high school prospect (which could induce the more desirable player to follow). Ironically, individuals with similar talent could find themselves in different recruitment categories, and those who ultimately proved to have the most talent could come from the ranks of the overlooked.[2]

Preconceptions And Expectations

High school athletes brought to college a set of ideas about what they would find there and what their lives would be like. In many ways they anticipated a continuation of their high school situation, only on a more grandiose level. As Tyrone explained:

> In high school, I thought in college I'd be cruising around the park in my car every Sunday looking at the womens. . . . Every time I go home my boys ask me, "Man, how much money have they been giving you? You must be getting a lot because I've seen you on the TV." And that's what I thought back there too, that's what I expected.

High school players thus expected that their future social lives would be rich. They had visions of themselves as "big men on campus," with high social status and popularity because of their team membership. While some were apprehensive about leaving their families behind, they foresaw their college lives as filled with fun.

Athletically, they had mixed expectations, depending on their level of high school attention and recruitment. The inundated players expected to walk right onto the playing floor. As Slick recalled:

> When I came out I didn't look at anybody else as an NBA player —I thought I was the NBA player. I's supposed to be in the game 30 minutes—playing all day—until I got tired, and then I'd come out when I'd feel like it.

The sought players had more modest expectations. Many of them came to the University because Coach gave freshmen a chance to play, and they were hoping that they would see some playing time. The overlooked players were just grateful to have the chance to be there; they had the lowest and most unclear images.

Their final set of expectations concerned their academic lives. Much of the recent literature examining the correlation between athletic participation and academic performance at the collegiate level has posited a negative relationship, suggesting that athletes enter universities either unprepared or uninterested in academics, having the advancement of their athletic careers as their sole intent (Cross 1973; Edwards 1984; Harrison 1976; Nyquist 1979; Purdy, Eitzen, and Hufnagel 1982; Sack and Thiel 1979; Spivey and Jones 1975; Webb 1968). Contrary to this negative image, most of the incoming freshmen we observed entered the University holding higher aspirations and more idealistic expectations about their impending academic experience. They were optimistic about their likelihood of "getting an education" and graduating. Their idealistic orientation and optimism derived from several sources. First, they had been exposed to numerous cultural messages that a college education would enhance their upward mobility and benefit their lives in many ways (cf. Semyonov and Yuchtman-Yaar 1981). These messages were reinforced by their high school coaches, their friends, and their families.

Second, college coaches reinforced these messages. During recruitment the coaches stressed the positive aspects of a college education and the importance of graduating (cf. Cross 1973). The athletes accepted the rhetoric (what Tannenbaum and Noah, 1959, have called "sportuguese") of the sports personnel, but they never really considered what a college education entailed. Thus a third factor fostering their optimism about academics was their naive assumption that after attending college for four years they would automatically get a degree. They never anticipated the amount or kind of academic work they would have to do to earn that degree. They did not realize the focus on analytical thinking and writing they would encounter. As one freshman reflected, he expected that college courses would be an extension of his high school experiences:

> I didn't think about it much, but when I did, I thought it'd be more or less the same here as it be back in high school, no big change. I be passin' all my courses there, but I still be goin' out every night.

Their optimism was based largely on their "successful" academic careers in high school ("I graduated high school, didn't I?") and on their belief that as college athletes they would be academically pampered ("I heard you can get breaks on grades because you a athalete"). Arriving freshmen commonly held the following set of prior expectations about their future academic performance: (1) they would go to classes and do

the work (more broadly conceived by them as "putting the time in");
(2) they would graduate and get a degree; and (3) there would be no
major problems.

Of the entering athletes we observed, 47 percent requested placement in preprofessional majors in the colleges of business, engineering,
or arts and sciences, indicating their initially high academic aspirations
and expectations. As a sophomore, James gave the rationale underlying
this choice of major:

> You come in, you want to make money. How do you make
> money? You go into business. How do you go into business?
> You major in business. And you really don't think about the fact
> that you're going to end up having to take all these business
> courses. It seems the thing to do at the time.

Despite warnings from coaches and older teammates that it would
be difficult to complete coursework as demanding as this while playing
college ball, they felt that they could easily handle the work. These
individuals planned to use college athletics as a stepping-stone to career
opportunities. Early in his freshman year Clyde, a polite, respectful
candy-ass from a middle class black family in the South, stated:

> I goin' to use basketball to get an education. Sure, I'd like to
> make the NBA someday, but you've got to have a realistic plan
> as well as an unrealistic plan. Right now I've got to have some-
> thing to fall back on if I don't make the pros.

Another group of freshmen, who had no specific career aspirations
beyond playing professional basketball (45 percent), were "clustered"[3]
(Case, Greer, and Brown 1987) by coaches in more "manageable,"
athletic-related majors such as physical education or recreation.[4] However, most of these individuals believed that they, too, would get a
degree. Though they had no clear academic goals, they figured that
they would somehow make it through satisfactorily. Somehow these
matters had worked out in high school, and they felt that college would
be no different.

Only a few individuals from the sample (eight percent) entered
college with no aspirations of getting a degree. Either these individuals
were such highly touted high school players that they entered college
expecting to turn professional before their athletic eligibility expired,
or they were uninterested in academics but had no other plans. Their

main concern, then, was remaining eligible to play ball. They never seriously considered the possibility that they would be barred from competition because of low grades.

Early Experiences

Upon arriving at the University, these former high school players found things quite different from what they had anticipated. This realization unfolded slowly, at first, but became clearer eventually. Let us look at the experiences these athletes encountered upon entering the University.

SUMMER

Freshman basketball recruits arrived at the University at a different time of year than other entering freshman. They were given two weeks or so to rest and relax after their high school graduations. Then, in June, they were expected to report to school. Older players followed this schedule as well, so that they arrived back from visiting their families at the same time. Upon their arrival these new initiates were greeted by Coach and his assistants, some of whom they already knew from their recruiting experiences and/or campus visit. Next, they were introduced to other team members who were hanging around the gym or the athletic dorm. Finally, they were taken to see their room and their roommate, usually another freshman from the team whom the coaches thought would be compatible in personality and background.

In addition to their coaches and peers, new recruits were immediately introduced to the boosters. A round of team barbecues, meetings, and dinners were held in the summer to introduce new players to the important members of the supporting community. At these social occasions the boosters fawned on them and flattered them, telling them how great they were, and how great a future they would have with the team. Outside of these gatherings individuals were sought out by particular boosters who became their special sponsors and close "friends," who invited them to their houses and out to dinner, and who slipped them small amounts of money from time to time. The more highly sought the recruit, the more numerous and wealthy his special friends would be. As a freshman, Buck described his perception of forming relations with boosters:

> Just about every player on the team 'as got someone who invites him out to dinner, who looks after him and who likes him more than the others. Those are the people whose house he can go to and sit around and just relax, get away from the other guys, put his feet up, and they'll take care of him. Those are his "sugar daddies."

Boosters provided jobs for all incoming players. Most of these were not very glamorous—pumping gas, selling doughnuts, construction, yard work—but they enabled the players to earn some spending money for the summer, and if they saved, to put some away for the school year as well.

These young, impressionable freshmen were overwhelmed by the boosters. They had never before met such rich people. Although they tried to conceal their awe in public, in private they gawked and exclaimed to each other about the fancy houses, expensive cars, and jewelry. When boosters asked them out and paid attention to them, players were strongly affected. Young, new to this scene, and highly receptive, they became convinced that the boosters had a sincere interest in and affection for them. Along with the coaches and other players, then, the boosters formed an integral part of the new recruits' athletic community and early experiences.

The summer months, before the rest of the students arrived on campus, were a special and formative period for incoming athletes. They worked at their booster jobs and were the only students living on campus. In the dorm, the basketball players provided each other with constant, intense company. They ate together in the athletic cafeteria, they hung around in the evenings and on weekends, and they played a daily pickup game in the late afternoon. Thrust together into each others' sole company, they developed strong bonding and cohesion. As a freshman, Ben described his feelings about the summer experience:

> By the time the three months were over I felt like I was there a year already, I felt so connected to the guys. You've played with them, it's been 130 degrees in the gym, you've elbowed each other, knocked each other around. Now you've felt a relationship, it's a team, a brotherhood type of thing. Everybody's got to

eat the same rotten food, go through the same thing, and all you have is each other. It's the best of times, the worst of times. By the time the year starts you feel like you're a part of the other guys. At this point you can't wait for it to begin, you're getting so anxious.

Through their experiences over the summer, new athletes were inducted not only into a group, but also into a subculture. From the older players they learned what to expect in college life, how to handle situations they might encounter, and what to think. This was fairly casual during the summer, as nothing much was happening. They also made special friends within the team and began forming individualized relations with various members of the coaching staff.

SCHOOL BEGINS

Early August brought the arrival of the football players who returned for pre-season practice. It was followed, in late August, by the return of the remaining student body. Suddenly the quiet campus was transformed into a whirlwind of hectic preparation for the start of the academic school year. The returning students enlivened the campus, but, even more, the returning football players enlivened the athletic dorm. Within two days the dorm population jumped from 15 to about 125 people. All around them were people from roughly similar backgrounds to themselves, at the University on scholarship and facing the dual roles of student and athlete. This was an overwhelming but happy occurrence. Basketball players found people of similar racial and socio-economic statuses, who may have come from the same regional area or type of community as themselves. Away from home for the first time, like many freshmen (cf. Moffatt 1989), they found living in the dorms a stimulating social experience.

Their early academic experiences were similarly positive. The first academic phase lasted from the onset of school in late August until the beginning of practice on October 15. During this time athletes were academically unencumbered by the time and energy required for practices. It was a time to be students. They had quit their booster jobs and were ready to turn their attention to school full time. Yet athletes' academic experiences did not start out like other students'. Unlike other students, athletes did not look over course descriptions, schedules, or general education requirements. Rather, they were registered into specific colleges (business, engineering, arts and sciences, etc.), majors, and classes by Coach Mickey, the assistant coach in charge of academics.[5] They were usually (although not always) consulted in the selection of their college and major, but rarely asked about which courses they would like to take. Some athletes remarked on this occurrence, noting that it was different from what they had expected, as Slick's comments as a freshman showed:

> They never even asked me what major I wanted. They just assumed that I would be a rec [recreation—physical education] major. They're probably right, but you get a certain message when they don't even ask you.

More commonly, they simply assumed that this was the way it was done, and thought nothing of it.

Upon arriving at their classrooms, freshmen athletes noticed a fairly sizable number of other athletes in their courses. They would not recognize until later that they were purposely being academically cushioned their first semester by being placed in the classes of professors known as "friends of the program." As fans of the team, these professors were knowledgeable of and sympathetic to the demands of college athletics. They provided extra assistance to athletes in working on tough assignments, and took the demands of their traveling and game schedule into consideration. In this way the coaches hoped to ease athletes into their school experience and give them some passing credits to fall back on should they encounter academic difficulty later. Being surrounded by other athletes in their classes tended to reduce athletes' interaction with regular students, a fact they occasionally bemoaned but did little to change. Yet their professors were fairly kind, and seemed generally interested in their well-being. Athletes spent these first few weeks in a surreal but happy state, waiting for practice to begin and trying to get by in their classes.

In the first few weeks on campus, athletes' early idealism was strengthened. During the summer months Coach had repeatedly stressed the importance of "getting that piece of paper" (diploma). He cared about his players as people and wanted them to build a future out of their college experience. In fact, one of the main reasons athletes' parents encouraged their sons to attend the University was because of Coach's integrity and values. A church-going man, he was a strict authoritarian with intense personal conviction who did not tolerate rule-breaking or misbehavior. Yet he had a kind heart and cared about his players intensely, both on the court and off. He ran a straight program and emphasized doing things the right way and the hard way.

Once the school year began, freshman athletes attended required study halls nightly, were told how to get tutors, and were constantly reminded by the coaches to go to class. Rob, interviewed during his freshman preseason, showed his idealism through his expectations and beliefs:

> I'm here for two reasons: to get my degree and play basketball. I don't think it's goin' to be no problem for me to get my degree. I want to graduate in four years and I think I will. I think that's really important to Coach too, because he always be mentioning how important the degree is and everything.

Overall Early Impressions

By the middle of October athletes' impressions of college life were a fusion of their general cultural expectations, their specific ideas formed during recruiting, their summer months on campus, and their first few weeks of school. This was a positive time for them and they were understandably optimistic and idealistic. People were wooing them and they were surrounded by new sensations. Out of all the individuals we observed, only one player was so overcome by homesickness that he left to return to his home and family. Any negative feelings or serious questions they might have had were relegated to the realm of the irrelevant.

These athletes' world was pleasant and exciting. They were on a major college campus and they were playing basketball with established, famous players. A whole crowd of "millionaires" was telling them that they wanted to be their friends and falling all over each other to do things for them. They lived in a dorm full of elite athletes who represented a world of potential friends. Their professors seemed sympathetic toward and interested in them. A whole new life was opening up to them, and they were excited about it. Best yet, October 15 was around the corner and soon they would be playing real college ball.

They had come to the University to have it all: the sports, the social life, and the education. The way things looked, it seemed like it would be no problem.

3
The Athletic Role

WHILE COLLEGE athletes' careers got off to an auspicious start, these early carefree days would not last long. They hungered for October 15, unaware that the start of the official practice season would be the start of their disillusionment. From their optimism of early Autumn, they would begin to learn the nature of college athletics, a learning process that would involve more than they had anticipated. They would learn not only how to play college basketball, but also how to think, act, and interact as college athletes. They would become socialized to the life, scene, and subculture of college athletics. This process had its incipient start in the preseason period, but would not fully reveal itself to newcomers until October 15, the day when their lives as college athletes began in earnest.

Role Differentiation

These freshmen had been leading a casual life. They worked their summer jobs, hung around the athletic dorms, mingled with the boosters, and went to classes. They did not view their lives and experiences as separated into distinct roles. As in high school, they fulfilled their responsibilities with, at most, moderate difficulty, addressing each demand as it arose. Then came the radical shift. On October 15, they began to practice in the gym under Coach's official supervision. Gradually, and at a diverse pace for various individuals on the team, they began to perceive a greater specialization to their lives and activities.

They started to recognize that their lives were segmented into three primary roles: *athletic, social,* and *academic.* Their socialization thus progressed from the initial stage of becoming familiar with their surroundings, to learning their roles, the role-set members within these, and the types of relationships that these roles would bring.

Athletic Role Experiences

PHYSICAL ASPECTS OF PRACTICE

With their expectations at a feverish pitch, freshmen athletes joined their older teammates in the gym at 3:00 P.M. on October 15 for their first official practice. Coach, looking like an angry bull, shouted out commands to them as they went through a series of drills. Gone were the days of playing free-form pick-up games. There would be no scrimmaging for now. Instead they worked with the medicine ball, an oversized water-filled basketball that they had to pass to each other while running up and down the court. They ran and passed, raced around the gym, threw balls against the wall, ran figure eights, and completed a series of other debilitating drills that would leave them exhausted at day's end. Though they had been practicing all along and running wind sprints and miles, nothing fully prepared them for this preseason conditioning program. As a freshman, Damon described his early impressions of playing and practicing:

> When I first came to the University I thought the training for athaletes was going to be easy because I had came from a hard basketball coach. I also thought I could breeze by the practices because I am a good runner, but that is definitely not true. We had been playing all summer long, but the first day of practice had finally came. All the players were in the gym to play. But this day Coach was in there too, and I said to myself, "This is when the real him goin' come out." He was tough on us. He never let up. I ran so hard and so long I couldn't even spit. He was the hardest coaching man I've ever seen or heard about. I was not used to running like this every day, after day, after day. I started to feel that if athaletes had to go through all this training, then playing basketball was not worth it.

At night the players tumbled into their beds. They were too exhausted to do much more than eat and sleep. The next day it was back to the practice floor again. Damon continued:

After we started running all the time, I finally got used to it. But then he put in the yelling part. "Run, run, play defense Evans. Run, run, get on the ball. Damn Evans, can you move your feet, son?" Coach yelled so much for the first two weeks that I heard him in my sleep. This was not what I thought athaletics at this school was all about.

Even the seasoned players found the onset of official practice a difficult change. During his junior year Tyrone remarked:

October 15 comes, we don't do what we want to do. The man's out there now. He's watching. You have to show him you've learned what he done taught you.

Every day these vigorous workouts continued, with weekends bringing the dreaded "two-a-days," an especially grueling two and a half hours in the morning, with a break to eat and digest lunch, followed by another couple of hours of practice in the afternoon. This preseason practice period became cumulatively wearing, as Apollo recalled:

It's unbelievably hard. You try to go two-a-days, get up as early as regular students, go to school, then go to practice for two and a half hours like nothing you have ever strained. When you go back to the dorms, you're so tired. The first few days is all right. But then after you've been doing it for weeks and weeks, . . . it's brutal. 'Cause you be so tired. Fatigue is what makes a lot of those guys say, "Fuck it, I'm goin' to sleep." You don't feel like sitting there and reading a book. You're not going to comprehend that much anyway 'cause you're so tired.

College athletes soon discovered that the salient aspects of their everyday lives were fatigue (cf. Edwards 1984) and restricted time for studying, which caused many of them to think about giving up and ceasing to care about their academic work. Thus, rather than using the little free time they had to catch up on their studies, they usually chose to spend it socializing or just sleeping.

For many new recruits, this early experience with the official practice season produced a sense of disorientation and role distance. College basketball did not live up to their inflated expectations, especially in the beginning. The competition was tough and they were suddenly thrust into an arena where they were new, unknown, and surrounded by more established players. One overlooked player described his reaction:

> All these guys that was on the team, they was a star on they team. At least started. They used to tell they stories. I didn't have no stories to tell. In high school I didn't make all-conference or all-nothing. I made all-bench. It felt kind of weird.

Compounding this intimidation was the grueling period of intensive work and training that had to be endured before any of the glamor of public attention could be realized. One player who felt that he would not measure up to the challenge dropped out as the season neared. Another player, Clyde, discussed his feelings about dropping out:

> During the first 40 days of the year it was brutal, especially with the two-a-days on weekends. Coach called it "40 days of hell." That was the roughest part. I thought I was goin' quit plenty times. But my brother told me there's nothin' back there for me now—"You're a man now, you're in college, you have to work." So my dream is to make the NBA for my father. Go to the NBA, make money, and set my mother down so that she don't have to work no more.

LEARNING ROLE PLAY

As freshmen, they also had to adjust to a new status: low men on the team. They had to start at the beginning, which, for some, was a difficult adjustment. As Slick reflected:

> Coming from high school I thought I knew the game. I scored 48 points every game. But here it's, "No, that don't mean nothin'. It's got you here — it's sold you. That's what paid your tuition, 'cause I had to read four pages on you. What that's telling us is that we can work with you. Now I'm gonna teach you how to do it better."

This initiation began with a reintroduction to the fundamentals of the game. Coach and his assistants worked with freshmen on techniques of passing, dribbling, shooting, and rebounding. They discussed the zones on the floor and the passing lanes. Recollecting on this near total re-training, Tyrone remarked:

When I came to college I thought I was a player who could score, rebound. I could run, I could shoot, I could pass. But now, once I got in the college atmosphere I can't no longer run, I can't no longer pass, I can't no longer shoot. That's because Coach go, "Wait, son, you can't do all this. You gotta learn how to do this." Then they go through the training. "You've got to jump up in the air [mimicking], put your hand in a 45 degree angle [demonstrating], and arch toward the basket." When I pass, I like just throwing it to somebody. He say, "No, son. You grab the ball with two hands and pass it." And running, I just barely move. "No, son. You lift your leg up and run."

Fitting into the team concept and learning the nature of the offense and defense was also part of this socialization process. Instead of using the more traditional "X's and O's" approach, Coach taught players to intuitively react to opposing offenses and defenses by going to certain spots on the floor and playing roles. As a senior, Danny described the importance of this training:

You must learn what's going on. You must learn the offense or you'll never get on the floor. You could be the greatest player, but if you don't know how to react and go to certain spots you won't be out there. And Coach hates sitting there watching somebody out there just running. So you're almost like robots— you know where to go.

Throughout this period they were introduced to Coach's favored style of play. In contrast to their previous experiences, they could no longer play in a loose, undisciplined manner, but had to take controlled shots or not shoot at all. As a junior, Lamont compared the difference:

They don't discipline how you play in high school. There are shots I took in high school I wouldn't even think about taking out there.

Throughout this process, Coach drilled the individualistic, "hotdog" qualities out of them and shaped them into team players. This involved a transition from playing a rounded game, being involved in all aspects of ball handling and shooting to a more specialized, role-oriented game. Freshmen came from high school thinking that they could continue to play their old "playground" style of game, but they were taught otherwise:

> In high school you think the only way to make the NBA is to shoot the ball. But Coach says, no. In college they're teaching you how to play a specific spot. And you better do it or you ain't gonna play. The NBA is a big business. They stress a lot on this. The NBA gonna pay you to do one job. They're much more specialized even than college ball.

Beyond relearning the fundamentals and learning the offense and defense, then, players were resocialized as role players. Apollo discussed how the coaches reoriented freshmen:

> They capitalize on what you do good. If you're a good shooter, they're gonna stress all the time, shoot that ball. If you're a good rebounder and a medium shooter, "We need you to get the ball." If you're a versatile player they will stress on something that you can do real good and they'll just bury it in your head that you can do it. "Son, you're the greatest passer in the world." And you go out there and say, "Oh boy, I'm goin' make me some good passes." "Say, son, you can shoot with the best," you're gonna feel comfortable shooting.

Discarding generalized competence in favor of specialized expertise was thus a joint result of Coach's demands and the players' hopes that they might be preparing themselves for a future professional career (the omnipresent NBA dream). Near the beginning of his sophomore year Tyrone discussed his recent meeting with Coach and the new role he saw himself playing on the team:

> This year I have to play rebounding. Coach say, "Washington, son, the NBA know you can shoot. Let's see you rebound. Let's see you do it. You've gotta get nine this year or we in trouble. Nine every game or we ain't gonna win." So in practice what you think I'm gonna be working on? Trying to get the damn ball.

Offense and defense. Anywhere that ball bounces, Washington gotta be there. I go out there and get all bucked up 'cause now I've got this new role I've got to play.

The emphasis on role playing forged these formerly individualistic players into a group that could integrate well with each other into a squad on the court. This involved a transition from the mechanical solidarity of doing it all to the organic solidarity of specialization and interdependence. Later in his sophomore year, Tyrone described what this meant to him:

Right now I'm in a stage, I'm working on becoming a complete player. I'm pretty sure I'm gonna be before I leave here. I don't care who shoots, I'm gonna get the ball when I can; I'm gonna dive for it when I see it.

When I say complete player, I mean a team player. When you come in as a freshman you don't think they're gonna stress on your being a complete player. You think they're gonna stress on your being an individual. . . . In college ball, you learn that you have to rely on so many people.

This shift in their style of play served to further bring home the blunt recognition that their former high school "star" status had been replaced with the lowly status of freshman. Many new recruits, who had relied on their athletic prowess in high school to provide them with a source of identity and status, now found themselves "riding the bench," waiting for their turn. Instead of playing whenever and for however long they wanted, they had to be grateful for getting any "P.T." (playing time) at all. When they went into the game, they were no longer the center of attention but peripheral players. Compounding their loss of star status and identity was their loss of the home crowd of significant others who had reinforced that self-image and supported their sense of confidence.[1]

STRIPPING DOWN AND REBUILDING OF THE SELF

Changes in athletes' style of play were accompanied by significant changes in their selves. Freshmen underwent a rigorous resocialization process involving the stripping down and rebuilding of the self. This parallels Berger and Luckmann's (1966) view of secondary socialization, a rejection of the old reality and legitimation of the new reality. Such transformations are particularly common and effective within highly controlled bureaucratic or social environments, especially in the rigidly isolated and regulated atmosphere of total institutions (Goffman 1961a).[2] While the arena of college athletics is not a total institution, it is characterized by many structural and behavioral similarities.[3] Within this quasi-total institution, identity transformation occurred through a two-part process. Coach worked to transform and rebuild athletes individually and collectively.

The stripping down began soon after the athletes' arrival, with a series of private talks. Focusing on their new lives and obligations, on their new opportunities and responsibilities, Coach made his expectations clear to them. He exhorted them to eliminate their undesirable traits; he worked to drill out of them things like fighting, arrogant and disrespectful attitudes, wild behavior, and inappropriate demeanor. He did this by pointing out the negative characteristics he saw and disliked in each player, at the same time encouraging them to develop more positive characteristics. Two players, Hank and Tyrone, recalled these talks:

> They cut you down, they found out what you really like. You're a pretty good guy. But if you got one of them ole Billy-bad-ass attitudes in the background, they goin' break that first. They goin' to get to that good guy and they goin' show you how to go with it. "Hank, there's a certain charisma in you. You can get along with anybody." And they worked with me for three years. Now it's "Happy Hank." They break that old ghetto-like scene out, they move you away from this old style of living.

> You find out what you are made out of and what the world is looking at you. "Son, you're not this—you can't be no hippie. Take that hippie band off your head. Get that earring out your ear. This is you." This is me, huh? And they build you. "Son, you get stronger, you'll be a killer." So what you do? Go in there and try to lift up everything you can see.

Most athletes' impressions of what their University basketball experience would be like came from their brief recruiting visit and from watching the team play on television. This left them fundamentally unprepared for the rugged renovation in their identities their athletic role socialization would entail. Apollo reflected on the changes wrought in him by Coach and how these were accomplished:

> He tamed me down a lot, no question. Mostly through his talks and reasoning. He was always able to reason and I listened. He might not 'a thought I was listening, but in the long run he seen I was. He'd call me into his office and talk to me many times— all the time. He had the ability to make you believe the things he was telling you.

Another player, in reflecting back on the effects of this rebuilding, suggested that Coach's tailoring transformed players into some version of himself:

> There're times I'll catch myself coming out of Coach's office, then go see Apollo, and it's almost like they're the same person. He pretty much builds the image of hisself somewhere along your mind.

Coach's private talks were reinforced by individually tailored strategies for specially handling each player. Like other coaches (see Feinstein 1986), he used psychology and "mind games" on his players. He sized them up and worked on a fluid and evolving plan to evoke the most from each of them. Some had to be built up, others cut down. They all had to be kept at the peak of their motivation: neither too cocky nor too dejected. He described how he differentiated among various types of players and decided what approach to use with each of them. These included delicate, sensitive individuals, consistent achievers, moody and temperamental players, spoiled brats, underachievers, overachievers, and a whole range of others. Coach gave his philosophy for handling some of the difficult cases:

> There are some people that you have to strip down. Guys that have been pampered. They're especially jealous of other guys getting my attention. They're watching all the time what you're doin' for others, and they come complaining. Take Brandon. He was pampered by his high school coach's *total* attention and now he don't have that no more. He couldn't stay at [other programs] because there were other guys there who were getting all the attention. I told him, "Your high school coach destroyed you,

son. He gave you everything, and therefore you can't accept
being just one of the other guys now.". . . He's constantly trying
to get to me. Coming 'round in front my face, making sure that I
take a look at him, that he gets my attention. So when I see him
now, I just ignore him.

Other players, in contrast, did not require such strenuous and inge-
nious treatment:

There are some players that you don't have to strip down. Marcus
Howard, you don't have to strip him down. He goin' be Marcus
Howard every day. I used to yell at Marcus just if he made a
slight mistake just so the rest of the guys wouldn't say, "God
dang, you don't never say nothin' to Marcus." And believe me,
they know when you never say something to a particular player
. . . Now you take Evans. He is constantly looking for acceptance. Every day he says, "Coach, how'm I doing?" So I try to
help him by saying, "Now this is what you oughta do, this is
how you oughta slow yourself down." He's one of the few guys
who are constantly wanting to know how he's doing. And those
kind of people I think you can help more than the ones that don't
say nothing.

While Coach's strategy in handling his players was clear to him,
they often could not see the plan behind it, and were upset by their
treatment. As one player complained:

I'm lookin' for some encouragement from the man, but he doesn't
even try to motivate me at all.

Yet this was part of his carefully orchestrated strategy of handling
players. He had to manipulate them to the precise point where they
were committed enough to their athletic role and future that they held
it as their first priority and sacrificed everything to it. At the same time,
he had to keep them from entertaining dreams so grandiose that they
neglected their classes and university-related responsibilities because
they were dreaming of jumping to the NBA every day. Buck described
how Coach motivated him:

College coaches give you that dream when they're recruiting you.
Anything that guy say, you'll believe it. He's not your Mom, not
your friend, but that man who came and got you out your
mother's house. And what he's telling you is you've got a chance

to fulfill your dream. And let's not get pig-headed about it, but you do get a little hungry. If he raw dogs you your dream is there but your confidence is not there. It's a balance he has to hit. They do it in private in their office when nobody's around so you don't tell everybody else. And when you walk out of his office and two of your friends say "Hi," you may say "Hi" back but you don't see 'em. "I'm NBA. I'm gone."

Coach continued stripping down and rebuilding players through a series of collective public shaming rituals. During these degradation ceremonies, he would openly denounce players in front of the whole team. He would rant about the attitudes or behavior of "certain parties" or "hopeless cases," and threaten them with ineligibility, benching, suspension, or non-renewal of their scholarship. No players, not even the candy-asses, were immune from these tirades. These sessions were serious, intense, and, due to the force of Coach's personality and institutional authority, intimidating. Sometimes he would chew them out after a practice if he felt they hadn't listened to him or had deviated from his game plan. Other times he railed at them if he had heard reports from boosters or other people that they had behaved inappropriately in public or at someone's house. Gross and Stone (1964) have suggested that such instances of deliberate embarrassment may be intended as both displays of power by the perpetrator and as negative sanctions against the embarrassed. They may cause their recipients to feel all the negative feelings associated with embarrassment: weakness, inferiority, low status, moral guilt, and defeat (Goffman 1967:101–2). In their structural resemblance to military hazings and the humiliations imposed on new members of extremely cohesive work groups (cf. Vaught and Smith 1980), they symbolize rites of passage into an established social world. These public and private assaults on their selves jarred athletes into dislodging from their old self-centeredness and made them ready for molding.

Coach also used these degradation ceremonies to set the mood for the team, building their confidence up or tearing down what he perceived as an excess of cockiness and inattention to immediate concerns. Buck described how the whole team was influenced by Coach's mood of the day:

However he walk onto the court feeling that day, you got to pretty well be prepared to go with it. If he's up, you gonna have a okay time. But if he's in a bad mood you know you gonna go through a sorry-ass dragging and you might as well just accept that fact.

Tyrone and James described how Coach used the NBA dream in meetings to motivate and/or puncture them:

> You work so hard. He [Coach] say, "Son, you keep this up, you're a first round NBA player." Or in a meeting he may say, "Everybody here think they're a NBA player. I'm gonna tell you my honest opinion. Such and such, such and such, and such and such really have a chance to make it." So you're gonna feel good when he say your name. Like, "Hey man, I ain't spinning my wheels after all." Or else you're gonna feel depressed if he don't.

> Coach keeps that idea in your head that you could be the next Michael Jordan, you've got this and that. He manipulate you in that way. A lot. During the summer in a team meeting in the locker room he said, "There are 14 guys in here with the ability to play basketball if they really want to work." And then a few weeks ago he called us nothing but a bunch of dreamers, and that only one out of this whole room would probably have the chance to play pro basketball. That's just statistics. He'll throw the dream shit on you to get you up, then he'll throw the realistic shit on you to cut your ass with it, then he builds you back up.

For Coach, the aim of this stripping down and rebuilding went beyond trying to mold players into an integrated, high performance team; he sincerely wanted to help them mature:

> When I talk to players I'm talking about just growing up as an individual, coming to school, gonna see some different things and learn how to handle it. Every one of them will become their own man by exercising their own choice. That's what I told they mother and father when I was in they house—"When I take him from here he might be a boy, but when I send him home in four years he'll be a man."

One of the ways he did this was by working to instill discipline and respect in them. As he noted:

> I think this game is strictly a game of discipline. The guys that are the most disciplined are your better people and your better

teams. And I think discipline comes from respect, which partly comes from fear. But fear can be good and bad. That's why I'm looking for respect more than fear. The toughest part of the job is to be both a disciplinarian and also make them [players] feel I'm a nice man.

PROFESSIONALIZATION

Another major change athletes encountered once the season officially began involved the professionalization of their sport (see also Sack and Thiel 1985). In high school, and even during summer pick-up games, they had played for fun. With the onset of practice they soon learned that this previous frivolity would be absent. As Damon remarked, it was more like work:

> You have to put your time in. I guess you could call it work. You have to go through the motions all the way through whether you want to or not. In high school it was, "Oh boy! It's sixth period. Let's go play some basketball!" You had a kick to it when you went to play that's not there anymore. It's more like I've *got* to go out there and do this.

College athletics, they found, was characterized by an occupational atmosphere (see also Ingham 1975; Porto 1985; Sack 1985). Their exchange of physical labor for college tuition made athletes conceive of themselves as quasi-employees of the University, their signing and scholarships regarded as features of their employment contract.[4] There was constant talk and awareness among them of business, finance, and profit. They knew that the University mounted its athletic program to achieve a profitable entertainment product. College athletics was an arena of big business, much like professional basketball except on a smaller scale. The talent was more diffused, the setting was educational rather than professional, and players were paid in scholarships rather than salaries, but they knew they were making money for somebody. The University expected its athletic program to support itself by bringing in enough contributions to completely cover the cost of scholarships and recruiting. Ticket sales could then be used to help pay the coaches' salaries. On a grander level, there was the hope that a prominent and successful team would attract more donations to the school's general fund, and attract a wider pool of applicants whose parents would contribute to the financial welfare of the University.[5]

Through a variety of remarks made by the coaches and older players, young freshmen became aware of the *commercialized* nature of college athletics (see also Coakley 1982; Edwards 1984; Eitzen 1979; Hoch 1972; Lance 1987; Sack 1977; Underwood 1980a). They learned that "there's a lot of money ridin' on us." This awareness first dawned when they heard about money being offered by other schools to recruit star athletes. It blossomed when they came into more contact with the boosters who supported the program. The longer they stayed in the program and hung around the older players, the more they recognized that the commercial nature of the athletic enterprise pervaded every aspect of their experience. They knew that the lack of a minor league system gave colleges the exclusive monopoly on young basketball talent. Colleges and the NCAA maintained a firm grip on this period of ballplayers' lives because they cashed in on it for large television and other revenues (see Weistart 1989). As one player explained:

> They know they got to make it look like they doing something to solve the problems in college athletics because if they don't, someone might finally say, "This system ain't working," and then basketball players might not be forced to go to college that don't want to. And then there go all they money.

Universities' attachment to attaining and holding the commercial benefits associated with big-time athletics caused other facets of athletes' experiences to pale in comparison to their athletic requirements. They knew the money that they brought in was ultimately more important to the University than the integrity of their educational experience. As Marcus expressed:

> You hear the stories about how much this booster just gave to the program, or how much the school got from bein' in the tournament or one of the schools in they conference bein' in the tournament. With that kinda money hanging over the program, how's a coach goin' to tell you, "Don't come to practice if you got a really important paper to do." The University's got too much at stake to let the coaches off the hook, and who has to carry the brunt of the pressure at the bottom? The athaletes. That's who pays the price.

The commercialized nature of the sport led to a great deal more emphasis being placed on *winning* (cf. Lance 1987; Odenkirk 1981; Underwood 1980a). While sportsmanship was valued, it did not occupy the same level of importance as winning (see also Vaz 1982). Everything was evaluated in terms of games won and lost. When Coach first took over this floundering program, to have a season that was considered successful, the team had to win a majority of their games and beat their cross-town rivals. After the first season with its tournament victories, the stakes rose. Having a winning season required at least 20 wins and an invitation to the NCAA tournament. This escalated by the third year to the expectation that the team do well in the NCAA tournament. Like people pursuing other careers, the athletes on the team wanted to perform well. Their personal desires paled, though, next to this institutional pressure to win. As Clyde explained:

> In college the coaches be a lot more concerned on winning and the money comin' in. If they don't win, they may get the boot, and so they pass that pressure onto us athaletes. . . . I go to bed every night and I be thinkin' 'bout basketball. That's what college athaletics do to you. It take over your mind.

Every year Coach went through a progression where he began the season trying to help the players get a firm grounding in the values and behavior he regarded as beneficial to them. He focused a lot of attention on their school performance, on their fit within the community, and on their adjustment to college. He instructed his assistants to oversee their classwork, their social lives, and their overall welfare. But as the year progressed and the season got underway, both he and his assistants became preoccupied. The demands of their jobs overwhelmed them, so that they lost the time and inclination to promote all aspects of the players' welfare. Between running the practices, obtaining and showing films on upcoming teams, traveling out of town on recruiting trips, meeting with boosters and reporters, and attending to the steady flow of crises that arose, they became totally absorbed in the core aspects of their athletic work. Everything else was cast off into a peripheral residual category. To take time and attend to other matters would cut into the critical demands they constantly faced. To not do everything they possibly could might contribute to a loss, and that could cost them all their jobs.

Moreover, the intensity of the athletic world caused them to diminish their interest in anything that did not directly relate to playing games and building the program. As one player observed, "I think even the coaches that care about academics the most can't afford to when the season is on." Thus despite their sincerely altruistic goals and intentions, the structural pressures coaches encountered engrossed them, precluding their attending to athletes' social or academic roles. Athletes' overwhelming by the athletic role, then, cannot be superficially attributed to the corruption or ill intentions of their coaches.

Athletic Role-Set Members

After their most critical athletic role-set members, the coaches and their fellow athletes, were another group of people who interacted with players primarily through their athletic role: the media, boosters, and fans. While new players had had some exposure to these people during the summer, it intensified greatly once the season began.

MEDIA

Most players did not see many members of the media before the season began. Occasionally, a summer press conference would be held upon the arrival of some highly touted high school player, but these were rare. For most freshmen, their first exposure to the media as college players came on October 15. For the first day of practice the local newspaper and television stations always sent reporters and a mini-cam crew down to the practice gym to get some footage and quotes for the evening news and daily paper. They filmed the scrimmage and conducted some interviews with a few veteran players.

Shortly after this the team scheduled its official "media day," where radio, television, and print journalists had the opportunity to interact with the players and coaches. This was a fun event for the players because they posed for action and still shots for promotional and other purposes. By this time, they had been watching the football players get all the media coverage, and they yearned for some themselves. Reporters were rarely seen again by players until mid-November, just before the start of the playing season.

At that time they once again appeared at practices, wanting stories about how the team was doing, how it compared to last year's team, and how various players and/or coaches forecast the upcoming season. From among the various media people, Coach had his individual likes and dislikes. He especially liked Del Ellison, the avuncular head sports reporter for the local television channel that carried his weekly show. Del was a slightly plump, gray-haired man in his fifties who was warm and kind. He was referred to affectionately as a "homer" because he represented the local interests and unabashedly rooted for the team while covering them. The most distrusted sportscaster was Gary Grant, the main stringer for one of the local papers, who often wrote critical articles. Many stories abounded in the team's subcultural lore of people he had "slammed" after interviewing them.

While Coach never explicitly banned his players from talking to any particular reporter, he tried to steer them away from doing depth interviews with journalists such as Gary Grant, or others who had done unfavorable features about players, coaches, or the program in the past. In addition, he gave preferential access to Del Ellison and his television station, by allowing them on the practice floor and into the locker room at times when other reporters were excluded. The ostensible purpose for this greater access was to allow the mini-cam crew to obtain footage that could be aired on Coach's Sunday morning half-hour television show. In effect, however, the station benefited by having filmed interviews and footage of practices and interactions from other days and events that they could show on the nightly news to scoop their competitors. This special relationship was based largely on the rapport between Del and Coach; this newscaster was a gentleman from the old school who never sought to create dirt or exposés, and who could be counted on to help the program present a favorable image to the community. In this way he had a symbiotic relationship with the program: to the extent that he helped the program develop a popular following, it created interest in the team and generated an audience for his show (see Altheide and Snow 1979). While the other stations occasionally complained about this differential access, the University's basketball program was the most popular team in town and they did not want to unduly risk alienating it.

Once the season began in earnest, team members saw media person-nel. Contact was usually confined to certain predictable times and places, however. Reporters did not follow players around and intrude into their academic or social lives unless they were doing a special

profile on them, and such coverage was cleared with Coach and the
public relations officer beforehand. They could generally be expected
to show up at games, some practices, awards presentations and banquets, and the weekly Monday media luncheon. In addition, Coach
had a weekly call-in radio show and a television show, to which he
often brought one or two players.

The most intense media barrage occurred on game days. Players
were usually not excessively bothered by reporters before games. Reporters were among the crowd that began assembling two hours before
the game, along with the main boosters and the members of Coach's
inner circle, and they milled around, setting up their equipment and
engaging in friendly banter with friends and acquaintances from the
program and other media people. They did not intrude into the locker
room during the halftime or immediately after the game, as this was
reserved for the team's inner circle (team trainers, doctors, managers,
assistant coaches, graduate assistants, academic advisers, and members
of the community or university who were close friends of Coach).
After the game, as the players filed into the locker room exuberant
from winning or depressed from losing, they collected into a group to
be addressed by Coach. They could be chewed out or praised, singly
or collectively (it often had no relation to whether they won or lost).

Once Coach finished addressing the team (five to ten minutes) he
headed back to the floor of the arena for his post-game radio show.
Sometimes, if things were too heated in the locker room, or if he had
to leave immediately to catch a plane for a recruiting trip, he sent out
his first assistant to do the show for him. Once he left the locker room,
however, the media descended, en masse, for their interviews with the
players. As they pressed into the area they created a tight crowd,
because the locker room was composed of only three rooms, one lined
with benches and hooks for hanging clothes (no lockers), a second
where players could lie down and get taped, and a third containing a
sink, toilet area, and group shower. Team members who had not
played dressed quickly and left. Players who were not being interviewed undressed, showered, changed into street clothes, and also
departed. Those focused on by the reporters were trapped in the
bench-lined room as they tried, slowly, to undress and make their way
to the showers, all the while dogged by reporters. During this time
they were asked questions about the game, about their lives, and about
their teammates. There was no pause to grant them either physical,
mental, or emotional privacy, and the crush was intense.

Generally speaking, players' relationships with reporters were polite and friendly but not close. These ranged at the extremes from concerned and kindly to distant and non-trusting. Some reporters were around more than others, and some players were more interested in the media than others. Local print and television reporters were more regular than the national media, but the radio announcers spent the most time with players, as they were part of the traveling squad and often rode with the team on the bus to away games. Yet even during these encounters, reporters usually rode in the front of the bus and spent most of their time talking to the coaches. Every media person had his or her favorite player, with whom they would talk more often, or whom they respected. One of Del's favorites was Lionel, a middle class black member of the L-7s. Lionel was a walk-on, a non-scholarship player who participated in all of the team's activities, yet, at first, paid for his own tuition and lived in the regular dorms. Although he was less talented than the scholarship players and got into games only in the closing minutes when the team had a guaranteed lead, he was a popular player with the students and fans. He symbolically represented victory, and displayed sustained effort with minimal reward. He was also well liked because of his good-natured, easygoing personality. As a communications major, it was Lionel's dream to go into broadcasting. Consequently, when he graduated, Del gave him a job at the station working with him. This opportunity came about not only because of Del's relationship with Coach, but out of the special friendship and mutual respect between Del and Lionel.

Reporters, thus, did not flock around all players equally, but had favorites they solicited on a fairly regular basis. The star athletes were among their first choices, but they soon learned that some of these individuals could provide poor interviews (they were "bad copy"). Shy players were also shunned by reporters, except when they had performed incredible feats during the game. Cocky players who were willing to speak out in a bolder fashion were quickly discovered. Players who were interested soon learned what kinds of comments attracted media coverage. As Tyrone said:

You put on a good performance one night and when they stick that microphone in your face you blow out a big proportion of that game and everyday they'll want to run in and go talk to you 'cause you're gonna yak. And it's gonna make they paper look good.

Slick explained:

> They like to hear things like a lot of background—human inter-
> est—Mom and Dad. If you say stuff like I had a poor night, I
> didn't feel so good, they're gonna write three words down. But
> if you say things about your personal background they're writing
> like crazy and you can be sure you'll see it in the paper the next
> day.

Players varied according to their own interest in attracting media
attention. Some consistently enjoyed seeing their name and words in
the paper. Apollo described why he sought attention:

> I always liked to play to the audience, even in high school, even
> though I didn't get much time. I'd feel the excitement of the fans
> cheering and I'd use it to help pump me and my teammates up.
> It's a very emotional game, basketball. But I never did get much
> "pubs" [publicity], I was always behind most of my teammates.
> So when I got to college I was tired of that. I wanted to get some
> of the pubs myself.

Other players, in contrast, regularly declined interest in getting media
exposure, as Clyde explained:

> Some of the things I heard in interviews or read in the newspa-
> pers that my teammates said. [Pause] I'm not saying it was wrong
> for them to say that. I just wouldn't say it. As far as the media
> goes, I always just dodged it. I never would give them an answer
> that would lead to another question. I answer enough not to be
> rude, but if I'm quoted, I have my butt covered.

Some players had ambivalent feelings about press coverage, being
attracted to it but wary of it. They went through fits and starts of
courting and rejecting reporters. Others changed their feelings about
media coverage, becoming interested in it early, when it was a novelty,
and getting bored or disenchanted with it later. One player explained
why he had retreated from his earlier role as a media favorite:

> I was the kid that everybody knows—that was my role. I stayed
> with it a little while but gradually it went away from me. I didn't
> no longer want to be the guy walking around with his chest out
> going, "I'm Delray Morrison."

A final group of players was uninterested in the media at first, only to develop an interest in and aptitude for it later. These players were uncertain in their early years about their talent and role on the team, not moving into a leadership position until they became juniors or seniors. In the beginning, then, they did not feel like they had anything worthwhile to say to the press. They came into a position of speaking for the team, when they were selected as captain or elected most popular player.

Despite their natural propensities to court or withdraw from media attention, there were some kinds of self-presentations that Coach tried to lead them toward or away from in their interviews. This was never approached formally, but rather in reaction to a specific instance. If players handled the media discretely and knew how to avoid making the wrong kind of impression, Coach left them alone. Only when players said something Coach found offensive would he bring them into his office for one of his private chats. Tyrone described how Coach steered players toward the team's party line:

> The media is lookin' for you to say "I." They like to hear you boastin' about you personal exploits, for you to talk about you. Most coaches want you to talk about the team—"Don't ever state just 'I.'" They read that and they pull you in the room. "When you start going 'I,' 'I,' 'I,' the other team members shy away from you. Say 'we,' 'we,' 'we.' You compliment the other players. I don't want to be reading about you 'till down at the end if that's who they're interviewing."

Through these and other talks the players eventually learned how to represent their program, how to avoid hurting themselves, their coach, and their fellow players, and how to manage the front that was desired. They learned how to talk sportuguese, shielding inside secrets and misbehavior from outsiders, while presenting a positive, uncontroversial, and often bland public front. They had to learn how to present the collective image of the team, emphasizing others' achievements before their own, and teamwork before individuality. They had to learn how to field questions that were often repetitive, mundane, or provocative, and respond politely. But because Coach was not totally authoritarian about the media, players did have more leeway in presenting themselves to the press than at some other teams (cf. Feinstein 1986).

When they were interviewed at practices, banquets, on Coach's radio or television show, or at other times, it lacked the intensity of having just played the game. Only in the post-game melee did they have all their emotions aroused, the physical drain of having played a gruelling game and the surge from the emotional interaction with the crowd. At this time, the media represented one more source of pressure, excitement, and aggravation added to the whole scene. Reporters conveyed to players the feeling that the whole community (or sometimes the whole country) was watching them, that their actions were more important than those of the ordinary person, and that being in the limelight of public attention was where they belonged. They were attractive to the media because they were basketball players, and that became their overridingly salient feature. The intensity of the media attention they received was thus important, drawing their inner focus and sense of self to the athletic role to a greater extent than it had ever been before.

BOOSTERS

Boosters made up a second important group of athletic role-set members. Players' contact with boosters before the start of the practice season consisted mostly of a meeting or dinner with some rich booster during their recruiting visit and a small round of parties shortly after their arrival in town. They had more extended relations with one or more boosters over the summer who favored them, or who had provided them with a summer job. Not all players were fortunate enough to be selected by a booster as their favorite. Darian described his first impressions of the booster scene:

> When you're young and you watch it on the TV it all looks so good, but then you get there and certain players are having so much done for them, other players are struggling, other players don't know what the hell's goin' on. Some are trying to adapt. You don't see all this when you watch it on TV, you see that's where I want to go *play*. That's all what's in your mind.

During the summer only a small circle of boosters (around 25 people) were rabid enough about the team to remain actively involved; most let their attention lapse, picking it up again in the fall. New players, then, with only their summer experience to draw on, had a vastly underestimated image of in-season booster involvement with the team.

Early Season. On October 15, when the practice season officially began, members of the hard core booster group were in attendance. The balcony in the practice gym housed the interested and curious. Those three or four boosters with a "special" relationship to the team (who gave large amounts of money and socialized with Coach on a year-round basis) had the privilege of being on the floor of the practice gym, where they could chat with players, the assistant coaches, the team manager, the trainer, or one of the graduate assistants. Their access to the sanctum of the inner elite signified to them, and to those less fortunate watching from above, that they were "members" of sorts. They were permitted a vision of the team denied outsiders (although their access was not complete, as there were other team meetings—the chewing outs—to which they were not invited).

This was, then, a source of status coveted by many but attained by few. Beyond the status boost they received, attending the opening practices marked a time of excitement and anticipation signifying the launching of another season and all the hopes for a successful year that it brought. It also symbolized the renewal of contacts with old friends, since the core group of active boosters allocated a significant portion of their lives spending time at games, practices, going on road trips, traveling to tournaments, attending team functions and banquets, and socializing with team members.

During the off-season this group was fairly dispersed, but the start-up brought everyone back together, and there was a strong feeling of camaraderie. Much of this friendly tone was set by Coach through his warmth and openness to outsiders (some of which he considered to be a part of his job, but much of which was genuine). Talk was exchanged, then, about what people had done during the off-season, and boosters caught up with the new things in players' and coaches' lives.

Yet players' contact with boosters outside of school was still limited. It was a few weeks into the practice season before more extensive relations began. By November, the players were starting to see more of the boosters. Coach had a program where his assistants lined up individual players or pairs of players with boosters for dinner on Sunday nights. No meal was served in the dorms this night, and Coach wanted to make sure his players ate adequately. At another level, this also increased the contact between boosters and players, which Coach sought to do whenever he could, to promote boosters' feeling of involvement with the team. Players soon learned that these dinners involved dressing up, being on their best behavior, and spending a considerable portion of the night socializing with boosters. Some players, especially the younger ones who were innocent and receptive, enjoyed these get-togethers. Apollo recalled his early years:

> I used to kind of like it 'cause I used to always learn something, every time. I learned most of what I know [about rich white people and their culture] by just looking and listening—observing.

Many of these freshmen held idealistic attitudes about their relationships with boosters as well. As a senior, Clyde reflected back on his feelings and attitudes toward the boosters during his freshman year:

> My freshman year, I came here with a big smile, big expectations, wide eyes, and a lot of dreams. And I openly accepted a lot of people into my life, a lot of boosters. I liked meeting new boosters. I thought you got to see who is really nice, and the togetherness of everybody. I liked the picnics, the way they'd talk to you, all that attention. I thought they were really interested in me as a person.

Other players did not feel quite as comfortable around this group of rich white boosters. Interacting with boosters felt awkward to these players, many of them teenagers from poor backgrounds, because they saw boosters as people who were above them in the ways that we traditionally judge status in our society: race, income, age, educational level, and occupation (Bogardus 1959; Hodge, Siegel, and Rossi 1964). As Damon expressed:

> Where I'm from the whole town is black. I never did see no white people before I came here. And there's only so much I can take of that. I don't feel so comfortable around white people.

Still other players had a combination of reactions. Tyrone recalled:

> When I first got here the atmosphere around me—what's up, what is this? We'd be goin' out to eat in all these fancy places like I never seen before. And these boosters was cutting up they steak

in little pieces, I was putting big hunks in my mouth. I was uncomfortable. I wasn't used to none of that. It wasn't me.

Playing Season. Whether players felt comfortable spending their time with boosters or not, the demands on their schedule grew as they moved into the playing season. Now, in addition to the regular Sunday nights out, they were frequently required to go to team meetings or out to dinner with boosters on weekday nights. Freshmen often had a hard time understanding these demands on their presence:

> There's a team meeting over at the Rich's tonight. Why? Why aren't we meeting over at the dorms? [At the Rich's] it means we all have to get dressed up and it shoots the whole night. Okay. Why? These are the questions the players don't even ask.

A further problem players incurred from spending so much of their time attending booster dinners, functions, and meetings was a drain on their time for schoolwork. When a booster function was announced, they had no choice but to attend. As a result, their homework assignments, from reading, to writing term papers and take-home exams, to studying for in-class exams, were often neglected. A conversation between two older players and a freshman shows how new players became socialized to this reality:

> BUCK: I didn't go out to eat with nobody since last basketball season. But as soon as the season starts, and the TV cameras and the newspapers come, they're gonna be calling up, saying, "Let's go out to eat."
>
> BEN: Why don't you do the right thing and say, "Why do you just care about me between November and March?" Why do you go out?
>
> BUCK: Because if you don't Coach'll "go off." . . . I don't want to fuck around with these boosters but I know I have to, because if I don't, they'll say, "Buck Moseby said no, he didn't want to be associated with us." If they want to take you out to eat five times a week, you've gotta go.
>
> BEN: But what if the guy's not nice, if you don't like him? I'm polite, I have good manners. I could say it nicely. I wouldn't go.
>
> JAMES: But you would have to go.

BEN: Really? I have to? That's teaching me something. That would trip me out. If I didn't want to go then I would go in and tell Coach.

BUCK: He'd say you've got an attitude problem. He'd say (mimicking), "Now people are trying to give you a free meal, and you don't want to do it? I can't believe that!" And then that's another check on his bad side for you. And that's one thing for sure you don't want to do.

Cultivating Booster Relations. As the players spent more time at the University, got more familiar with the booster scene, and were socialized by older players about the boosters' intentions, their attitudes toward the boosters began to change. They began to differentiate between different kinds of boosters and the way they were treated by them:

They have some that's interested in Jesse as a student, then they have some that's interested is Jesse as producing or promoting the University's basketball team. You can tell the difference just by talking to them. The ones that's interested in you as a basketball player, alls they talk about is basketball. Who's doing what, what happened then. Those that's interested in you as a person, they ask how's your classes, what books you're reading.

Older players also gave them advice on how to react to boosters and how to handle them:

Danny helped me out a lot, told me what was really up with them, how they are. That it's just a status symbol thing to them. As much as the people in this community act like they care about you, they don't give a damn. If they see you in the street once your four years are up they'll pass you right by. Right now they'll take you out to eat, and everything else, 'cause it's basketball season. That's all that matters to them.

When they went out with boosters or over to their houses they increasingly felt coerced. They did not enjoy the feeling that they were not sought out for their personal qualities, but rather for their status as team members. This tended to make them feel like objects instead of people, as James explained during his sophomore year:

You have to spend all this time with people that just want to be with you for a status symbol in the community so they can say they know the University basketball team. All they ever talk about is basketball, and you get tired of talking about basketball. But you're in demand, and you have to go when they call. And like when I got in that fight [with an opposing player during a game, and was ejected], that was the biggest attention getter. People all wanted to be seen with me afterwards.

Darian also expressed his feelings:

Sociable people use you as a prop. They have you over for dinner so they can feel like they know you when you're running up and down the court. Having you at their house gives them a sense of being someone.

Players thus got the feeling that these people owned them, that they were the property of the booster club. They felt that they had been transformed into promotional agents and their selves into products. As one player poignantly expressed:

This college life ain't nothing like I thought it was going to be. It's put me through too many changes at a young age that I wasn't ready to go through. I thought I was coming here to play ball, but I find I'm a PR person now.

In Hochschild's (1983) study of airline stewardesses, she suggested that these service personnel are socialized and expected to do "emotion work": no matter how they are feeling, part of what they offer to customers is a pleasant and friendly demeanor. Their feelings, then, were a commodity to be offered. Like Hochschild's stewardesses, these athletes represented a commodity to be offered. But whereas the stewardesses were commodifying their emotions, athletes were commodifying their selves. On demand for the fans, media, and especially boosters, they had to drop whatever they were doing or had planned to do, and set themselves forth as polite and personal objects of admiration and possession. They were the glorious heroes of the media, but at the same time they were the powerless playthings of the team's lowliest financial supporters.

Yet they were not alone in their self-commodification. Coach possessed the highest status and was in the greatest demand. As a senior,

Rob summed up the players' general perception of what many boosters wanted from Coach:

> It becomes a social status, especially for the big money boys. A lot of them would be, like, who can see Coach the most, who can take him out to lunch the most, who can be seen with him in they house or at they country club the most. Like you go over to one booster's house, they say, "Oh yeah. June called us up to tell us they had Coach and y'all over." So you know they be talking.

Despite the generally negative sentiment the players held toward boosters as a whole, there were still some of them with whom they felt close and with whom they maintained intimate relations. This was for personal reasons as well as because players needed the boosters. One player explained the function of a "sugar daddy":

> A guy that you lean on a little bit. You need a little money, he'll set you out with a little cash. You go eat, he'll buy you a little food. You get in a bind, you call him. Somebody you can go to. He's a guy that shows that he's very fond of you and you're pretty fond of him. And he takes care of you.

While every player had at least one sugar daddy, the team stars and most popular players had more. After graduating, Apollo reflected back about his sugar daddies:

> When I was at my height I had a lot—about seven or eight. There was just two I was really close to. Two or three. Then it whittled down and whittled down. It's hard to please all of them. You get tired. Like one wants you to come to his son's birthday party, come to dinner with his wife. When you've got seven or eight, that's more things on your time. But you do more work, you get more benefits. You can call it a job.

Contradictions and Confusion. For players, relations with boosters were sometimes clear, but other times confusing and mystifying. Many players, especially those from the poorer backgrounds, had an image of college athletic life that included being "taken care of" by boosters. They expected that they would not have to suffer for their physical wants. Others were not sure what to expect. Coach held to a pretty hard line about accepting things from boosters. He lectured the players regularly about not having their hands out to boosters for several reasons. First, some gifts could constitute a violation of NCAA regulations, and he was fairly straight about following these rules. Second, he did not want the booster community to develop an image of his players as being beggars. He preferred that the boosters give of their selves to the players, and confine their financial gifts to the University's program. Third, he had moral feelings about what it would do to his players to be asking boosters for money, and he wanted his young charges to mature into responsible and decent adults.

When players needed things, then, they were not sure what to do. One player described why college athletes found themselves in situations where they needed to ask boosters for money:

> Living in the dorms, everybody has to eat all together and when they want you to, or you don't eat. Maybe you're tired and you have to go up and lay down. You may have to lay down the whole evening and get up and eat later. But you can't eat if you don't have no money. So you've gotta go dragging over there, force some food down, pretend like you're full, go up there and take a shower. By the time you lay down the little food you ate just done dissolved, and you're sitting up there hongry as hell. And you get on the phone, "Is there any way I can get me two dollars, five dollars, something to go eat?" You always looking for money.

Boosters made frequent offers to players asserting that if they needed money or anything else, all they had to do was ask. Yet, these offers often contained mixed messages. Clyde described how he found himself in trouble when he took a booster up on his offer:

> And then he [a booster] offers to lend me his car. And so the next time I needed it I asked him to borrow the car. He lent me the car and gave me 15 dollars for gas. And then he goes and tells Coach that I asked to borrow his car and I asked him for money. So now I'm in trouble with Coach.

Situations like these made players feel betrayed by boosters, and destroyed their impression that these boosters had any genuine feelings for them. Compounding this, they came to discover that boosters could be fickle, and often switched their allegiances from one player to another:

Some will jump on you bandwagon, "You're my favorite player," or "I seen you on TV," and this and that. And then they'll jump off onto somebody else when some new freshman come to town. They'll talk about how he's a great player, whatever, and they'll be on him, "Come on over to my house." It was like being on show and tell, like, you know, being put on display.

In all, and despite their best efforts to curb these, players' relations with boosters were terribly consuming of both their time and their selves. For youths newly removed from their parents' houses and their local communities (and the protected enclaves these represented), dealing with boosters could generate both confusion and anxiety. They were forced to interact in a culture very different from their own, to show respect for people who often disgusted or bored them, and to cope with boosters' constant demands on them. These experiences and changes were often difficult and unsettling. As Jesse sadly expressed:

Suddenly, just out of high school, they put me in a man's world. I'm a product now, and I'm unhappy because I don't know what the hell's going on.

FANS

While fans fell into the same general category as boosters, fans lacked the personal contact boosters were able to achieve. Boosters got close to the players, knew them individually, and were recognized by the players. They got this kind of closeness by contributing to and joining the University's booster club, by attending its functions, by hosting meetings or dinners at their houses, and by inviting individual players out to eat with them. Mere fans did not usually achieve this level of acquaintance with players because they did not give money to the program and, hence, had neither the access to the team nor the ability to have players delivered to them on request. Fans, then, were people who liked or followed the team from a greater distance than boosters. This distance usually robbed them of individuality in the minds of players; they were conceived as an amorphous blur of people whom players encountered in certain types of structural situations and who made predictable types of demands on them.

Like boosters, fans could be counted on to appear prior to and after games. They usually wanted one of two things: to talk to players, or to get their autographs. Since fans, by definition, did not know players personally, the only kinds of conversations they could engage athletes in were role conversations; they asked them about basketball-related topics. While this was expected and fine, Mark described how it was usually repetitive and boring:

> They come up to you and they're either shy, they don't know what to say to you but they know they want to talk to you. So they stand around and you got to help them out to make conversation, which is a drag. Or else, they have some specific idea in mind they want to talk to you about. And it's about basketball, for sure. How can you say the same thing for the twentieth time and make it sound fresh?

Most of these conversationalists were adult men. The autograph seekers, in contrast, were generally kids and teenagers, occasionally girls. This was an inherently more interesting crowd for players, since most boosters were adult men and they saw plenty of those. Players talked loosely and casually with autograph seekers in the one- to two-hour period before the game that they spent hanging around the sports arena. They were fairly relaxed then, and could socialize with friends, boosters, and fans. At a certain point, however, they had to go into the locker room to get changed into their uniforms, and as that time approached they became noticeably less conversational. After they came out of the locker room, to the fanfare of cheerleaders and the band, they had twenty minutes to warm up and shoot. They did not like to talk to outsiders too much once they were in uniform.

After the game they emerged from the locker room to a throng of people that varied in size depending on whether the game was won or lost and by the time of the season (the crowds built up as the season progressed, if the team was doing well). This group included players' parents, girlfriends, and friends, members of the inner circle, and various boosters and fans. After playing hard and being badgered by the media in the locker room, many players did not want to spend much energy on fans. They wanted to get to their cars and get home, or to find their friends, parents, girlfriends, or whomever they were planning on socializing with for the remainder of the evening. The last thing they wanted was to fight their way through a crowd of fans who wanted autographs or who wanted to talk to them about how the team had performed or how they had played individually during the game. As Marcus described:

> You come out and you see the people out there, and of course it feels good if you won and there's people waiting to congratulate you, but you're also tired as hell and you want to go be with your friends. The first few fans you get stopped by are all right, but after a bunch of them, you don't really have the patience for it anymore.

This crush was always the worst for the team's stars or for the players who had performed outstandingly during the game. Lesser players who received little attention but who had played unusually well were often delighted to be thronged by fans after the game and were particularly gracious. Lionel emerged one night from the locker room full of "high fives" for his friends, exulting with the exclamation, "Hey, I got time [playing time]!" That night he must have signed 50 autographs. Because he was rarely sought, his attitude resembled this freshman's:

> I love signing autographs for people. If somebody is interested enough in me and my team to want my name on a piece of paper I'll sign 50 of them for him. I'm proud.

Players who had reputations as "good boys" could also usually be counted on to oblige with autographs under any circumstances. Other players did not feel the need to bother with this tiresome public relations, and gave off an air of moodiness as they left the locker room that seemed to effectively keep most fans from invading their personal space.

The other main place athletes encountered fans was when they went out in public. Their forays into the public domain were limited during the season, when their time and location were tightly controlled by the demands of their class, practice, and booster schedule, but they got out more during the off-season. When they left campus, they usually went out to eat, to a mall to buy clothes, to work at their summer jobs, to a movie, or to a club (disco) for an evening's recreation. At these times they were readily recognizable, and were approached by fans. For the most part, fans were polite and sensitive to intruding on players' private lives. They stared at players, pointing at them and talking about them. They asked for autographs, making polite small talk while the autograph was being written. More intrusive individuals initiated conversations with players. These were less welcome because they were time consuming and repetitive. As Buck described:

If it's the season, you can be sure they'll ask you about the last game or the next game, or how's your injury. If it's the off-season, they'll ask you about the next season, or the new recruits, or how's your injury. It's boring, because you've heard it all a million times before, and it don't have anything to do with who you really are.

Worse than this were the instances where players were confronted by a belligerent fan who demanded to know why they or another player were not playing well, or why the team lost a particular game or road trip. As Marcus described:

During the season when we're losing, people come up and ask us what's wrong with Daryl. Why isn't he playing, what's wrong with him. How they would get him to play better. We know, but it's none of their business—he's a part of us. He's a moody person, he's not mature yet. He chokes on the pressure because he don't want to be a star. So we don't tell them anything, we jus' tell 'em a line.

These inquisitors were usually armchair coaches who second guessed Coach and wanted the satisfaction of being able to air their opinions to someone in the program.

When players went beyond this small range of locations, they exposed themselves to more intrusive public scrutiny. Those individuals who ventured into community swimming pools, community athletic arenas, or any other public place where they planned on relaxing in one location for a considerable period of time usually came to regret this decision. They spent their entire time there being mobbed by fans, and lost whatever semblance of privacy or relaxation they had hoped to achieve.

Fans were thus a mixed blessing. On the one hand, players dreamed of making it to the level of big-time college athletics, in part, because they wanted the status and recognition that comes with fame. They enjoyed having fans who admired them and who treated them with deference. Once they ascended to the level of stardom, however, the recognition and attention they received became overly intrusive on their lives. Their contacts with fans lost some of its original novelty and appeal, and became recast in their minds as an annoyance and nuisance.

4

The Social Role

LIKE MOST newly entering students, freshmen athletes were on their own for the first time. Arriving on campus, they expected to establish their independence and get involved in college life. They brought with them a diverse array of hopes, expectations, and images of their upcoming college social experiences.

Hopes and Expectations

Some athletes, especially those from poor, ghetto backgrounds, viewed college as a means of upward social mobility. Of all incoming athletes these individuals had the highest expectations for their college social lives. They expected to receive, immediately, the noticeable trappings of success: a fancy dorm room, good food, the latest sports equipment, shoes, and attire, and a lifestyle complete with cars, girls, and money. Along with these material comforts, they surmised, would come a great deal of status and prestige in the college community.

Athletes from middle-class backgrounds held a high level of expectation for their college life as well, but their anticipations were based on an image fostered by the media, rather than the dominant ghetto culture. Many of their generalized images of college life came from films and television, as Damon explained:

I had a stereotype of a major university—like Animal House—live parties, vicious frats, big frats, life on campus, real live.

Not all athletes, however, came to the University expecting the high life. While they may have held an image of major college life as encompassing all of these characteristics at one time, many athletes re-evaluated their expectations after they made their recruiting visit. What they saw during that visit was, by most individuals' accounts, disappointing. The University's athletic dorm was neither new nor plush. The social life was not fabulous. For some athletes, however, this was not so terrible. As a freshman, Damon said:

> I knew when I saw this school that it would be okay for me, because if I'd a gone to a real big school with a lot of frats and parties I would'a partied all the time with my friends after basketball and I'd a probably never really found time to study.

In contrast to the generalized and culturally derived expectations of their peers, these athletes held a more particularized image of the University. Yet despite this group's more subdued expectations, nearly all incoming athletes we observed held a common set of social expectations: to make friends widely on campus, to hold a high social status for their athletic position (as they had in high school), to find collegiate romance, to engage in some escapades, and to be integrated into the mainstream of college life. It came as a great disappointment to find out that this was not to be.

Isolation and Alienation

Instead of being "big men on campus," incoming college athletes found themselves isolated from the center of college social life. The athletic dorm was at the opposite end of campus from the other student residences. They ate all their meals in the athletic dorm, had their training table there, sat in required study hall there, and ended up spending most of their spare time there. They were also cut off from the rest of the students by the demands of their schedule. For example, they had classes in the morning, required practices or informally re-quired pick-up games every afternoon, and loosely enforced curfew every night. This cut down on their ability to spontaneously socialize with other students. As Buck explained:

You might go to class in the morning with a bunch of regular students, and say, one of them suggests, "Why don't we all go over to the [local pub] for some lunch and a beer?" Well, maybe you would like to go out with those guys, but you have to think, "I've got a practice at three o'clock, and if I drink a beer now, I might be tired later," or "If I get started having a good time with these guys I'll just have to quit pretty soon because I have to get to the locker room by two-thirty to get to the gym by three o'clock." And so you don't go, even though you might like to, because you have this other thing that you always have to do.

Demographically, athletes were further separated from other students by racial and socioeconomic barriers. The University drew its students from the white, middle and upper class suburban areas surrounding most of the nearby cities, while most of the basketball players were black, and from the ghetto and lower to middle class neighborhoods located in the inner cities or rural areas of nearby states. Culturally, this left them with little in common with these students. Finally, they were physically distinct from other students because of their size and shape. Imposing and occasionally intimidating in physique, many ordinary students viewed them as either frightening, or too tall to interact with comfortably. This saddened them considerably. During his junior year, Marcus articulated his feelings about wanting to be part of the campus social life:

Everybody always thinks that athletes just come to school to play. They don't care about nothing else, they don't care about nobody else. But we want to be a part of the frats, be friends with them, help the community like they do. We don't want the girls think- • ing that we want to rape them. We feel like outcasts. We're black, we're athletes. Other students move away from us at test times, think we're going to cheat off them. That makes me feel bad. It makes me feel bad when we walk by and they cover up, they don't talk to us. I don't want them to be scared of me. We want to be a part of the campus, socially as well as athletically and academically.

Other players also expressed the feeling that they were thwarted in their attempts to become integrated into the campus social life:

> We look out the window every Friday, Saturday night and they're having a good time, here we are up here in our room. We could go over there, but we'd be talking to me and him [each other].

When they did go to these parties, they often had unpleasant experiences. Darian recounted:

> We're on this side of the campus and they're all on the other. We went to one party and we were the only black people. I thought everything would be like in high school—they'd accept us. But when we walked in some guy said, "Oh, oh, here comes trouble."

Other times, at parties, athletes felt that people were interested in them only as a commodity, not as real people. Yet they found that being athletes brought some superficial social benefits. As Ben explained:

> You're in the limelight. People are gonna want to be your friends, want you to come to their parties, make their frat houses look good. Just so they can say they had you there, or so other people can see you there and be impressed. But I guess that's an advantage. You can go to their parties, drink their beer. I wouldn't be invited to their party if I wasn't an athlete.

Darian explained how this popularity was fickle:

> Sure, they'll invite you to their parties when the season is on and you're in the papers and on TV every day. Or when the team is winning. We don't get so many invitations when the team is losing.

For some players, this lack of a social life was no great loss. Clyde contrasted his college social life with what he had experienced in high school:

> Back home I just stayed home mostly, watched TV, did my homework, went to a few dances with my girl. If I wasn't doing homework I was usually playing ball. I went out, but I'm not sacrificing a fabulous social life, it's not like I'm missing anything.

Yet despite these obstacles, some players did manage to develop a social life moderately resembling the commonly held image, complete with parties and girlfriends. This was more likely to occur for the white players or middle class black players. As James, a white middle-class player, described:

> I think—I mean I know—I really overdid it on my social life last year. That's why I'm on academic probation right now. But I was young and I was away from home for the first time. So I guess I just kinda went wild, getting invited to all those parties. I figured it was my reward for all that hard work in practice.

When the lower class and black players attained success in their social lives on campus it was usually for one of three reasons. First, they had an especially outgoing or charismatic personality, such that students of all kinds were captivated by them. This was the case with Apollo, who could articulately and humorously express himself. Wherever he went, he seemed to attract a crowd of friends. Second, they were able to interact comfortably and make friends in a largely white environment. As Buck explained:

> I went to a mostly white high school, and my best friend in high school was white. People were always wondering what we were up to. So I feel comfortable making friends here. But take Daryl, for example, he doesn't like white people. His whole school and his town was all black, and he doesn't feel comfortable around white people at all.

Third, lower class black players' social lives turned on whether they played a pivotal role on the team. Tyrone, a highly recruited starter from a ghetto described the social life for black athletes on campus:

> On the University's campus? Mediocre. It's a white campus. White girls like this face, though. If you're that highly publicized player they'll go into their act. But most of them say "Hi" and keep walking. So it's, let's go to the discos to find the womens.

For most players, then, the social life was disappointing. They were no longer highly popular on campus, as they had been in high school, merely for their athletic participation. As James explained:

> See, in high school, girls want to go out with the jocks. Jocks are the main attraction. But in college they want to go out with the frat boys. And most of them is the same people. The high school

jocks turn into college frat boys. They wear their frat sweater instead of their letterman sweater.

These college athletes were thus different from high school athletes by virtue of having remained in the athletic role. This distinction served as a clear base of social stratification. While the high school athletes whose parents could afford to send them to college went on to pursue academic or business careers, scholarship athletes were still playing ball as their ticket to college admission. Though their scholarship status was not a stigma, other things were. They not only lacked the positive status of fraternity membership, but were also labeled with the pejorative "jock" image. Athletes bristled against being thought of as jocks, and made a clear distinction between what they were and jocks. As Marcus explained:

> It really bothers me when people call me a jock. I say, "No I'm not. I'm a student-athlete." And when they call our dorm the jock dorm, I say "Wait a minute, that's the athletic dorm.". . . There are athletes who are jockish, and some who are not. The jock image is that they don't care about nothing but athletics. They don't care about people's feelings, don't care about school, about how they look, or nothing. They use their popularity as athletes to get women, and if things don't work out, they just drop them.

James elaborated,

> A jock is the stereotypical person. Just loves sweat. It's a negative thing. You love your sport and that's it, and you're dumb as hell. A lot of the football players are jocks. They'll pride themselves on just fucking some girl right outside the dorm, right on the hood of a car. 'Cause they're wild and they're stupid. And that's the stereotype. But there's more to me than just a basketball player.

In forging their college social lives and identities, these athletes had to deal with both the loss of their prestigious high school status as well as being cast into the pariah jock image. As a result of all these factors, most athletes had limited relations with non-athletes. Some were more successful than others in making friends outside of the athletic dorm, and the majority of athletes had at least a few friends from classes or other campus activities, but these associations were not extensive. Their primary social reference group consisted of the other athletes who shared their living accommodations.

The Athletic Dorm

Coming to college and finding themselves housed in an athletic dorm was a new experience. Athletes were used to some sort of family life; their dormmates became both surrogate family and cellmates. Most reacted to the arrangement of being housed in an all-athlete residence hall with mixed feelings.

As noted earlier, there was the initial solidarity of being thrust together in a time and place with no other students on campus. During the summer months the basketball players bonded into a cohesive and familial group. Alone in the dorms, they had extensive daily contact. Aside from their jobs, they had unlimited free time in which to play basketball, hang out, and get to know each other. Once the football players moved in around mid-August, they were soon added to the group. Referring to the combined group of both teams, Lamont said:

> We live together. We see each other every day. We eat with the all the basketball players, and with the football players too. Even the ones I don't know too well, I feel connected to. And if one of them got in a fight, even if it was someone I didn't like, I'd go to their defense. 'Cause we're all student-athletes, we're the same.

The athletic dorm also provided players with a place where they could retreat to get away from the rest of the student body. Being from different racial and socioeconomic backgrounds than students throughout the rest of the campus, athletes often felt like they did not fit in at the University. They had to act a certain way around the boosters, and present their fronts to the professors and other students. The athletic dorm served as a refuge where they could let down these fronts and engage in backstage behavior. As Marcus said:

> Being in an athletic dorm, there's a different atmosphere from the regular dorm. You have to watch what you say, but you can be more confidential with athletes. They're more from the same class as us. All of us being athletes, we have more in common, more to talk about. It makes us feel more confident.

Clyde expressed it this way:

> I feel I can't go out and act black when I'm around white people.
> I cut out my cussing, try to talk slower. But around the dorms I
> can act myself. You gotta have somewhere to act black, some-
> where to communicate with other people like you. Especially
> with the boosters, you have to really act straight.

Yet despite their greater commonalities with dorm members, athletes
found the social milieu within the dorm restrictive. As Frank expressed:

> There is no atmosphere, you can't feel comfortable. You are
> living by rules in a dorm, rules you don't catch on to until you be
> there awhile. For instance, who do you hang around with in a
> dorm? You got to hang out with somebody who grew up almost
> the same way you did. Or else you can't talk to them. Finding
> the right companionship when you get to the school is very
> important. You can't be "bad" in the dorms or you'll find yourself
> in a world all by yourself, and one day you'll be yelling, "Help,
> help," and somebody will say "No, remember you bad."

The closeness bred by athletes' common situation and their isolation
from other students intensified the interaction of life within the dorm.
There was bonding, but there was also pressure to conform, to "fit in:"

> Living in the dorm the privacy is limited. 'Cause everybody in
> that dorm going to know something about you before you leave,
> and it ain't through the media. The athaletes are around you 24
> hours a day. They know what routine you're going through.
> You've just got to fit in once you go to a jock dorm. You've got
> to sometimes play the role that you don't care. You can't be the
> good guy every day. Some days you have to go back to where
> you feel comfortable and just play the ghetto-type person. Or else
> it gets to not be reality no more.

Relations with Teammates

For players, then, their teammates were the dominant members of
their social role-set. They may have had a girlfriend, and that was
important, but the people who formed their closest friends and with

whom they spent the most time were their peers, their fellow student-athletes.

One of the most salient characteristics of their relations with their teammates involved the sponsorship bonds that were forged between new players and seasoned veterans. Raw and naive upon first entering college, new freshmen did not know what to expect or how to react to their surroundings. Older players, from sophomores on up, took the role of advisers or mentors, and socialized them to the ways of the college experience. With the exception of one or two players who dropped out of the program early, all the freshmen we observed were adopted by older players and given guidance and aid. These links were forged by players according to emerging social relationships. Much like other students' friendship cliques (Moffatt 1989), players quickly sized each other up and assessed who they thought would be compatible with their background, values, and lifestyle. This evaluation was helped by the coaches, who decided on players' rooming arrangements based on the impressions they formed of players during the recruiting process. Since they assigned players into the rooms and suites available to the basketball program on the basis of these perceptions, each of the cliques described in the introduction tended to be congregated into its own suite. Once friendships began to coalesce, older players helped and advised the younger ones on a variety of topics. As Apollo explained:

> I pick out my favorite guys and I try to help them. Watch them, try to encourage them in their game. What's goin' happen, be prepared for this, it ain't goin' always be like that. I pick a favorite out but I don't take him everywhere. Let him fall into his own situations, like I did. That was the best way. You'll figure it out. It don't take long. Watch him, he's a good guy, try to take Doc in his classes, what they're like, what Coach is like, how to get by when Coach is on him, how to get him off.

Different types of advice and socialization also took two more specific forms. One of these involved role modeling for younger players. Individuals enjoyed helping to forge others in their own image. During the course of our research, we observed two senior players, who were roommates and best friends, socialize a pair of freshmen. These freshmen grew into the model of the older, and eventually departed, former players. During their junior year they, in turn, picked out two freshmen roommates and chose to adopt them as their favorite players and pet projects. They helped and socialized these players, such that the newcomers eventually grew to fill the role of the original two. They thus symbolized a virtual third generation within the space of four years, carrying on the legacy of attitudes, behavior, and position vis-à-vis Coach and their other teammates held by the first pair. Clyde, one of the last group of freshmen, described his initial treatment by this middle group and how he felt about it:

> They're right in the same suite right next door. And Darian took algebra and told us if we need help in the class we could come next door and he'd help us. And he knew how it was 'cause like when he was a freshman he was scared, didn't know who to respect or nothing. And so he influenced me. When I need help I can go over there. I really admire them two.

This extended to giving away clothes or possessions to help mold the new players into the right image. As Darian, a member of the middle pair, explained:

> Danny and Rob took us under their wings. They told us what to expect, about college life. Stressed when we go to the games, be as neat as possible, like a businessman would go to they job. They even gave us some of their clothes to help us out in the beginning when we didn't have much, so we could look good and present the right image. I guess we got our dress code from them.

For other players, this socialization took more of a warning form, of advice to abandon potentially damaging behavior and conform to the ways of the team. Tyrone described how he got drawn into socializing a young freshman:

> I'm not the type of guy, normally, to be giving people advice. But you look after every one of them. You catches yourself doing that. Frank, his first couple of weeks here, he got caught two times stealing. I had to tell him this. I caught myself giving him this whole rap session—"You can't come up here stealing." You ask me this now and I say why am I telling him this? But I *had* to for some reason, 'cause all the other guys weren't relating to him.

But relations within the team were characterized by division as well as unity. While the group became cohesive when facing outsiders, they often broke down into factions or cliques among themselves. Buck reflected on the nature and origin of these cliques:

> In high school the guys are all from the same neighborhood, but in college they're from all over. All the different states. People from the same areas stick together. People from the same kind of background stick together. People who party or do drugs stick together, and those who don't stick together.

As Buck observed, cliques revolved around their members' shared attitudes, values, backgrounds, and lifestyles. Other factors, such as academic and athletic ability, were not salient. Some cliques (especially the bad niggas and the whiners) liked to go out more, used drugs recreationally, placed greater emphasis on their social lives, and preferred immediate gratification. Others (the candy-asses and the L-7s) hung around the dorms on the weekends, watched TV, went to bed early, saved their money, and (many of them) belonged to religious groups. To Coach, these latter were the "choir boys," and the former the "weedsmokers." A regular churchgoer himself, he encouraged his players to behave in a responsible and moral manner, publicly decrying the rowdiness and irresponsibility occasionally practiced by the bad niggas and the whiners.[1] Yet underneath this moralistic demeanor, he also related strongly to the tough, ghetto boys. He had pulled himself up from a similar background and could relate to their perspective and problems. He went out of his way to recruit such players, not only because they were tough on the court, but because he thought he could handle them: he could relate to them and tame them. Yet he handled the two types of players, candy-asses and bad niggas, differently. He was tough to the latter, trying to win their respect by playing their game. He was gentle to the former, encouraging them with support.

This difference usually resulted in his developing closer off-court friendships with members of the candy-asses, and he would often call them into his office and quiz them about the actions of the others. In particular, he asked them to reveal what they knew about those individuals' social lives, their habits and pastimes, and other tidbits about them that might have made it into the dormitory "grapevine." What resulted was the widespread perception that some players were "snitching" on others. This action polarized the camps even more, and created several instances of bad feelings between individuals. At one point two players, Apollo and Rob, got into a fist fight in the locker room one summer over the snitching issue, and bad feelings continued to loom between them after that. Apollo stated why he thought the snitches were doing the team a disservice:

> You know, we all got to live together here, and we got to have some unity. I just wish the snitches would chill out and grow up, realize they don't have to go running up to Coach every time they hear something 'bout someone else. They need to mature, cause it's hurting the team.

Darian, an accused snitcher, explained things from his point of view:

> You get called in, he ask you questions. Sometimes we answer them, sometimes we don't. It's only our opinion anyway. But those players call you snitches; it's a type of jealousy. You getting called in so you snitching. And then they shy away from us because they don't trust us, or they think we the Coach's pet.

While snitching was clearly divisive among the team members socially, there were some who thought the factionalization it bred also had an influence on team play. Darian expressed his opinion that the balkanization was deleterious:

> If we don't have that solidarity, that unity, it can hurt us. I feel like we ain't had too much of that last year. And this year we've already had fights. Everybody wants to be that superstar and not sacrifice for their team; everybody's an individual on this team. People are selfish on the court. They should be giving up a shot that may be a little bit out of their range instead of shooting all the time, not playing any defense.

Slick showed how this divisiveness could extend onto the court by discussing his personal feelings for one of his teammates and commenting on how it would affect his play during games:

> We've got a lot of guys with a lot of different attitudes, who think they is hot shit, like Tyrone. I can't even talk to him now. Don't you think it's hard for me to go out there and play with him on the team? I might come down the court and see Tyrone and I wouldn't want to pass to him.

James cast it in terms of group relations:

> There are definitely groups, and it affects your play. If you pretty much get along with everybody on the team, you're going to have a good year. But if there's half the team who like you and the other half who don't like you then y'all going to pretty much keep the ball between the side who like you. It may not show, but it's gonna be there. You're gonna pretty much look for your friends.

Yet at the same time there were others who felt more optimistic about the situation. They felt that there was a separation between what happened in the dorms and on the court, that people acted in a more serious and responsible manner on the court. Marcus commented that, "Once we get into a game they forget about the fights and try to win." By this he did not imply that the players got along any better, but only that they put their feelings aside temporarily and fused together in a common desire to win. Then, when the game was over, they could go back to feeling however they liked about each other. Optimistic players suggested, then, that when faced with a threat from outside, the team developed cohesion, but with the removal of that threat it returned to its normal state (see Simmel 1950).

In fact, while there were divisions within the team, there were no strong antagonisms between the groups. Most members from the various cliques had good relations with those in the others, it was just that they were closer friends with the individuals in their own clique. Any really serious antagonisms that arose were an individual matter. In sum, then, the team's unity was greater than its divisiveness.

Peer Subculture

Personal differences notwithstanding, basketball players experienced significant encapsulation. The uniqueness of their experience compared to other students, and the intensity of their contact with fellow student-athletes, encouraged their reliance on this peer group as their sole reference point.[2] The peer group not only offered them a solace where they could retreat to interact with others who shared similar backgrounds and travails, but also carried with it a subculture replete with norms, values, a store of shared knowledge, mythologized heroes, specialized argot, common hopes and dreams, role models and role behaviors, and a set of accounts designed to facilitate those behaviors. The athletes' peer subculture contained within it all the knowledge of the difficulties college athletes face, all of the multiple and conflicting demands placed on them, and all of the responses that had been forged throughout the years.

Central to the peer subculture was athletics. As Jesse exclaimed:

> In a athaletic dorm where you've got all athaletes, what are they goin' be talking about? It won't be Reaganomics, believe me. It'll definitely be *Sports Illustrated*. You put them in this big building with just ordinary people, what do you think they'll be talking about? Ordinary things.

Damon discussed the collective orientation of the peer subculture, framed by its location in a segregated athletic dormitory:

> Sure, they always say that the reason [for housing athletes in one dorm] is so they can have the training table in one centralized place, so they can feed the athaletes the same, and stuff like that, but I think it's really mind control. Athaletes carry two images in they minds. One image is, "My Momma send me to school to be a engineer and in order to be a engineer I've got to go to class every day and study hard." The other image is, "I come to school to play basketball, I didn't come to school to study that hard." But Coach don't want you thinking about you economics class. You've got to be thinking about North Carolina. If you was hangin' out with a group of just regular students you goin' to be more into reality than to have all these jocks over here dreaming in all they dream worlds.

The peer subculture generated by the focused, intensive life of the athletic dorm thus served to mold each individual athlete into the composite of the generalized college athlete. Coach did not have to reinforce their focus on athletics; the athletes themselves influenced each other to continually turn toward their strongest area of common interests.

The athletes' peer subculture also carried within it another set of influences. While there were many white players living in the athletic dorm, the majority were black. This dormitory was a black ghetto encased within the overwhelmingly white environment of the University. It was thus a place which reinforced their blackness, and was central to the fashioning of the athletic subculture. The power of black culture, and the broader connection between race and athleticism generally, could be seen in its dominance of the athletic subculture. After a while, many of the white players began to adopt elements of its language, music, and gestures.[3] Thus while the team was only two-thirds black, its culture reflected a stronger influence of black values. This could be seen in the behavior and collective attitudes the players displayed.

Athletes formed and disseminated collective attitudes in two ways. First, they reacted together to situations in which one or more of them found themselves, so that their opinions and actions were very much a product of the group assessment (or at least, that of their clique). Second, they drew upon collective norms and values already existing within the peer subculture that had been formed by older players, and applied them to their present situations. Their development of new solutions to collective problems and affirmation of old ones reinforced these attitudes and behaviors within the peer subculture. Individuals' interpretations became collectively shared, and collective interpretations were adopted by individuals.

One of the main topics focused on by the peer subculture was the athletic role. Athletes discussed various dimensions of this role and the ways they dealt with it, from boosters, to coaches, fans, the media, games, other teams, other players in their league and the professional leagues, their hopes and dreams, their futures, and those of other players. Together they underwent the intensive and collective process of being exposed and socialized to the structures and experiences that made up their world. Only they understood the incredible demands placed upon them by this role and, at the same time, its incredible allure. It was not through the structural demands or their experiences alone that they were drawn to capitulating to the demands of this role. The peer subculture gave them an arena where they could vent the feelings they developed from these demands and rewards, from the intensity of the overwhelming experiences they faced. Only through the collective reinforcement of others also feeling the demands and being drawn to this arena did they all decide to follow the same path and let the importance of this role escalate to its full peak.

At the same time, the peer subculture helped to frame their attitudes toward their other roles. Although they entered college with different academic expectations and goals, the peer subculture tended to collectivize them. It also helped them deal with their feelings of need for a social life, and to decide where it could be fit in and where it might have to be sacrificed.

Role Conflict

College athletes often felt a conflict between their athletic and social roles. They had not experienced this competing pull in high school. Back home their time spent in practice had not been excessive, and they had a sense of having ample time and freedom to engage in all of the activities they wished. In college, however, they soon learned that there were strains and pulls between the demands of their various roles and the time and leeway they had to act within them. The conflict between their athletic and social roles took several forms.

First, they often felt that Coach took an overly controlling role with regard to their *social lives*. This began with generalized indications about the amount of time they could spend with women and friends during the course of the season. Most of the players complained about the constraints they felt on their social lives:

> Basically, we're not supposed to have a social life, especially during the season. During the weeknights that's forbidden, weekends: two-a-days, season: games, and you're supposed to be resting for the games. He fixes it so you have hardly any social life. He makes you tired as hell, he makes you watch a film, go out to dinner with boosters, show a recruit around. Rather than being with your friends. But I like girls, I like to have fun. And I feel like after I've been to class all day and been to practice, I've got to have some free time on my own to do what I want. And Coach don't want me to do what I'm doing. He wants me to sit around the dorm.

Another player echoed this sentiment:

> Girls? Forget it. Girls go on the shelf for the season unless you're married.

Yet some players realized that Coach was not totally authoritarian about this rule, acknowledging that, "He's smart enough to know

when to look the other way about girls when he has to. After all, we're
not monks. We're college guys."

Yet ironically, Coach took a different view of his control over their
romantic lives:

> On a major college campus it's very hard to control. I tried to do
> it the first year, and it's just too much. There are football players
> here, and there's too many other people involved over there to
> ask questions. There are rules—girls are not supposed to be there
> after a certain hour, but you can't really control something like
> that. . . . You don't have the control because you've got so many
> people in that dorm and they're all athletes. You can go over
> there and say don't do this, don't do that, and as soon as you
> leave, it's just right back again.

Athletes thus followed the usual practices of college students with
regard to partying and fraternization with members of the opposite sex
in the dormitories (see Moffatt 1989). On weekend nights there were
often women in the halls and in the rooms, complete with towels
blocking the bottoms of the doors to keep marijuana smoke accumu-
lated inside from escaping into the halls. Occasionally, people would
gather in one room of a two-room suite. Someone would remain in
the other room and keep his door open so that he could serve as a
lookout in case one of the coaches or someone else unexpected came
around. Women in the dorms came from all over town. Some were
students; most of them were white. There were few black women on
campus. Others were girls players had met around town or at discos,
or after games or while they were out shopping or on some other
business. Many of these from the part of town where the black
population was concentrated, and where players went to meet women.
Rumor had it that fast women from this neighborhood occasionally
came down to the dorms uninvited, hoping to meet and party with
athletes. Only some athletes engaged in this revelry, however. Some
had steady girlfriends whom they dated on weekends, others just did
not get into the swing of things. And athletes often liked to get out of
the dorms and off campus on weekend evenings, so they spent time at
the "cribs" (apartments) of their friends (former athletes, married athletes, students) who lived in the neighborhoods immediately surrounding campus.

Players thought that Coach, beyond suggesting limits to their ro-

mantic liaisons, constrained their freedom of association by telling
them who were and were not desirable individuals for them to select as
friends. Players groused because coaches "tell you to quit hanging
around so much with certain people on the team because they are a
bad influence on you." Buck cited this as the hardest part of adjusting
to college life:

> For me, it was having to listen to somebody tell me what to do.
> I know what's right and wrong. I don't need nobody saying
> don't go there, or don't be around this person or that person.

Apollo echoed this sentiment:

> He tries to control your whole life. That's one of those parts that
> I know a player hates, when he gets into that aspect of your life
> —your girlfriend, who to hang out with, where you can hang
> out—and he gets into all those things.

While the players accepted Coach's authority over them to a certain
degree, they had a collective feeling that there would be limits to the
extent of his control. When he overly encroached on their social lives,
his behavior violated their intuitive sense of legitimacy and they reacted
against it. Second, they felt that their athletic role intruded into their
social sphere and caused them a *loss of privacy*. Whenever they left the
protected enclave of the dorms or campus and went out in public they
had to be careful of the image they projected. As members of the
University's basketball team, all of their behavior represented the program. Early on, Coach impressed upon them the restrictions this responsibility entailed. As Rob stated:

> I was in the public eye. A college basketball player has to repre-
> sent not only himself but the University, because you've got to
> think about the media, what they can do if they see you drinking
> a beer in public, or getting into a fight, how that make your
> school look, how that make your coach look, how that make your
> team look.

This suddenly transformed everyone they might see into a potential
observer. As Buck explained:

> When you go out in public you represent the team with every-
> thing you do, because everybody's always watching you. Coach

knows everything you do because boosters and fans report back
to him about anything that they don't like or don't think you
should be doing. Apollo got into big trouble one time because
he was horsing around and jumped into someone's pool with all
his clothes on. And some booster lady saw it and reported it to
Coach.

Not only did this entail restricting their behavior, but it required
athletes to graciously do things that were a bother to them. They had
to spend time with boosters or recruits when they would rather be
alone or with friends. When out in public they were potentially open
to being invaded by autograph seekers. At these times they had to
relinquish their privacy and take on the role of the athlete. As Apollo
said with frustration:

Sometimes you just didn't want to bother with it, it wasn't that
exciting to you, like a lot of autographs. After you've signed so
many you don't like it as much. It's a highlight for them and I try
to please them. All it is is patience. It'll be gone soon enough, so
just take your time and take care of business. Even though I'd be
saying in my mind, "Damn, wish these motherfuckers was gone,
let me eat, my burger getting cold." I guess that's part of the
price you pay also. It's another intrusion on your privacy—a
whole lot of your privacy.

A third dimension of this conflict lay in players' *loss of autonomy*.
Their actions were viewed and evaluated not only by adult boosters
and fans, but by another significant audience for them—children.
Youngsters often picked a player from the team as their favorite and
followed everything that player did with avid interest. They read about
him in the paper, watched him carefully at games, went to public places
where the team was appearing, and generally idolized him. Everything
he did had the potential to influence their lives. These forms of attention constrained their overall persona, because they felt the obligation
to provide a positive image for youth. As Marcus lamented:

There are so many rumors around about us, because we're so
quiet and nice and everybody want to know what we're doing.
We can't hardly go out and have fun in public like a regular
college kid because of all the attention on us. Young kids, they
look up to us as somebody nice, and maybe they'll go around not

smoking and drinking and breaking into houses and stuff like that. It's a lot of pressure to be a role model but it's rewarding.

Finally, athletes felt the conflict between their social and athletic roles with regard to their *time commitments*. In college, players found the demands on their time rigorous and pervasive. Back in high school their time was largely their own, and they could allocate it as they desired. But in college, their free time was suddenly constrained. As Tyrone remarked:

> In the ghetto, time is no essence—you can sit in the park, kick back, chill out 24 hours a day. It's a spur of the moment life. But in college, oh man, they can really control your time, no doubt. If they don't want you to leave and want to keep you 24 hours on the schedule they can do that. All they have to do is hand out copies to every player telling them where to be at 2:30, 3:30, etc. . . . Because you are on the clock once school starts. It's like, put it where you can see it 'cause I'm going to move every second. Something is up, 10:50, I've gotta go. See y'all later.

These demands on players' time often interfered with what they wanted to do in their social lives. Suddenly they were relinquishing things they really wanted to do, things they had taken for granted before that they could do. Buck offered the following lament:

> In college I can live a pretty good easy-going life up until October 15. I can go away for a weekend if I want, I don't have to play ball. But I know when October 15 comes everything is for real. You can no longer just do what you feel like doing on the spur of the moment. When you finish classes you can no longer have your own time. If college was more like that, college sports would be a whole new different story. Instead, it's "Go down to the gym, and you better be there."

While athletes expected their playing schedules to be demanding, they were unexpectedly overwhelmed by the number of athletic-related functions they were required to attend. They were frustrated and upset that they had to put these functions and people (boosters, fans, media) ahead of their friends, girlfriends, and selves, and most freshmen had a hard time accepting this reality.

All of these forms of role conflict served to reinforce to them that their athletic role was the superordinate one, and that their social lives were being relegated to a less important status. This was a surprise to them, and differed greatly from their high school experiences and the image they had held about college life on first entering. In high school their sports participation had been rewarding and important, but it had not eclipsed their social lives. As Damon remarked as a freshman:

> My main reason for coming to college was to play basketball, but the biggest part of me is my social way of life. Basketball has always been something I chose to do with my time, but not something I had to do. And I always had more time to go out with my girl or party than I had to be spending in practice.

Coming to college put athletes into a different position. Suddenly their basketball role was the central organizing principle of their lives and they had to schedule social activities into their time. Yet their social selves remained very important to them. As Tyrone said:

> Your social life, you're going to find time for that, believe it or not. That's when basketball is not important. When you do find a woman and you find the right one, it tends to help you a little better, as far as being an athlete.

However, their living situation (in athletic housing), their relations to authority (their coaches replaced their parents), their social identities (they were college athletes instead of high school students or just teenagers), and their social milieu (they were primarily surrounded by other student-athletes) all served to accentuate the centrality of the athletic role and to change their self-conceptions. This role conflict was difficult and confusing. How were they to make the time for their social selves? How were they to accommodate to the escalation of their athletic role demands? How would all these changes in their life situation affect their core selves and identities? These were questions that they came to grips with over an evolving period of years.

5
The Academic Role

ATHLETES COMING to the University underwent a process of resocialization not only in the athletic and social realms, but also in the
academic realm. Athletes brought to college a diverse, albeit naive,
array of hopes and ideals about their impending academic experiences.
Confident that playing basketball and being students would not prove
problematic, many set lofty academic goals for themselves. Their idealism and optimism were reinforced during the early weeks of school
before the start of official practice season. At this time they had the
luxury of acting like normal college students to a greater extent than
they would ever have again.

Early Impressions

One of the first things they noticed were the attitudes and behaviors of
their professors. Placed in courses with those who were friends of the
program, first semester freshmen concluded that their professors were
either easy, caring, or both. During the early part of his freshman year,
Clyde gave this evaluation:

> Some of my professors are nice. When they give assignments they
> always look at me 'cause I be sittin' there looking like I don't
> know, so they ask before I leave, "Do you understand?" If I
> show I care by coming to class they are extra concerned about
> you. And one of my history professors gave the coach a couple

of guys that might be able to tutor me. The others is just regular.

Their optimism was reinforced by the beliefs Coach espoused in his early contacts with them. They listened to what he had to say about academics and regarded him as someone who was sincere in his caring and interest for them as people. They sensed his ideals, and the young players especially thought he would help them achieve all of their goals. As a freshman, Damon said:

> I think he really wants the best for us all around. On and off the court. There's no way we could get exploited by a coach who cares this much about us as people—only by a crooked coach. Every now and then in practice he mentions how important the degree is and everything. And when we have hard practices, two-a-days, he say, "Get to class in the morning. Make sure you go to class tomorrow." So I trust him that everything he's asking us to do is for our own good as well as his.

They thus saw his interests as being highly supportive of academics. Coach expressed his feelings and philosophy about academics:

> I want to win worse than anybody else in the world, that's one thing. But by the same token I want to win in all aspects. I want to win as a basketball coach, I want to win as a teacher, an instructor on the floor —teaching them the finer points of the game. I want to win in the fact that my students are guys who go to class and work and try to get a degree. That to me is winning. And when they get that piece of paper I've won again. I've got a lot of winnings I want to do, and it's not all on the floor.

Indeed, he spent considerable time talking to his players and assistant coaches about the importance of academics. He instructed his assistants that they were responsible for making sure that the players were not cheated out of their educations. One day after a particularly vivid dream that he interpreted as symbolizing his responsibility for the academic welfare of his players, he gave an impassioned speech to the assistant coaches, telling them that "the blood would be on their hands" if the University's players went through college without getting the education they deserved, and that if the players failed to get it, the coaching staff should take this failure personally.

While he delegated the day-to-day mechanics of dealing with the academic domain to his assistants, he pondered ways of making policy that would get athletes to put more time into their studies. He fretted about their involvement and efforts in the classroom. One day he mused:

> I worry about whether or not these guys are going to get up and go to class the next morning. I'm going to have to make a rule: starting next semester, anybody that cuts three classes, I'm going to have to ask the professor to drop 'em from the class. And if they drop below twelve hours they're not a full-time student, they're off scholarship. If I have to go that far. I hope they don't make me make rules I don't like.

But he never went that far. He yelled at them a lot, he preached at them, he cajoled them. He required them to go to study halls nightly, and he put the assistant coaches in charge of monitoring these.[1] He had high goals for his players, and he knew that the system could easily take advantage of them. As he often said, "I don't want to go to Kentucky Fried Chicken, and see my former basketball players in there working."

Athletes' early experiences thus strengthened the academic goals they had abstractly set for themselves before coming to college. They were impressed by Coach's seriousness and dedication to education. This reinforced their desire to attain the full thrust of their multi-faceted college experience. They would play basketball, but they would also be students. As a first semester freshman, Buck aptly expressed this attitude:

> I don't see any problems in playing basketball and being a student. I'm all over making the transition from high school to college. I'm here for four years. I know that only one percent of the whole team goes to the pros. I'm looking at a degree. You get that degree, you can work. Still have fun playing basketball, but the degree—money's what it is. . . . Sure I have the dream, but I can't let my academics get away from me.

False Security

Several factors lulled athletes into thinking that a cushion of security existed in the academic sphere. They believed that they would be

protected and insulated from potential problems. Among the first
cushions were the impressions of college athletics they brought with
them. Like their social expectations, their imagery of college academic
life was partly influenced by various cultural myths. During his freshman year Ben mentioned an idea he had heard before he came to
college:

> I heard you can get breaks on grades because you're an athlete.
> That's what people think—I wonder if it's true. I don't know,
> 'cause it's my first year.

Just as the coaches settled new athletes into their dorms, jobs, and
booster relations, so too did they settle them into their classes. The
assistant coach in charge of academics enrolled players into their college, their major, and their classes. He was responsible for making sure
they were taking courses that fulfilled their distribution as well as major
requirements, and he took care of the mechanics of enrolling them in
classes.[2] The players, uninvolved in academic decision-making, had
little direct contact with professors (beyond simple class attendance),
academic counselors, or academic administrators. As a result, the players did not learn how to handle these academic matters, nor—in many
cases—were they interested in doing so. They did not worry that these
academic decisions were being made for them, or that they did not
have to process their own academic paperwork; they took it for granted
that this was the way things were. As James stated during his sophomore year:

> The day before class you go up to the office and they hand you a
> card that got your schedule all filled out on it. You don't say
> nothin' or think nothin' 'bout it, you just go. And it kinda make
> you feel like you not involved in it, 'cause you don't have nothin'
> to do with it. Like it's they's job, not yours.

Some athletes were even proud that they had someone to take care
of this for them; it signified that they were too important to do it for
themselves, that they had a more vital job to perform. With other
students, however, they did not usually mention their ignorance and
academic detachment. It was a source of embarrassment for two reasons: first, they felt awkward about having the privilege of a coach
doing their administrative work for them (just as they were embarrassed to admit that the basketball secretary typed their papers), and
second, they were a bit ashamed by their ignorance—that they did not

know how to take care of it for themselves. This reinforced their bond with each other and their isolation from other students.

Having someone take care of these academic matters gave them a clear message, and it was not the one Coach manifestly intended. Athletes developed a false sense of security, a feeling that someone was looking out for them academically and would make sure that they were given another chance if they needed it, a feeling that they could foul up and not have to pay the consequences. This feeling was exacerbated mid-way through the semester when, as decreed by the NCAA, the assistant coach sent out notices to all athletes' professors asking for a progress report on them. This form letter asked professors to evaluate athletes on their submitted work, their attendance, and their attitude toward the class. If a problem was reported, the coach gave the professor a call and discussed it with him or her. He negotiated with the professor about what remedial action could be taken, he made promises on behalf of the athletes regarding their future performance (and then tried to strong-arm them into upholding these), and it was he, ultimately, who developed a relationship with members of the faculty. Throughout this, the players sat back, sometimes unaware that this was happening. They became more aware that discussions were in progress when they received some direct notice from the professor that they were doing poorly in the class or that they were in danger of flunking. At this point they approached the academic coach about the situation. They then sat back, waiting, hoping he could clear it up for them. On many occasions this was possible, either because the professors were sympathetic to the tough demands placed on student-athletes, or because they were willing to be reasonable once the lines of communication were opened. Rarely did an athlete take the initiative to go see his professor on his own or to develop a personal relationship with him or her. The response of most athletes, then, was to detach themselves from the whole process. While a few of the more serious students complained about being removed from selecting their courses, and felt that this belied the rhetorical emphasis on caring about academics, most welcomed the supervision.

They thus accepted the situation that taking care of academics was somebody else's responsibility, not theirs, and that they did not have to put much effort into worrying about it. This further reinforced the importance of their athletic identities and eroded the significance of their academic role.

Freshmen athletes' sense of false security was made complete by the final assumption that their athletic role-set members dominated over their academic role-set members. The coaches wielded power and influence over their professors and the academic administrators, they believed, and would make sure that they were "taken care of" academically. This belief was strengthened by the autonomy held by several big-time athletic programs within their universities, making the supervision of athletes and their special problems an issue of the athletic rather than academic sphere (Weistart 1989). As Slick stated:

> I never could understand how Frank can play. He flunked outta one school and done transferred three times. He never go to class. The coach can probably do something if he really wants a player to play. He is it—he can fix your career, your academic.

This perception about the differential power of their coaches compared to professors or academic administrators also led athletes to distance themselves from their academics and to diminish their effort in this realm.

Classroom Experiences

Athletes soon found that their college classes were hardly an extension of their high school experience. Rather, classes were very different from those of their high school days. This would become an area of difficulty and disillusionment that drove them away from self-involvement in the academic role.

One of the earliest things athletes noticed about University academic life was the attitude most students took toward classes; they were serious and they cared about their grades. This offered them the first inkling that academics might not fall into place as simply as they had anticipated. Near the beginning of his freshman year, overwhelmed by all he was encountering on campus, Damon gave this impression:

> Back home I used to go out and party every night, even during season. But here I see, grades are more important than partying. They say, like, when you get up here, that partying life's gonna be over with, 'cause you've got basketball, grades, you go on road trips, and when you come back you've gotta get your books.

Their early impressions of life on the University's campus struck them as more focused and intense academically than what they had experienced in high school. In his second semester at the University, Damon wrote about his impressions:

> The big difference between the schooling at [the University] is the grades. The subjects a freshmen are taking here at [the University] are very hard. Back in high school a D was fine to make, but not at [the University]. Most people who make D's will most likely take the course over or drop the class so the grade will not show up on their transcript.

Players had a variety of reactions to encountering this attitude on campus. Some were intimidated. They felt unfamiliar with the type of people who cared so much about classes and grades, and began to doubt their ability to perform in the same academic arena as them. Others felt alienated. They could not relate to this extreme focus on competition and academic standards of evaluation. They started thinking of themselves as different from other students, as athletes who did not belong in the academic sphere of the University. Still others were inspired by this attitude. The players with the highest academic aspirations may have felt worried about themselves or unfamiliar with the terrain, but they welcomed the chance to enter the University and "get an education." Yet even in this early period, they were still discovering the nature of the academic arena.

Athletes' initial optimism began to weaken once the season began and they were more intensively drawn into basketball. Their exhaustion from practices and their preoccupation with the upcoming season caused their class attendance and regularity with work assignments to become sporadic. They began to resemble other, older players in their laxity. Around mid-semester, their professors received the inquiries from the academic coach. Now they became "athletes." If they had any hope of being judged as individuals rather than as members of a social type, this labeling eradicated that opportunity. This generic identity that was cast onto them brought both good and bad images to the minds of their professors. After this, athletes believed that many professors regarded them as jocks.

Their coaches' inquiries about their academic progress were not the only indicators marking them as athletes. Often, they wore athletic or team clothing to class. They were most often taller than other students and more muscular, a fact not hidden by the scanty nature of most athletic tee and muscle shirts. They were also frequently surrounded in their classes by other athletes. Arriving in a group, they often occupied the rear of the classroom, and appeared uninterested. They perceived, then, that professors treated them differently from the general student body. While a few professors did give them greater interest and toler-ance—i.e., extra tutoring sessions, relaxed deadlines, relaxed academic standards (cf. Raney, Knapp, and Small 1983)—there were others who took the opposite approach. They stereotyped all athletes as dumb jocks, and assumed that none of them were interested in academic work. Many athletes attributed professors' harsh treatment to jealousy (that they could go on road trips, be media celebrities) and/or grudges. As Marcus explained:

> Some try to make it harder on you. Some are out to get you because they feel like you're living like a king and it shouldn't be that way. With those guys it don't matter how hard you try. They gonna flunk you just 'cause you a athalete.

In these cases they "rejected the rejecters" (Sykes and Matza 1957), using persecution as a rationale for disengaging from academics. This differential treatment served to reinforce their perception that they were athletes more than students. Therefore, when they returned to their dorm rooms at night, exhausted and sore from practicing, it became easier for them to rationalize, procrastinate, and "fritter" (Bernstein 1978) their time away instead of studying.

Athletes also became disengaged in academics because of the con-tent of their classes. Many individuals placed in the more "manageable" physical education or recreation majors, even those who were fairly uninterested in academics from the beginning, felt that their courses lacked academic or practical merit and were either comical, irrelevant, or demeaning. As a sophomore, Buck articulated the commonly held view:

> How could I get into this shit? They got me takin' nutrition, mental retardation, square dancing, and camp counseling. I thought I was goin' learn something here. It's a bunch o' bullshit.

Athletes placed in pre-professional majors (business, engineering, arts and sciences) or those enrolled in more advanced or demanding courses to fulfill their requirements, often found themselves unprepared and unequipped for the difficulty of the work expected. They could be taking required or serious upper-division courses in their major as well as filling distribution requirements, in addition to an elective or two chosen because the coaches thought these would be easier courses. Many players were greatly surprised by how hard their courses were, and how different they were from their high school classes. Recalling his high school academic experiences, Clyde remarked:

> You could get B's and C's by just showing up. I never really had to try or to study. I would go to practice, eat, and go out. I never even wrote a research paper until senior year, and then when I got to college it was all research papers.

Darian commented on what he found the toughest, academically, in college:

> Math. The writing and the reading. Everything. The normal basic things—put together papers like you was the teacher. Can't just throw anything down. And it's not as easy to bullshit on the essay questions.

Continuing his essay about the life of a college athlete, quoted earlier, Damon wrote:

> Before I came to [the University], I thought this school was going to be just like high school. For example, at my high school back home, the teachers would give little reading assignments because they new most of the students would always go out. They would also make sure everyone done the reading before we went on to the next subject. The teachers really cared if the student got behind, so sometimes they would teach individually.
>
> Another thing I thought about [the University] was the test we took. I thought it would be a lot of test during the semester because of the little reading we would do. I was used to taking about 14 test a semester for each of my classes. But when I came to this school, all this things I thought were wrong. First of all, college is nothing like high school. In high school you go to the same class everyday. But here, we go to certain classes on certain days. Another thing thats different here than high school is reading assignments. Here the reading assignments are about 3 to 4

chapters, and thats just for one class. In high school that was about as much as all my classes.

The main thing I realized was that the teachers don't waight on the student to read the assignments. But by the next time the class meets, they ask if you understand the assignment. If you say yes, then most of them would give a pop quiz, like my English teacher. English is one the hardest subject a freshmen will take. Another false thought I had back from home was test. The teachers would always emphsize how much we have to remember things on the test. Like here, for example, in Sociology you really can't memorize things because you can always remember the multiple choice answer but you have to defend your answer. And most of the things on the test are asking for your own thoughts.

Another major difference in high school then college are the caring of the teachers. Back home the teachers really cared if the students got behind, so theirfore they help individually. But here I can not really say the teacher's care because if you get behind its your problem not theirs. The one good thing I can say about teacher's are, they will send a person who needs help to a reading or writing lab or they will advise you to get a toutor.

Although many college students are disillusioned by professors' impersonal attitudes toward them, the lack of supervision from guidance counselors, and the difficulty of the academic work (Moffatt 1989), most athletes are especially untrained for the demanding calibre of college work. Many of the individuals recruited came from rural areas where the schools were not academically sophisticated, and they had not experienced the kinds of assignments commonly given in college. Another reason was that the University, like many Division I schools, had lower admission requirements for athletes than for the rest of the student body (cf. Eitzen and Purdy 1986; Sack 1984). The administrators defended this policy on the grounds that they were offering students who were academically less qualified, but who had other areas in which they could contribute to the University, a chance to get an education and achieve upward mobility. The result was that many of the athletes did not stand on equal footing with other students, and had a difficult time keeping up with the work. Yet even those athletes who came to college with respectable test scores had trouble completing the assignments. For most of them, their athletic experiences in high school had given them more rewards than their classes, and they had developed neither the study habits nor the skills necessary to compete in a serious academic arena (cf. Edwards 1984). Thus, because of their backgrounds, motivation, and the way their athletic experiences overwhelmed their attention, many athletes had inadequate skills, knowledge, study habits, time, and interest to produce academically competitive work.[3] In addition, just as the season got underway, the fall semester concluded, bringing final exams. This juxtaposed timing made it even more difficult for athletes to complete their course assignments and study for tests. Their anticipated rewards from the academic role were often replaced by a series of disappointments. Marcus described how his failures brought feelings of frustration and inadequacy:

> When I first come here I thought I'd be goin' to class all the time and I'd study and that be it. But I sure didn't think it meant studyin' all the time. Back in high school you just be memorizing things, but that's not what they want here. Back in high school I thought I be a pretty good student, but now I don't know.

Athletes did not have an easy time accepting these kinds of feelings. When faced with them, they often chose to withdraw from the scene. Buck described his reaction to experiences of failure:

> My first semester, in Anthropology, I flunked the first test, so I said, "To hell with it, I'm not going to try." I gave up on a couple of classes.

Athletes' experiences in the classroom were very different from their preconceptions. The work was harder and they were not taken care of to the extent they had imagined. Because of the intense competition in the athletic arena, they became obsessed with success (Harris and Eitzen 1978). Their frequent academic failures (or, at best, mediocre grades) led to their embarrassment and despair, which caused them to engage in role-distancing (Ball 1976) and to abandon some of the self-investment they had made in their academic performance. It was better not to have tried at all than to have tried and failed.

Yet a new type of freedom accompanied the disenchantments. Unlike high school, their attendance at classes was not compulsory, nor did they have to attend all day. James reflected on this change:

You're a lot more on your own. You don't have your mother coming in there in the morning saying "It's time to get up, go to class, go to school." It's harder because you have to make your own decisions. In college, classes are a little too carefree, in a way.

Being able to skip classes placed a greater responsibility for self-motivation on them. As they observed the activities and behavior of many older athletes toward academics (lack of respect, lack of effort), many gradually adopted a less serious attitude also. They relaxed their attendance standards, and began to "ditch" classes when they were tired, distracted, or unprepared. During his sophomore year, James articulated a common pattern of gradually slipping behind in his attendance and classwork until his problem became compounded:

> When I first started school I went to all my classes because I was used to going all day, every day. Then when the season started and I got caught up in everything I began to slip. I didn't do well. Every semester I say to myself I'll do better this semester; this one'll be different. But I've been fucking up so bad in my classes now I'm just embarrassed to show up any more. It just keeps getting worse and worse.

Road Trips

Compounding the emotional distraction of the season was the physical removal athletes experienced during road trips. Most freshmen took their books with them on the road, hoping and trying to keep up with their work while they were away from school. With great effort they were able to get some light work done. As Rob described:

> Yeah, I did get some work in a few times. You don't have all those other distractions on the road that you have when you at home. Ya know, I wasn't going to call anyone from my hotel room, because I knew I had to pay for it. So there was times when you can read. I mean, I didn't do any serious homework on the road, but I did get some reading done now and then.

After their first year, however, most players stopped taking their books along with them because they knew it was futile; the conditions made it too difficult to study. Marcus described these in more detail:

> I quit doin' it. I mean I wouldn't take a book 'cause I knew I wouldn't study. An' I would try to study, but your mind would be on practice. Because when you travel, you would travel a day before the game. You be travellin' like all day, and airports take a lot out of you. I hate being on the road. I don't like hotels. It's rough. Then you go to practice. And then Coach would tell you, "Get a good night's sleep; get somethin' to eat." So you go to sleep and you think you'll study then. No, you're thinkin' about the game tomorrow. Then you get up in the morning. Eat breakfast. You sort of tire from yesterday's practice. You wanna relax, but you're gonna be ready. And then you gotta go to shootin' practice at 12. And that's 12 to 1, maybe 1:30. An' you come back over, you eat a pre-game meal. There's time to study then but you've been working out, got hit, maybe you're a little sore, and you just want to lie down, relax, and get ready for the game. An' then it's time to play the game. You're tired after the game. You can't study then. And then it's time to go to another city to play another one. An' then you gotta go practice again. So I had to stop takin' the books, because there's no way you can study on the road . . . I don't like the road because you get behind in class and the students, they think that you're skipping.

Not all of the players were as conscientious about their schoolwork. Most did not mind missing classes or getting away from assignments. They made fun of Mark (an L-7), whom they claimed took his books along on road trips, even though he did not crack them, to promote his image with the boosters as a serious student. They, in contrast, did not take their books. As Ben explained, there were plenty of reasons not to feel guilty:

> No one opens books on the road. We have fun on road trips. In a hotel, you feel like you're free, like you're on vacation. Just laid back in a nice comfortable hotel, good bed, no worries in the world, watch cable TV, eat the best food. There's school going on back at [the University], but I'm not worrying about that; I'm 500 miles from school and it's legitimate for you to be there and

not thinking about school. It's an adventure to be in a hotel, especially at our age. That's our reward for all that hard work. Lay around and relax.

When players returned from the road Coach usually ended the trip with an admonishment to the entire team to "Be sure and go to class." It was hard to readjust their perspectives to being back on campus, back as ordinary students, especially with the continuing onslaught of home games. Only the ones who really tried were able to accomplish this mental transition. The others never really became students again until the end of the season.

Finishing the Year

By mid-March then, or later, depending on their success in post-season tournament play, the games were over. It was time to become students once again. One cycle was finished and another was to begin. For the serious students this was "catch up" time. The bounds of their season represented the bounds of their lives as students. Just as the beginning of the season had plucked them out of fall semester's end, out of finals, so did the end of the season coincide with the waning of spring semester. One player remarked that October 15 is the turning point where basketball ascends from second place into the first priority. Season's end marks the point of turning back, where athletes can become students once again. The most academically inclined athletes turned their efforts to their classes at this time, trying to make up what they could, to complete their coursework and study for finals. Yet this was very difficult. As Danny expressed:

> When the season's over you get a big sigh of relief and you say I'm gonna relax. So you might relax and not play basketball, but you also got the idea, "Well I'm gonna relax at school too." And that's what you really wanna do.

After the last game Coach always assembled the team and congratulated them on their good season. He encouraged them to spend time in the weight room over the summer, building up for next year. He made remarks directed toward certain individuals, giving them suggestions on how to improve their game. And then he also said, "Stay in the books." By the timing and tone of his remarks, most players interpreted this to mean that they should stay eligible. After this the team generally dispersed, with the players and coaches going their separate ways. Players might not see the coaches for days or even weeks unless they came up to the basketball offices.

Thinking rationally, most players realized that this was the time to throw themselves into their academic work. They should go to class, study, and complete their coursework. Ironically, however, it did not usually happen this way. Many athletes did not use their newly found free time to focus on academics. Some of the serious and dedicated ones did, but the majority turned to their neglected social lives. Without the constant presence of their coaches monitoring and haranguing them to at least go to class, this vestige of their academic conscience abated.

By the end of their first year most athletes began to grasp the complexities of this system. They realized how difficult it was to fulfill the requirements of their academic role. They recognized, then, with varying degrees of sadness, that their college careers could have no more than limited academic potential.

Broken Security

Athletes entered the academic realm with a high degree of confidence, expecting to achieve success. Much of this expectation was based, especially after their early experiences, on their blind faith in their coaches. As they became progressively socialized to the academic role, a lot of their confidence disappeared as their trust in those coaches eroded. The security that they had once felt was shattered by several related realizations.

LIMITED INTEREST

First, they realized that their coaches had limited interest in the academic sphere. The allegiance they paid to academics was more than lip service, yet less than they alleged. While they cared, they did not care enough to follow through and make sure that academic policies were followed or academic concerns given priority. Nightly study halls degenerated, as the assistant coach monitoring them was often in his office with the door shut, and rarely checked on them. Rather than studying, they mostly clowned around. Thus, the admonitions and threats Coach voiced in practice were never backed up with any action. Eventually the players learned that if they could get past his threatening, they could do as they pleased. James, who had expected the coaches to keep him in line academically, described his disappointment in discovering that this assumption had been erroneous:

> When I first came in, from what they were saying, I thought they'd keep on my ass. Like if I wasn't going to class I'd have to go out and run bleachers or something. . . . I've finally realized that there's not gonna be nobody to wake you up in the morning, to make sure you're goin' to class. Nobody's gonna send you runnin' if you don't do all of these things.

The safety net that they thought was being provided by the coaches monitoring their progress in class also turned out to be imperfect. In fact, James, enrolled in the business school, found out with only three weeks left to go in the second semester of his sophomore year that he was on the verge of flunking out of school. He would not even have discovered his imminent dismissal had he not seen one of the business school counselors to arrange his enrollment in summer school. That this came as a shock to the coaches as well as to himself led him to believe that they had been remiss in their responsibilities toward him:

> Coach Mickey [the academic coach] stuck me in the business college and I thought he knows what's going on over there. But he don't even know about drop/add. I thought everything was all right or I would'a heard about it. Then, all of a sudden, I'm flunking out and everybody is freaking out. Mickey is pissed off, Coach is mad. Up until just now they weren't even worried about it. They never checked, and now it's the last three weeks of the semester.

James had been irresponsible about keeping up his grades for almost two years but had never received a formal reprimand or warning, such as being placed on academic probation. The event precipitating his near expulsion was failing a class because he had never withdrawn from it correctly. Although the assistant coach had followed the normal arts and sciences withdrawal procedures, he did not know that permission from the dean was necessary to drop required business school courses.

Being threatened with expulsion made James clearly realize how close he could come to the ultimate academic failure without his coaches even knowing about it. As he expressed:

Practically all the stuff he talks, that he's more interested in scholarship, scholastic-wise, than he is athletic-wise, is a bunch of bullshit, because he's just not interested in it. They don't check with you until the last week of school. All's they're worried about is the 24 credits a year that you need to keep you eligible. Now they're talking how you're supposed to be your own man, doin' it, when before, they wouldn't let you tell them anything about how to do it and it was, "We know what's best for you, don't interfere."

Once players got past the starry-eyed idealism of their first year it increasingly dawned on them that the academic speeches of the coaches were largely rhetoric. They saw that despite coaches' real or feigned interest in academics, when the crunch of the season came, the pressure on them to win was so great that they pushed aside everything else ("They can't afford to be thinking about our academics"). Athletes also realized that to their coaches, "getting an education" was synonymous with "getting that piece of paper." There was no ostensible emphasis on learning. Rather, the coaches' goals were to get the best players they could, and to keep them eligible to play. Because of the pressures they felt to win, as well as the constraints on their time, they were interested mainly in the athletes' graduating rather than in the kind of education they got. Thus, while Coach could afford to speak and feel as idealistic as he wanted, he was not the one planning athletes' schedules, talking to their professors, or having to make the difficult decisions. It was the academic coach who decided whether to enroll them in a hard course that they needed for their major (that they might not pass, or that they might pass with such a low grade that they would fall onto academic probation) or an easier one that would keep them academically eligible to continue in college and on the team (without necessarily advancing them toward graduation).

LIMITED POWER

Second, athletes' sense of security was broken by their realization that their coaches had limited power. As freshmen, athletes regarded their coaches as demi-gods, capable of wielding compelling influence over all spheres of life. The longer they remained in the program, the more likely they were to question this belief. James saw this for himself. He continued to believe, until nearly the end, in the peer subculture lore that the coaches can save those athletes they really want to, and that they are willing to sacrifice those who are not critically important to the team. As he exclaimed on the verge of his expulsion:

> There are 20 to 30 football players in the same place as me—they're gonna be dismissed. But they're gonna keep the ones they want and let the others go. The ones that they think are bad for their program don't come back. If they want you, they'll keep you goin' in and out of offices until you show enough interest that they keep you.

When his coaches tried, at the last minute, without success, to salvage him from expulsion, he realized that his athletic role-set members did not actually dominate the academic role-set members. In the end his parents saved him by going directly to the provost to plead his case.

LIMITED INTEGRITY

A third crushing realization involved athletes' perception that their coaches had limited integrity when it came to their academic lives. While they started out trusting their coaches completely, nearly all athletes ultimately came to feel that this trust had been abused (by the academic coach in particular). This realization dawned on some individuals during their sophomore year; others did not become aware of it until their junior year or later. They kept blithely moving on from semester to semester, assuming that everything was going according to some academic plan, until they had occasion to discuss their academic progress with someone outside of the athletic realm. There, most athletes were crestfallen to discover that their courses had not put them on track to graduate. As Marcus exclaimed dejectedly:

> Now here I am, a second semester junior, I been takin' classes every semester, and they tell me I'm 75 credits short of graduation. Nearly three years here and I ain't got more than 45 credits toward my major. And I'm only a rec major.

Darian also complained:

> We don't like their filling out our schedules anymore. Sometimes
> they don't even know what to put you into. Maybe Coach Mickey
> doesn't, even. We've come to the conclusion that he is just put-
> ting us into classes and not even getting us set up to get our
> major. You can take four years of college and not even work up
> to your major . . . . I don't know about those coaches. Sometimes
> I think they look at us as their bread and butter.

Academic Role-Set Members

Three groups of people made up athletes' primary academic role-set
members: their professors, their fellow students, and their parents. It
is telling that their interaction with members of each group was limited.

PROFESSORS

To athletes, professors represented a somewhat distant and removed
group. Largely white and middle class, they came from social backgrounds that many athletes regarded as superior. Athletes were further
awed by their education, status, and title, always referring to them by
their doctorate and last name. They brought to the relationship an
initial degree of intimidation.

Few athletes got to know their professors to any significant degree.
They did not stay after class and discuss ideas raised during the class
period, nor did they come to the professors' office hours to get help,
ask for clarification of points, discuss their special situation, or any
matters related to them or the class. They never called professors when
an exam was impending or a take-home was out to check out their
ideas or ask questions. In fact, the only times most professors had an
opportunity to interact one-on-one with their student-athletes was
when an athlete was in trouble and was sent by the academic coach to
ask the professor's permission to drop the class.

Further, athletes did not select their classes by continuing with
professors whose classes they had previously liked (they did not select
their professors at all), although they often found themselves re-en-
rolled in classes with professors who were known as friends of the
program. The professors they tended to get to know, if any, then, were

those predisposed toward them and their situation, or those whom they took repeatedly to satisfy their majors.

In interacting with their professors, athletes tended to be somewhat shy. Out of deference to professors' status, they rarely made complaints or demands, like other students, but rather adopted a more retiring role. They showed only a limited side of their selves to their professors, and rarely got to know them very well as people. A few of the more academically motivated athletes, those who persevered in the serious majors, eventually approached one of their professors to discuss their progress toward completing their requirements. This was usually when they realized that they had made significantly less progress toward graduation than they had imagined.

STUDENTS

Athletes had the opportunity to meet regular students in their academic classes (as opposed to their physical education classes, which were populated mostly by other athletes). They varied in the degree to which they reached out and made friends with those students. Generally speaking, athletes enrolled in arts and science majors made more student friends; athletes in business and engineering had less in common with their classmates, and the physical education majors encountered fewer regular students. Having relationships with regular students broadened athletes' social lives, as they were invited to parties outside the athletic dorm and spent more time socializing with non-athletes. However, since the number of athletes in arts and science majors was relatively low, and it decreased as they progressed through college, this still represented a relatively small portion of the team members. Most of the remaining athletes knew relatively few regular students and associated primarily with each other.

Athletes who hung around with their student friends found these types of interactions rather different from their interactions with athletes. As Clyde said:

Hanging around with the guys, you don't get the feeling from them like you will with, like say, a normal student, like some of my friends who are normal students. I don't sit down and talk about a lot of my schooling with them, yet they'll just go off and rattle about what they're doin'.' And here I am, I'm too embarrassed to do that, and I find myself lying, and saying I've went to class today, which I didn't, just to say that I did, so they won't think certain things about me. And then I find myself even lying to my parents, saying, "Yeah, I'm all right, don't worry." But I'm not, it's the other way around. And that makes me feel like shit.

Being ashamed and lying to student friends about behavior that they could openly admit among fellow athletes drove a wedge between athletes and other students. When they were with regular students they felt stupid and inadequate, like they did not belong. For all of these reasons, they tended to withdraw from their associations with regular students and to cocoon themselves in the ghetto of the athletic dorm.

PARENTS

Although athletes' parents knew them as fully rounded individuals, athletes tended to regard their parents (among others) as belonging to their academic role-set. As the above quote indicates, athletes' parents were often concerned about their academic progress, and questioned them about school in their phone conversations or, if they lived close enough, when they came to campus for games. Buck described his normal phone conversations with his mother:

The first thing she'll always ask about is, "How you doin' in school?" Then, only after that, she'll ask me how'm I feelin' and how'm I doin' in playing. 'Cause my mother worked very hard to support my brother and me, and what she always wanted was for us to get a education.

Their families were thus an active force keeping them involved in the academic role. This was significant because most athletes considered their family members very important. On the other hand, their families were far away, and they did not see them or talk to them very often. They lacked the compelling immediacy of the other people and pressures surrounding athletes daily.

Overviewing athletes' academic role-set members, we see that their relationships with these individuals were characterized by a limited degree of contact. Athletes had few associations with their professors, their relationships with other students (when these existed) were sometimes problematic, and their parents were generally removed from the scene. As a result, athletes lacked the strong reinforcement from their academic role-set members that they derived from both their athletic and social role-set members. This further served to weaken their ties and commitment to their academic role.

Role Conflict

It did not take long for athletes to realize that there were conflicts between their academic role and their two other roles. Ben summed it up succinctly when he exclaimed:

> It's either cut off my social life, or flunk out of school, or not go pro.

ACADEMIC-ATHLETIC

The most obvious conflict lay between their athletic and academic roles and obligations. This was especially problematic because they had to balance the two, or they risked losing them both. The naive early idealism of their freshman year gave way to disappointment and growing cynicism as they realized the difficulties involved in getting their academic work done. They soon discovered that handling both roles was not always possible. A primary reason was the *time conflict*. Some athletes discovered that courses they needed for their majors were offered in the afternoons during practice time. This effectively precluded athletes completing natural science or engineering majors because of the required afternoon labs. Many other non-recreation majors faced similar obstacles.

Games and road trips also served as a hurdle to athletes' academic progress, as they often coincided with exams and term papers. Going on the road meant, further, that athletes needed adjustment time before and after leaving: time to make up the work they had missed, and time to do the work that was currently assigned. Most athletes found this impossible, especially during the season, with all its distractions.

When they were not being pulled away from their studying by home and away games, banquets and booster obligations cut into their academic work. As we have shown, they often attended two or three dinners a week and had to spend time getting dressed up, socializing politely after the meal (they could not just eat and run), and waiting for transportation to and from the event. While class attendance was ostensibly optional, practices, booster functions, road trips, and games were definitely not. Thus, much of their time was controlled by members of their athletic role-set rather than by athletes themselves. As a result, even players like Darian who were serious about academics had trouble finding adequate time for school work, as he explained:

> You don't have no time for academics, basically. Like last weekend I thought I'd get a chance to catch up on my studying, but he [Coach] brings in a new recruit, he wants us to show him around, play with him for a couple of hours, you shower, there's a football game on, you know I want a little recreation, come back, and it's time for bed. It's like academics and athletics are two jobs.

Yet unlike students who went to school and worked on the side, athletes could not put their jobs aside mentally when it came time to concentrate on school. The basketball intruded into their consciousness when it was time to engage their academic role. Marcus explained:

> At night when you're in your room and you're supposed to be studying, you're thinking about the last game, or the next game, or what's happened in practice, or what's gonna happen in practice. You're thinking basketball. If you have a test the next day, forget it.

Clyde echoed his sentiments:

> Many times I'm in class and I'm thinking about who I gotta guard, you know, what play we're gonna run, or tryin', you know, to remember the film. I may go through the whole class daydreamin' about a game. And then I go out and I haven't learned anything.

Athletes also faced a conflict between their pulls toward *immediate versus long-term reinforcement*. Athletic participation gave them immediate positive feedback for their efforts in the form of adoring fans, media attention, praise and rewards from the coaching staff, and the admiration of their peers. These were very intense forms of gratification. Academic participation, in contrast, was something that would not pay off for them until some time in the future. Before they could reap any benefits they had to finish four years of college and graduate. Even then, their reward would be a job (hopefully) and a secure lifestyle. This was hardly a challenge to the allure of a possible professional basketball career, despite the slim odds of their making it. Most athletes came from backgrounds that favored the immediate, rather than deferred, forms of gratification. Yet even those who came from middle class families soon succumbed to the orientation toward the immediate, and succumbed to the ethos of "cashing in" on the rewards for all their hard work in the present time.

A third dimension to their academic-athletic role conflict lay in their *coaches' inner conflicts*. They had begun their college years thinking that their coaches would inspire or help them remain committed to academics. They had heard the rhetoric about academics and believed it. Ultimately, however, their coaches' actions belied their words; athletes realized that the coaches, too, were caught in a conflict, or at least a contradiction. Darian described the indicators which signified to him that his coaches did not sincerely care as much about academics as they professed:

> Being a athalete you need help to get through. And, like, we've got to go to Coach to get our tutors, and if a guy don't really care about his academics he won't go. I think if the coach really cares about academics he ought to be checking on you—"Hey, you need a tutor," but we've got to go. And another thing. One time I had a paper that was really hard that was due. So I said to Coach Mickey, "I'm gonna be a little late to practice because I have to go to the library to do some work on my paper." But he told me, "You'd better be in the gym by three o'clock." I think if they was serious about academics, they would cut you some slack on that.

Their coaches' attitudes and actions had a great influence in heightening the role conflict for them. While coaches demanded that athletes keep up with the obligations of the athletic role, they were expected to fulfill school responsibilities on their own time. This bred a cynical attitude among athletes toward their coaches. As Marcus said:

> Only reason coaches care about if their kids get a degree or wind up on the streets is because it helps them. If they don't get their

players to graduate ain't nobody else going to come to their schools and that's gonna make them look bad. That's the only reason I think they care about academics.

Thus, by the end of their first year, most athletes realized that they did not have enough time to perform as well as they wished in these two roles. Darian, who cared a lot about academics, remarked:

If I was just a student like most other students I could do well, but when you play the calibre of basketball that we do, you just can't be an above average student. What we try to strive for is just to be average students. 2.75 was my best GPA. You just don't find the time to do all the reading.

Recognizing the role conflict thus made them see beyond the rhetoric to the reality: that academics came at the expense of their social life, not their athletics.

ACADEMIC-SOCIAL

With the athletic role dominating players' social and academic roles, these latter two roles (and their role-set members) then competed against each other for athletes' remaining time and energy. Unlike their participation in athletic-related functions, which was mandatory, the amount of relative effort athletes invested in their social and academic lives was left to their discretion. Nearly all athletes took their social lives, or recreational time, as a basic personal necessity to which they felt entitled. The academic role was more variable in importance.

All athletes wanted to have a social life and do well in their classes, but they followed different patterns in deciding how deeply they would cultivate these two roles. Several factors affected their decision. First, their prior *academic orientations* influenced the seriousness of their commitment to the academic role. This was somewhat tied to their future goals, for while all athletes held strongly to the NBA dream, some had more clearly developed fall-back alternatives. Most of these required a college degree. Second, athletes' *commitment* to academics was affected by their early positive or negative experiences in their classes. They all did more poorly than they had expected, yet some managed to form relations with students or professors. These relationships helped them learn how to get more academic resources from the

University by going to see professors, going to review sessions, or
revealing their sincere interest in school. These athletes usually managed to stave off the more severe early forms of academic humiliation
and failure. Third, their attitudes were affected by the general tone of
the *peer subculture*. Faunce (1984) has noted that concerns and standards about academic achievement are anchored in social relationships.
The peer group's anti-academic character had the effect of lowering
everyone's academic interests and goals. James explained how this
occurred:

> Everyone's attitude just kind of spreads to each other, 'specially
> in that dorm. If someone says they're goin' blow off class, you're
> goin' sometimes do it too. You may get up to go to your morn-
> ing class, but after lunch, when you're all together, someone will
> come in and say they're going out to this or that, or you end up
> laying around the room just talking, and that's it until practice.
> So you get more careless about what you do, and about your
> standards too. Like Ben handed in a paper written by his high
> school girlfriend and got an F on it when he was smart enough
> to do it himself and get a better grade. 'Cause everybody's look-
> ing for the easy way out.

Fourth, and most importantly, their involvement in the academic role
was influenced by their *friendship networks,* or cliques, within the athletes' peer community. Differences in academic involvement and effort
emerged between the groups. Both the L-7s and the candy-asses cared
about academics and were willing to sacrifice a considerable amount of
their free time to do school work. Members of these groups were
influenced by each other to leave room in their plans for academics.
This came slightly more easily, as well, because they did not have as
demanding social lives as the whiners and bad niggas. While the L-7s
and candy asses usually had steady girlfriends and saw them exclusively,
the whiners and bad niggas were more likely to date around or to cheat
on their steady girlfriends. This absorbed a great deal of their time and
effort. The former also spent their time somewhat more sedately. While
they would spend weekend evenings drinking a beer, the whiners and
bad niggas were more likely to get high on marijuana, have a few
drinks, and/or an occasional snort of cocaine. Their kind of socializing
was more likely to take them further from the likelihood of studying.
Members of these groups thus liked to party more and accorded it a

higher priority. Comparing those with whom he socialized to the candy-asses and the L-7s, Buck remarked:

> They don't care about their social life as much as we do. It's not as big to them as it is to us. They let Coach intimidate them and get them, and he forces them into doin' that [school]. He's more buddy-buddy with them, and academically I guess they feel they have to do it because of Coach and the way he threatens them — his friendship and his respect.

Within the whiners and the bad niggas, the emphasis was on getting the most out of the college social experience. Individuals within these groups had serious career goals, but the tenor of their crowd did not reinforce them. Many of them derided academics and team members who put time and effort into it. Commenting on this, Apollo described how his peers reacted to his instances of academic effort and success:[4]

> When most of the other guys are making D's and F's, if I work hard and I get a C on a test, if I go back to the dorm and they all see I got a C, then they goin' snap on [make fun of] me. So most of the guys, they don't try. They all act like it's a big joke.

This attitude, common to all four groups, carried into the classroom, where uninterested athletes set a negative attitude for each other toward academics.

The whiners and bad niggas thus spent most of their non-athletic time going out to clubs or just hanging around. Candy-asses and L-7s, in contrast, placed more emphasis on the academic role. They stayed around the dorms, rarely missed classes, participated in class as much as possible, and emphasized the future rewards their deferred gratification would bring. The conflict between the groups was exacerbated by the favoritism the coaches showed toward the straighter ones.

Yet even those athletes who believed in their academic role and held academic goals generally considered their recreational, personal time more important. They were caught in a struggle between two roles, neither of which could be abandoned. In high school they had handled this problem by allotting little time to school while still managing to maintain an acceptable level of academic performance. In college, more effort was required to sustain the minimum threshold. As Apollo noted:

You get more involved with the school part of it as you go through. You don't really realize when you first get there what all is expected from you. You kind of think of it as a big high school. You don't think of it as you have to read, and you have to study, and you have to listen to the professor or you can't obtain it. In high school you can obtain it all from the teacher and not really look at the books. You can study minutes before the test and still pull off a C. In college you flunk every time doin' that. As far as the years go on, you learn. You have to.

While they came in expecting things to remain basically the same, they eventually learned what their academic obligations entailed. Their role conflict thus became even more intense as they progressed from one year to the next and learned the role. This conflict was engendered primarily by the growth and dominance of their athletic role, which took an all-encompassing position in their lives. They thus came to realize that this role was a "greedy role," forcing all other concerns and involvements to yield to its demands. Like Coser's (1974) notion of the "greedy institution," it exerted inordinate pressure on individuals to weaken or sever ties with any group or activity that might make successful competing claims on its assertions of supremacy.

6
The Gloried Self

THE MASSIVE expansion and intensification of their athletic role effected some fundamental social psychological changes in college athletes. This role not only demanded more time, more concentration, and more physical exertion, but also offered more in return. Through their membership on this high-powered, high-visibility team, athletes were raised to the stature of heroes. They became celebrities so famous they could not have privacy in public, they were sought after by reporters, and they became role models to community youth. In effect, they were thrust into the spotlight of glory. They found this overwhelming.

Athletes experienced this glory in many ways and developed a variety of means to deal with it. Yet from the team's biggest stars to the lowliest freshmen or walk-ons, it changed them in both subtle and noticeable ways. The experience of glory was so existentially gratifying that these athletes became emotionally riveted on it, turning away from other aspects of their lives and selves that did not offer such fulfillment. Out of the glory experience they thus developed "gloried" selves lodged in their athletic role.

Athletes developed gloried selves as a result of the intense interpersonal and media attention that accompanied their celebrity. It did not necessarily matter whether that celebrity was positive or negative; in our society we accord status and recognition for both fame and notoriety (Goldsmith 1983). Their developing gloried selves was caused, in part, by the treatment of their selves, by others, as objects. A "public persona" was created, usually by the media, that differed from their private ones. These public images were rarely as intricate or complex as athletes' real selves; they often drew on stereotypes or portrayed them in extremes to accentuate their point. And yet, the power of these media portrayals, reinforced by face-to-face encounters with people who held these images, often caused athletes to objectify their selves to themselves. They thus became initially alienated from themselves, through the separation of their self concept from the conception of their selves held by others. Athletes ultimately resolved this disparity and reduced their alienation by changing their self-images to bridge the gap created by others' different perceptions of them, even though they fought this development as it occurred.

The Allure of Glory

The glory experience was exciting, reinforcing, and ultimately transformative. Two self-dimensions were either created or expanded in the athletes we studied: the reflected self and the media self.

THE REFLECTED SELF

As a result of the face-to-face interactions team members had with people they encountered through their role as college athletes, their impressions of themselves became modified and changed. As Cooley (1902) and Mead (1934) first proposed, individuals engage in role-taking, and their self-conceptions are products of social interaction, affected by the reflected impressions of others. According to Cooley (1902), these "looking glass" selves are formed through a combination of forces; individuals react to the impressions they perceive others forming about themselves and also develop reactions to these judgments. These reactions are instrumental in shaping their self-images. They thus utilize what Rosenberg (1979) and Sullivan (1953) have called "reflected appraisals" in forging a new sense of self.

The forging and modification of their reflected selves began as team members perceived how people treated them and subsequently formed reactions to that treatment. One of the first things they all noticed was that they were highly sought after by strangers. Large numbers of people, individually and in groups, wanted to see them, to be near them, to get their autographs, to touch them, and to talk to them. People treated them as objects of awe and fascination. For example, one day Coach walked out of his office and found a woman waiting there for him. As he turned toward her she threw herself in front of him and began to kiss his feet. He described his reaction:

> I didn't know what to do. All of a sudden here was this woman kissing my feet and babbling on about what a great man I was, how much I had done for the black community, how great I was, over and over, and how much respect she had for me. I pulled her to her feet and told her that she didn't have to act like that to anyone, but all the while I was thinking, "Is this right? Is this appropriate? What has this thing come to? It's one thing for the media to go on about us, but something is wrong here if regular people are starting to act toward me this way."

More commonly, fans who were curious about team matters approached players and coaches to engage them in dialogue. These interactions sometimes made players feel awkward because they wanted to be polite to their fans, yet they had little to say to them. Carrying on a conversation was often difficult, as Apollo expressed:

> People come walking up to you, and whether they're timid or pushy, they still want to talk. It's like, here's their hero standing face-to-face with them and they want to say anything just so they can have a conversation with them. It's *hero worshipping*. But what do you actually say to your hero when you see him?

These interactions, then, often took the form of ritualized pseudo-conversations, in which players and their fans offered normatively stylized but empty words to each other.

When out in public, players were also often recognized and approached by total strangers who acted as if they knew them. These fans accorded them "cognitive recognition" (Goffman 1963), socially identifying them, and expecting them to respond in kind. As Marcus remarked:

> It's a real odd feeling to have these people be walking up to you like they some kind o' friend of yours. They call you by your first name, they want you to make conversation with them. Suddenly everybody in town's on a first name basis with you.

Players were particularly thrust into a "pseudo-intimacy" (Bensman and Lilienfeld 1979:94) with members of the public because of the nature of their sport: there were far fewer players on the squad compared with the football team, so people knew and recognized them all; they wore no face-concealing helmets; and there are parts of the game (such as foul shots) where they remained fairly immobile so that the television cameras had the opportunity to broadcast close-ups of their faces while they were in deep concentration. The public vicariously lived through these times with them and experienced an emotional bonding with players. Yet although it was a one-sided relationship, they expected players and coaches to reciprocate their feelings of intimacy. Through their celebrity, players and coaches frequently found themselves in "exposed positions" (Goffman 1963) where they were opened up to be engaged in personal interaction with others whom they did not know at all.

As we have seen in chapter 1, boosters jealously fought over the privilege of spending time with players and having them in their houses. Their polite, respectful, and interested treatment often confused players, as Tyrone stated in his freshman year:

> When I'm at some millionaire booster's house I always wonder what they are thinking. Why do they want me here so much? Why are they always smiling when they see me? What's goin' on? Am I that appealing to them?

It soon became apparent that boosters derived social status from associating with them, that boosters "basked in the reflected glory" (Burger 1985; Cialdini et al. 1976; Sigelman 1986) they captured from them. Players recognized that they were "glory bearers," so replete with glory that they could cast it onto anyone by their mere presence. They experienced a sense of the "Midas touch." They had an attribute that everybody wanted (fame), and it could be transmitted. Their ability to cast glory onto others and their desirability by others because of it became an important dimension of their new, reflected self-identity.

THE MEDIA SELF

A second dimension of the self created out of the glory experience was one largely influenced by media portrayals. Bensman and Lilienfeld

(1979) have suggested that in contemporary American society the media have dissolved the boundaries between public and private. Altheide (1984) has discussed the effect of the media as a fulcrum between self-feelings and the impressions, expectations, and behavior of others. He has argued that modern life is increasingly characterized by media attention, leading to the creation of a "media self," where the self is raised to the level of self-consciousness, the focus of the individual's own attention. Fenigstein et al. (1975) have called this a "public self-consciousness," where the self becomes perceived as a social actor who serves as a stimulus for others' behavior. Most athletes who came to the University had received some media publicity in high school, but the national level of the print and video coverage they received after arriving, coupled with the intensity of its constant focus, caused them to develop a more compelling and salient media self than they had previously possessed.

Radio, television, and newspaper reporters covering the team often sought out athletes for "human interest" stories. These features presented media-framed angles that cast them into particular roles and tended to create new dimensions of their selves. Images were created out of a combination of individuals' actual behavior and reporters' ideas of what made good copy. Players, then, were cast into molds through their media coverage that were often distorted or exaggerated reflections of their behavior and self-conceptions.

Team members often felt that they had to live up to these portrayals. For instance, first Rob, and then in later years, Marcus and Darian, were depicted as "good students," shy, quiet, religious, and diligent. Special news features emphasized their outstanding traits, illustrating how they went to class, were humanitarian, and cared about graduating. They knew that Coach appreciated this because it was good publicity for the team, but it affected their everyday interactions with fans, acquaintances, and friends. As Marcus lamented:

> Other kids our age, they go to the fair and they walk around with a beer in their hand, or a cigarette, but if me and Darian were to do that, then people would talk about that. We can't go over to the clubs, or hang around, without it relaying back to Coach. We can't even do things around our teammates, because they expect us to be a certain way. The media has created this image of us as the "good boys," and now we have to live up to it.

Other players were seized upon for their charismatic qualities. They had naturally outgoing personalities, the ability to turn on a crowd, to put their fist in the air, wave towels, jump up and down exhorting fans to cheer. They capitalized on this media coverage, exaggerating their antics to gain attention and fame. Apollo discussed this role:

> I was always the favorite of the crowd. I would play to the crowd, go into my act. I have a certain amount of charisma, you know, and I know how to use it.

But throughout his college years, the more he mustered that showmanship, the more it got away from him. It turned into a caricature of his original self. Whenever he was around others, he felt compelled to turn it on. The more the media presented this image of him, the more he portrayed this character and the more it consequently developed an outside life of its own. He could not act the way he wanted to, could not draw upon the complexity of inner feelings he often experienced such as reflectiveness, seriousness, or personal concerns. He discussed his feelings of constraint by his objectified media self:

> That Apollo image, it's out there. The media like to play to something like that, it sells papers. And so they come around expecting it. But they wrote about it so often that everybody is expecting me to be that way. It's okay, most of the time, but sometimes it bothers me. I never get to be a real person, to have another side. And, you know, sometimes I don't feel that up. I want to just be concentrating and minding my own business and not be into pumping everybody up on the team. And in the stands. And on the street. 'Cause it follows you everywhere you go.

Tyrone, who had a similarly high public profile, described how he felt trapped by his braggart media self:

> I used to like getting in the paper. When reporters came around I would make those Mohammed Ali type outbursts—I'm gonna do this, I'm gonna do that. And they come around again, stick a microphone in your face, 'cause they figure somewhere Washington will have another outburst. But playing that role died out in me. I think sometimes the paper pulled out a little too much

from me that wasn't me. But people seen me as what the paper said, and I had to play that role.

Particular roles notwithstanding, everyone shared the media-conferred sense of self as celebrity. This was as true for the players who saw more court time as for those who were substitutes, and as true for the candy-asses and L-7s as the whiners and bad niggas. Raised to the status of stars, larger-than-life, they regularly saw their names and statements in the newspaper, saw their faces on television, or heard themselves whispered about on campus. The enormous success of the program as a whole created a team atmosphere that was exceedingly rarified. This fostered such an abundance of glory that it distinctly separated even the team's least important and talented members from the lay public and generated media selves for them. Jesse described the consequences of this celebrity:

> We didn't always necessarily agree with the way they wrote about us in the paper, but people who saw us expected us to be like what they read there. A lot of times it made us feel uncomfortable, acting like that, but we had to act like they expected us to, for the team's sake. We had to act like this was what we was really like.

Ironically, however, the more they interacted with people through their dramaturgically-induced media selves, the more many team members felt familiar and comfortable with this image ("We know what to do, we don't have to think about it no more"). The media presented these selves, the public believed them, and so athletes continued to portray them. Even though they kept repressing and denying these selves, telling themselves that they were media constructions, something pressed for their legitimacy and acceptance. With time, they increasingly began to believe these portrayals, transforming their behavior into more than just "impression management" (Goffman 1959). Gradually, they evolved from role-playing into role-making (Turner 1978): infusing elements of their core self in the role, whether this was diligent and studious or flamboyant and charismatic.

Individuals' treatment through such public selves, as Mead (1934) first implied through his discussion of the role-taking interplay between the I and the Me, penetrates deeply to influence their private selves, those self-conceptions that spell out what kind of people they sincerely consider themselves. In many instances, as Hochschild (1983) has noted, it is easier to actually change one's emotions than to pretend to emotions one does not feel. They thus went through a process of gradually abandoning their "role distance" (Goffman 1961b), and became more engrossed or involved in their media selves. The recurrent social situations of their everyday lives served as the foils against which both their public and private selves developed. The net effect, then, of having these selves cast upon them and interacting with others through these, was that athletes eventually came to believe in them and to integrate them into their core selves.

SELF-AGGRANDIZEMENT

Athletes' encounters with the celebrated self-images reflected onto them by others, in person and through the media, affected them profoundly. Being cast as heroes felt exciting and gratifying. Presented with these images, and feeling obligated to interact with people through them, athletes added a new self to their repertoire: a gloried self. This self differed from their previous identities in its greater degree of aggrandizement. They may have dreamed of glory, but until now they had never formed a structured set of relationships with people who accorded it to them. Yet while they wanted to accept and enjoy this glory, to yield to its incorporation into a full-blown self-identity, they felt hesitant and guilty. They wrestled with the competing pulls of their inner desires for exorbitant pleasure and pride versus the normative guidelines of society inhibiting these. Their struggle with factors inhibiting and enhancing their self-aggrandizement yields insight into how and why they ultimately developed gloried selves.

Inhibiting Factors. Players knew they had to be careful about both feeling important and showing these feelings. As Fine (1987) has noted in studying preadolescent culture, the norms of our society dictate a more modest, self-effacing, posture. Consequently, they worked hard to suppress their rising feelings of self-aggrandizement in several ways. First, they drew on their feelings of fear and insecurity. While it violated the norms of their peer culture to reveal these feelings, many athletes were uncertain about their role on the team. Especially among the younger players and those who had received little recruiting attention, there were doubts about how they would perform. Even for the more established players, the uncertainty of a professional career or the suddenness of a career-ending injury always loomed. These fears haunted them, helping them inhibit, to some degree, their feelings of importance.

Second, they tried to discount the flattery of others as exaggerated or false. As Jones and Nisbet (1972:80) have hypothesized, "There is a pervasive tendency for actors to attribute their actions to situational requirements, whereas observers tend to attribute the same actions to stable personal dispositions." Basketball players, then, tended to evaluate their behavior less globally than their audience, and to interpret their successes as based less on their own outstanding characteristics than on some complex interaction of circumstances. When fans, boosters, or members of the media, for example, referred to them as "magic," "insurmountable," or "NBA material," they graciously accepted these attributions, without necessarily believing them. This did not, however, set aside their natural motivation to want credit for the positive consequences of their actions and avoid the blame for the bad consequences (cf. Taylor and Koivumaki 1976).

Third, their feelings of importance and superiority were constrained by Coach's actions and the norms of their peer subculture. For his part, Coach actively tried to keep players' self-aggrandizement in check by puncturing them whenever he thought they were getting too "puffed" (conceited). He "dragged" (criticized, mocked) them in both team meetings and individual sessions, trying to balance their confidence with humility. As one player explained:

> Sometimes Coach, he just drill on your dream—like, "No Tyrone, no way. You can just git that dream out your head. Just play ball. There's one out of one thousand make it." Every time the NBA is brought up too much they give you those crazy stats. They don't really want you going "I'm an NBA player—I'm gonna make it one day." They want you to concentrate on "I'm at this university."

Additionally, the players punctured their teammates by publicly ridiculing each other in their informal dorm sessions. According to each one, he was the best player on the team, and they had little praise for each other. It was not that they actually thought their teammates had no talent, it was just that the peer subculture accorded little place for "glory passing." As a result, except for the braggarts, none of the players publicly expressed how fantastic they felt and how much they loved being treated as stars. Instead, they mostly tried to suppress these feelings of excitement, intoxication, and aggrandizement, and not to let themselves be influenced by these reflected feelings of glory. As Darian remarked:

> You feel it coming up on you and you know you got to fight it.
> You can't be letting your head get all out of control.

Fourth, Coach helped them to normalize their experiences and reactions by casting them within the occupational perspective. His view was that adulation came with the job, and that this job was no more special than any other ("When you get past the glory part, although I know that strikes you so hard in the beginning it's hard to get past it, you see that this's just a work-a-day job like any other job."). According to his perspective, he had to spend time with and bestow special attention on boosters, to let himself be seen with them so they would feel connected to the team and donate money. Before games, at banquets and media events, and in public, then, he would stop and say hello to them, shake their hands, talk to them, and try to address them by name. Coach conveyed this sense of occupational duty to his players and assistants. They, too, had to "get with the program," to work the public and help support these people's sense of involvement with the team. All the attention they got from their fans was recast as something they had to service as part of their job. In public, then, players feigned intimacy with total strangers and allowed themselves to be worshipped, all the while being told that this was a job, like any other job.

Enhancing Factors. Yet as tired as they were, as repetitive as this behavior became, they knew that this was unlike any other job. Its excitement, centrality, and secrecy, which did not exist in the everyday world, made this arena different. As one assistant coach explained:

> The times were exciting. There was always something going on, something happening, some new event occurring each day. We felt like we were newsmakers, we were important. We touched so many more lives, were responsible for so many more people, and so many more people cared, wanted to know something from us. It was very intoxicating. Everyone even close felt the excitement, just from elbow-rubbing.

Athletes were also influenced in their developing feelings of self-importance by the concrete results of their behavior. Through "self-attribution" (Bem 1972; Kelley 1967; Rosenberg 1979), they were able to observe the outcomes of their behavior and utilize these to form and modify assessments of their selves. Thus, when the team was winning, their feelings of importance, grandeur, talent, and invincibility soared; when they lost they felt comparatively incompetent, powerless, and small. As the team's record throughout our research was overwhelmingly successful, team members reviewed the outcomes of their contests and the record of their season, and concluded that they were fine athletes and local heroes.

Interestingly, it is noteworthy that the process of social comparison (Festinger 1954; Rosenberg 1979) was not significant to team members' developing sense of self-esteem. Rather than comparing themselves competitively to other teammates (which occurred, but to a surprisingly minor degree) and feeling negative about themselves in light of the team's high success standards, players invoked the "normative" (Bandura 1971; Felson 1981; Kelley 1952) and "associative" effects (Felson and Reed 1986) in forging their self-conceptions. First, they used their athlete peers as a reference group to normatively set group standards of their behavior and self-worth. These group self-conceptions were extremely favorable and generated positive self-appraisals for team members, ignoring variations among individuals. Second, they made positive inferences about themselves based on their association with the team. Using it once again as a reference group, they basked in their own reflected glory and forged individual self-conceptions based on the performance of the team as a whole. Their tendency to forge self-conceptions based on collective behavior and membership rather than individual attributes was undoubtedly influenced by their participation in this team sport and their constant identification by themselves and others as members of the program.

One of the results of being the objects of such success, personal interest, and intense media attention, was that players developed "big heads." They were adulated by so many people and their exploits were cast as so consequential that they began to feel more notable. While they tried to remain modest, they all found that their celebrity caused them to lose control over their sense of self-importance. As Marcus described:

> You try not to let it get away from you. You feel it coming all around you. People building you up. You say to yourself that you're the same guy you always were and that nothing has changed.

But what's happening to you is so unbelievable. Even when you were sitting at home in high school imagining what college ball would be like, you could not imagine this. All the media, all the fans, all the pressure. And all so suddenly, with no time to prepare or ease into it. Doc, it got to go to your head. You try to fight it, and you think you do, but you got to be affected by it, you got to get a big head.

Although they fought to normalize and diminish their feelings of self-aggrandizement, they were swept away by the allure of glory, to varying degrees, in spite of themselves. Their sense of glory fed their egos, exciting them beyond their ability to manage or control it. They had never before been such glory-generating figures, never felt the power that was now being invested in them by the hordes of worshipping fans. They developed deep and powerful feelings affirming how important they had become and how good it felt.

The experience of glory was thus one that brought feelings of excitement, pride, power, and self-importance. Team members' elevation to the rank of major local (and even national) celebrities brought them an intensity of fame and status that overwhelmed them. These sensations were immediate and real; they flooded all team members' lives, overwhelming them with feelings of invincibility. With these powerful feelings came a transformation, involving the development and ascent of a self-dimension they had barely felt or glimpsed before: the gloried self. This arose through both their perceptions of the impressions others had formed of them (their reflected self), and the images of them portrayed in the media (their media self).

The Price of Glory

The glory experience involved the ascent of a self-dimension that was either new or developed from a previous, not so salient, role in athletes' repertoire of identities. Yet this burgeoning self did not develop without consequences for athletes' total constellation of roles or their relative dominance or centrality. The self-aggrandizement brought on by athletes' developing gloried selves was accompanied by an associated diminishment in other facets of their identities. The price they paid for being elevated came in the form of self-narrowing, or self-erosion.

They sacrificed both the multi-dimensionality of their present selves and the potential breadth of their future selves. Various dimensions of their identities were either diminished, detached, lost, or somehow changed. Let us look at some of their diminished self-dimensions.

SELF-IMMEDIACY

One of the consequences of athletes' ascendant gloried selves was a loss of future-orientation. In all their lives, from the most celebrated players to the least, these individuals had never felt the level of excitement, adulation, intensity, importance, and respect that they were currently experiencing (see also Messner 1989). As a result, their focus turned toward their present situation and became locked onto it.

This reaction was caused, in large part, by the absorbing quality of the moment. During the intensity of the season, the prominence of their basketball obligations and involvements were obvious. The responsibilities of school, when they were lying, exhausted, in their hotel rooms hundreds of miles from campus, or on their beds after a grueling practice, seemed remote and distant. Darian described his state of preoccupation:

> I've got two finals tomorrow and one the next day. I should be up in the room studying right now. But how can I get my mind on that when I know I've got to guard Michael Jordan tomorrow night?

Their basketball affairs were so much more immediately pressing, not only in the abstract, but due to the presence of others making specific demands on them, that it was easy for them to relegate all other areas to the realm of unimportance. Their scholarships demanded that they put their athletic responsibilities first, yet this had profound consequences for their selves. As Damon explained:

> A player a coach is counting on, that's all he think about is ball. That's what he signed to do.

Many of them ceased to think about their futures except as a direct continuation of their present. They abandoned any sense of long-term planning and deferment of gratification in favor of the enormous immediate gratification they encountered from their fans and celebrity.

What emerged was a self that primarily thought about only one source of gratification, athletic fame, that imagined and planned for little else.

Their absorption in the present was also partly the result of Coach's manipulations. He knew, as well as they, that only two percent (Leonard and Reyman 1988) of major college basketball players are good enough to succeed in the ranks of the NBA, and only a fraction more are absorbed into the other worldwide professional leagues. Yet he encouraged each of them to keep focused on their goal, to strive to be the lucky ones. This was part of the "psych game" he used to keep them performing at their highest levels of effort (see also Feinstein 1986). Thus they *all* clung to the hope that they would be the ones to make or break those statistics. For instance, Jesse, one of the less outstanding athletes on the team, expressed the attitude players commonly held toward their present and futures:

> You have to have two goals, a realistic and an unrealistic. Not really an unrealistic, but a dream. We all have that dream. I know the odds are against it, but I feel realistically that I can make the NBA. I have to be in the gym every day, lift weights, more or less sacrifice my life to basketball. A lot.

Players, then, who had entered college hoping to use their college educations to prepare themselves for professional careers, got distracted from those plans and relinquished them. The demands of their basketball schedules became the central focus of their lives and the physical, social, and professional dimensions associated with it took precedence over all other concerns.

Vaguely, they imagined that if they did not make it as professional athletes, they would be provided with a job by a rich booster. Although they were able to observe the older players leaving the program without any certain job opportunities, they were too absorbed in the present to recognize this. Ironically, they came to college thinking it would expand their range of future opportunities, yet they sacrificed the potential breadth of their future selves by narrowing their range of vision to encompass only that which fed their immediate hunger for glory.

DIMINISHED AWARENESS

Locked onto a focus on the present and smitten with a vision of themselves obtained through their celebrity status, all team members, to varying degrees, became desensitized to the concerns of their old selves. They experienced a heightened sensitivity and reflexiveness to their gloried self and a loss of awareness of their self-dimensions unrelated to glory. Nearly everyone they encountered interacted with them, at least in part, through the vehicle of their gloried selves. As this self-identity was fed and expanded, their other selves tended to atrophy and diminish in salience. At times, it was as if they were so blinded by the force of their glory, that they could not look beyond it. As Goffman (1967:43) observed, "Whatever his position in society, the person insulates himself by blindnesses, half-truths, illusions, and rationalizations."

This diminished awareness had several consequences. First, in becoming so absorbed in their gloried selves, athletes relegated concerns outside the realm of their athletic self to secondary, tertiary, or more distant status. This included commitments to friends, relatives, and school. For example, many athletes began each semester by vowing that this time would be different, but each semester it happened anew: they would "forget" to go to class. As Coach Mickey lamented:

> I've sat there and I've wondered, when someone knows the consequences, when they know that it's a small community that they're living in, when they know that they're being checked on by two or three different sources, why do they still forget?

Reflecting on this question, Buck mused:

> You don't think, it's not like you goin' to be a bad boy today, or you goin' to pull the wool over someone's eyes. You just plain ol' forget. You sleep through it.

For a while they could ignore the facts and the consequences of their behavior. They pretended that they really were going to class this semester, that they had not missed anything significant, that they were competently managing the other facets of their lives. Eventually, as the semester progressed and they fell more noticeably behind, this denial wore thin. They then moved into a process of neutralization, the specific forms of which were supplied them by their peer subculture.

Second, their gloried selves made them seem different. Their new personae were swelled, even in their interactions with friends. Players referred to this as being "puffed," and each accused the others of it:

Sometimes I can't even talk to Lew no more. He's so puffed in the head you can't get him to talk sense, he's lost touch with reality. It's like it's full of jello in there and he's talking a bunch of hot air.

What they sensed filling up the heads of these puffed players were the self-images created by the glory experience.

Third, their gloried selves made them act differently. Some players gradually ceased to reflect about the value of doing certain things; they just plunged into various acts because these fed their gloried selves. They distanced themselves from their old values and took potentially career-ending risks. For example, when James, who filled a substitute role, was "red-shirted" (given an extra year of eligibility) due to injury, he was willing to give up this desirable and protective status when Coach asked him to return. Despite his secondary position, he became easily convinced that the team could not function without him; like others, he had blocked off the warnings and cautions that stemmed from a submerged awareness of other needs and interests. This same lack of reflexivity and self-disclosure also prevented players with chronic injuries, those who were hobbling and could not jump anymore, from admitting to themselves that it was over, that their gloried selves had to retire.

SELF-DETACHMENT

For some individuals, and at times for all team members, the distinction between their gloried and their other selves became more than a separation; the distance and lack of reflexivity grew into a detachment. In the most extreme cases, some athletes developed a barrier between this new, exciting, and glamorous self and their old, formerly core selves. It became increasingly difficult for them to break through that barrier. They experienced a dualism between these selves,[1] as if they occasionally represented distinct individuals and not multiple facets of the same person, and an occasional shifting back and forth between them. Ultimately, for many, the different images became so disparate that they could not be fused. Alternatively, individuals got so swept up in their gloried selves that they lost control over their efforts to constrain and integrate them. The more these individuals interacted with others through this self, the more it developed a life and destiny of its own.

Apollo, for instance, struggled with some of these problems generated by his gloried self. Charismatic and enthusiastic whenever he was
in public, he generated enormous amounts of attention and adulation
by his outgoing personality. Reporters thronged to him because he
was colorful, lively, and quotable. In public settings he was always
referred to by his Apollo moniker.

Yet although he had deliberately created the Apollo identity, it
eventually began to control him. It led him to associate, at times, with
people who valued him only for that self, and it surfaced in interactions
with friends when he had not called it forth. It led him to detach
himself from responsibility for things he did while under that persona.
This was especially true of his dealings with other people through his
Apollo role. As he described:

> I had a summer job working for some booster at a gas station. I
> figured he wanted to show off that he had Apollo pumping his
> gas. I'd go into my act for the customers and the other employ-
> ees, how fine I was, lotta times show up late or not at all. I
> figured he wouldn't fire me. But he did. . . . Looking back, I can't
> see how I just up and blew that job. That ain't like me. That was
> Apollo done that, not me.

In other instances, he became so wrapped up in the Apollo identity
that, even when he wanted to, he could not shake it. This surfaced in
his relationship with his longtime girlfriend. As he reflected:

> I think some of the biggest problems I had with my girl, was that
> even when we were home alone, after all the crowds were gone
> and we could just be together, was that I still acted like Apollo.
> You know, struttin', braggin', bossin'—actin' like I owned her.

As Elliot (1986) has hypothesized, the tendency to engage in fantasy
self-imagery, as in conceiving of one's actions as the product of some
other person rather than persona, disrupts individuals' self-consistency
through a blurring of their distinction between fantasy and reality. Yet
behind that cockiness and bravado there was still a person who was
not putting on acts all the time. This self had been left behind by the
gloried self, become detached from it. A certain degree of bifurcation
was the result.

The second dimension, then, associated with developing gloried
selves, lay in the loss of critical, although sometimes subtle, aspects of
individuals' identities and self-conceptions. In order to feed the gran-

deur of their gloried selves, athletes ignored, modified, or abandoned parts of themselves that either hindered or failed to complement this powerfully gripping self-identity.

The Gloried Self

Aspiring high school graduates thus entered the world of college athletics and underwent a fundamental transformation. Thrust into a whirlwind of intensity, adulation, and celebrity, they reacted to the situation through a process of simultaneous self-aggrandizement and self-diminishment. Their gloried self expanded, overpowering all of their other roles and self-dimensions. This became the aspect of their self in which they lived, where they lodged their self-investment. They immersed themselves into this portion of their selves with a single-mindedness. The feedback and gratification they derived from this identity, then, dwarfed the others. They had not anticipated this happening, but gradually, as they were drawn into the glory arena, all of the team members were swept away by the taste of stardom and fame. Their commitment to the athletic role and its associated self grew beyond what they had ever intended or imagined. Once they experienced the power and centrality associated with the glory arena, they were loathe to relinquish it. They cast off their other aspirations, lost touch with other dimensions of their selves (even to the point of detachment), and plunged themselves into the gloried self.

Athletes' gloried selves originally arose as dramaturgical constructions. Whether via the media or face-to-face, people cast these identities onto athletes through their expectations of what they were or should be like. Athletes responded by playing these roles, partly out of their feelings of loyalty to the organization, partly due to interactional obligations they felt out of courtesy, and partly because they enjoyed playing them. But in contrast to other roles that can be casually assumed without consequence, athletes' actions in these roles increased their self-investment in them. Kornhauser (1962) has noted that making such a self-investment, or commitment, reduces people's availability for alternative lines of action. As a result, athletes' actions influenced not only their immediate but also their future behavior, profoundly transforming their self-conceptions. This refutes Goffman's (1959) notion that selves are merely masks without substance lying behind them, and supports the Meadian (1934) view that people have anchored selves that grow, decline, and change as a result of their experiences. The entire process, moreover, illustrates the relation between dramaturgical roles and real selves, showing how the former come to impinge upon and influence the latter.

This gloried self, then, like the role and program in which it was based, was a greedy self, actively seeking to ascend in importance and cast aside other self-dimensions as it grew. It was an intoxicating and addictive self, which overpowered other aspects of these individuals and sought increasing reinforcement to fuel its growth. Yet, at the same time, its surge and display violated societal mores of modesty in both self-conception and self-presentation. Athletes thus became embroiled in inner conflict between their desire for recognition, flattery, importance, the pulls to keep feeding this self-affirming part of them, and their socialization, that urged them to fight such inner feelings and behavioral urges. That their gloried selves succeed in flourishing in spite of the struggle they mustered against them is a testament to its inherent power and drive to eclipse other self-dimensions.

7
Resolving Role Conflict

WITH THEIR socialization to the college athlete status, basketball players became aware that their lives were compartmentalized into multiple, and enormously demanding, roles. Previous theoretical and empirical investigations into the interactive character of multiple roles have yielded competing explanations, ranging from the abundant energy to the scarcity approach (Marks 1977).[1] Most studies of college athletics have suggested that the scarcity model is the most appropriate for this realm, and that the multiple role demands are excessive in both their energy and time requisitions (cf. Coakley 1986; Lance 1987, 1989; Leonard 1988; Purdy, Eitzen and Hufnagel 1982; Sack and Thiel 1985). Our research also supports this model; athletes found that the role demands placed on them pushed them to the limits of their time and energy, and realized that they could not maintain the goals and priorities they had brought with them to college. Some resolution to this role conflict was in order.

Athletes reached the point at which they finally decided they had to adjust their roles and goals at different stages of their college careers. Some recognized the role conflict, and the impossibility of fulfilling all their role demands to their satisfaction, as early as the beginning of their sophomore year. Others recognized it sometime during the early or middle stages of their junior year. Nearly all had recognized it by the end of their junior year. They made these role conflict resolutions according to their perceptiveness, and the degree to which they became overwhelmingly riveted on their athletic role.

Coakley (1982) has identified several social psychological processes college athletes can potentially use in coping with their role conflict: integrating, synthesizing, withdrawing from, compartmentalizing, neglecting, or de-emphasizing selected roles. In resolving their role conflict, the athletes we studied forged a series of "role bargains" (Goode 1960) whereby they realigned their expectations.[2] No longer could they plan to accomplish all of their aims in each of these three roles. Some of them had to be modified, reduced, or abandoned altogether. In order to accomplish such a reconstruction, athletes had to assess their priorities, sometimes without conscious thought or decision-making. After two or three years in college, the knowledge and experience they had acquired enabled them to more easily re-evaluate the continuing worth of their initial impressions and ideals.

Such a reconstruction involved, in effect, the realignment of their roles. By raising, diminishing, or modifying their attachment to certain roles, they shifted the importance of these roles vis-à-vis others. This role realignment would be their final one as college athletes.

Most of the University's freshmen came to college conceiving of themselves primarily as athletes. Yet this did not mean that they saw themselves as unidimensional.[3] Quite the contrary: most of them, as we have noted from the outset, regarded academics and social experiences as an integral part of their past and future lives.[4] Most players hoped to accomplish the goals of all three roles. We will look at each role separately and discuss both the changes athletes had to make within them and how they naturally evolved over time.

Athletic

The athletes we studied all resolved the conflict between their roles by yielding to engulfment in the athletic role. There were no exceptions, no variations to this pattern by race, class, recruiting experiences, academic background, future aspirations, playing time, or talent. Despite differences in basketball players' entering role alignments, athletics always emerged over the course of their college experiences, not only as primary, but as the role which subjugated all others. The athletic role vaunted compellingly to the top and significantly overwhelmed the others for several reasons. First, most of the athletes we observed entered college primarily immersed in their athletic roles.

While their roles were much more blurred (they did not think of them as so separate) in high school (cf. Coleman 1961; Eitzen 1975) and there was not as great a gap between them, many individuals' early experiences had rooted their dreams and identity in the athletic realm.

Second, structural features of the college athletic arena promoted this role's dominance. All recruits were selected and brought to school by their coaches, housed by them, fed by them, enrolled in classes by them, provided with a per diem allowance by them while on the road, and directed in their athletic lives by them. Every part of their environment was constructed, overseen, and directed from within the athletic milieu. For these individuals, athletics was not just a part of their lives, it was the central organizing principle. The athletic role was also especially compelling because of its occupational character; basketball had come to take on the characteristics of a job more than a game. Athletes thus saw themselves, structurally, as employees who had to follow the dictates of their boss, who was lodged within the athletic realm.

Third, Coach held direct influence over players through the force of his personality. A persuasive individual, he could communicate effectively with both individuals and groups. At times he bent players to his will through the sheer force of his insistence. He supplemented this by reasoning with players, promoting his point of view through the force of his logic. Through his charisma, dominance, and compelling persuasion, he profoundly affected many athletes as individuals. He was able to sustain all team members' dream of a professional basketball career, whether they were celebrated stars or hopefuls still waiting for their chance to prove themselves. Apollo described how Coach managed to maintain his grip on players even after they had recognized the intent of his control efforts:

> He'll threaten you and threaten you, and after a while people realize that he's all talk and no action. But then he still gets over on you because he has such a good mind game that he can pull it off. He'll pull you into his office and make you think you can be as good as the pros—that you're as good as Adrian Dantley, and a bunch of other players. And then you'll do or think whatever he says.

Fourth, the athletic role's rise to dominance was supported by the athletes' peer subculture. Isolated from other students, athletes were incestuously thrust into each others' company. They relied on their peers for both constant companionship and guidelines for coping in this strange and new world. Once firmly ensconced there, they continued to rely on their peers for support; they alone could understand the many pressures and allures contained in the athletic arena. The peer subculture, which powerfully framed their interactions and provided guidelines for the interpretation of unfolding events, offered ways for them to both understand and resolve their role conflict. All athletes were strongly influenced by this subculture, no matter how strong their athletic dreams were. Peer norms reinforced total acquiescence to the demands, claims, and promises of the athletic role. The strength of this subculture thus bolstered the dominance of the athletic role.

Fifth, the athletic role overwhelmed athletes through the intensity of its experiences. Despite their projections, they were unprepared for the surge of feelings they would encounter. Playing on a nationally ranked team before an audience whose primary local allegiance was to their program, swarmed over by fans, boosters, and the media, they were transformed into celebrities. From the starters to those who spent more time on the bench, all players got the sense of being public figures who were admired and in demand. They were thus swept up into the vortex of this wildly exciting world and developed gloried selves anchored in it. Their gloried selves cleaved to the athletic role and cast off all other concerns that interfered with it. Clyde reflected on how he was affected:

> When I came to college I thought I had my head on very straight. No nonsense. Get my education, play a little ball. I knew I wasn't a standout in high school. But, I think it was the fifth game of the season, we'd had some injuries, and Coach told me in the locker room that he wanted me to start that game. I couldn't believe it! Me, starting with guys I'd been reading about in national basketball magazines. Now I remember, that from that point on, basketball started taking over my life. When I went to class I'd be always dreaming about basketball. When I lay up in my room at night, I'd be thinking about basketball. I think my eyes musta got about as big as basketballs! I started spending a lot of time in the gym, started missing classes. I think it was because I came here without the expectations of doing all those things, and all of a sudden I was exposed to it. I just got carried away by it.

MATURING IN THE ROLE

As athletes became socialized to the athletic role they experienced its progressive unfolding. Over the course of their college careers, it changed in character, as did they along with it. As they aged from freshmen to veteran players, their role on the team and with Coach changed. As upperclassmen, they held a position of greater responsibility. It was they who took the younger players under their wings and told them what to do. No longer were they the unrefined, green recruits; they had become integral members of the team's offense and defense. They knew where to go, what to do. They knew how to read Coach, what to expect, how to weather and interpret his storms. No longer did they glaringly stick out as rough, jagged individuals. They had been molded, shaped. Tyrone reflected on his changes:

> The first two years, "Woof, woof, woof, woof, woof," that's all he was. Right in front of me barking. Two years in a row made me realize one thing—you're goin' have to learn. And I have learned. He know I've learned. I'm at a stage where I'm pretty well much the public image; I know what's going on in the system, I know what to do to stay eligible, so it's like, "Okay, Coach, you can chill out on me. I know what to do." Now he's standing there barking across my shoulder at a guy called a freshman, called a sophomore. And I'm just easing past.

In order for Coach to mold players, he had to expend considerable effort on them, especially in the early years. Looking back on his relationship with Coach, Apollo remarked on it and how it had changed:

> In the beginning he was more influential. And I was 17 years old when that stripping and all that part went on back then. I still like playing basketball, but I no longer like Coach disciplining me the way he think he should. And he don't no more. But Frank? He's goin' get to Frank. What do you think Coach think? I'm goin make him stop stealing, I'm goin' make all that ghetto stuff leave him, and I'm goin' make him a man.

Players' relationship with Coach changed as they progressed through the role. They no longer needed the intensity of his attention, as Danny commented during his senior year:

You're a junior, you'd better do it good. You're a sophomore, you'd better show some kind of smart. You're a freshman, you'd better listen. If you're a senior, you're as good as gone. He's not goin' bother too much with you. You freshmens, you listen. You catch a freshman talking, sounds like the world's coming to an end. Each year you's supposed to be better than what you were.

THE BOOSTER CAREER

As players aged in their athletic role, their relationship to other members of the athletic role-set changed. Just as Coach no longer needed to expend as much attention on them, the boosters no longer seemed as intensely interested in them. Moving through the athletic role, then, involved dealing with the vicissitudes of the booster career.

That boosters might ebb and flow in their interest was something that players never considered in their early years of college. They were too busy being overwhelmed by boosters' attention, or complaining about boosters' demands. They simply thought, in the beginning, that boosters really liked them and would take care of them. They did not discover how wrong their belief was until it was too late. Darian, out of the program for two years, explained the situation as he described the experiences of a senior still in the program:

> Every time I talk to Clyde now I warn him, the boosters are gonna change. And he's feelin' it now. Some boosters that are real close to him, used to give him everything when he was a freshman, sophomore, and a junior, now, he calls, they blow him off, you see? And I tell him where it's at, but he gets upset about it. An' he's a pretty emotional guy. I keep tellin' him you gotta wake up, this can really affect you.

Ironically, just as the players were reaching the pinnacle of their playing careers, they had already passed the peak of their booster careers. Marcus explained the booster career curve:

> It's like making an investment, like a long-term investment or a short-term investment. It's like, coaches like to say, if I had a senior that was worth ten points, and a freshman that was worth ten points, they would play the freshman. And I think it's, you can relate that to the booster situation. I'm an important part of

the program because I'm a senior, but at the same time, I can only do so much in one year. This guy has four years to do as much or more than I have to do in one year, ya understand?

Various players described different patterns in the way boosters changed their treatment of them. While some felt that the withdrawal of attention was gradual, most experienced it as a sudden form of dumping:

> If I had a child, I would try to steer him towards something else other than athaletics, because it's a dream that we live as athaletes, it's a fantasy, and after your senior year I really recognized that the fantasy was coming to a end, and all the crowd cheering and the boosters there, it was all going to come to a end. And I'm glad I realized that early my senior year because they were looking toward the freshmen and the sophomores and the younger kids, and I thought that I was one of their favorites somewhat out here, and it's really, you really crash, you really come down to earth quick.

Athletes who had to end their careers prematurely due to a debilitating injury also found that their booster appeal came to a screeching halt. Apollo recalled his situation:

> I thought I had close relations with some boosters, but it turns out it wasn't the way I thought it was. I liked a couple of boosters a lot, and I liked their wives, but it turned out that they was just blowing smoke. I thought they really cared for me. But as soon as I went down on my knee, it was like unbelievable. They, like, turned the nigger off, and shit. And that kind of hurt me. No question, you are forgotten once you are out.

After receiving this kind of treatment at the hands of people who had been espousing friendship, athletes began to reappraise their estimations of boosters. They scrutinized their relationships with people more carefully to screen out those whom they thought associated with them just for status purposes. They began to define boosters as people who were associated with them through a money relationship:

> A booster is someone who wants to be seen around you because he's kissing the coach's ass, or he's kissing the University's ass, or he's kissing your ass. I didn't used to look on it this way, but

now I realize that the difference between a booster friend and a real friend is that the booster has a dollar sign hanging there in between you and him. And once you take that dollar sign away, the relationship ain't worth much.

As a result of these experiences and realizations, seniors had to detach themselves from caring about boosters. In his senior year, struggling with his feelings of betrayal by boosters, Clyde compared his old attitude toward boosters with his reconstructed one:

As I said, my freshman year I came here with a big smile, . . . and I openly accepted a lot of people into my life, a lot of boosters. Because of college experiences, though, I started noticing certain things about these people. And I didn't like it, but bein' that it's their lives and I can't make them change, the only thing for me to do is not associate with them so much. I'm not spending as much time with boosters simply because I don't want to be around that type of person.

Being cast adrift by boosters was thus the last stage of their growth in the athletic role. They had spent the energy and youth of their college years in this role, thinking, hoping, and expecting that boosters would pay off for them. Boosters represented one point to which they had pinned their hopes. When these "friends" abandoned them, their expectations were not entirely dashed, but they were weakened. Athletes came to regret the time they had wasted on these boosters, time that was so scarce and precious to them. This betrayal was particularly poignant for black players when boosters occasionally "found" jobs for white players.

Social

A large part of athletes' social role adjustments were thrust upon them early in their college experiences. While they entered college thinking they could do what they wanted, have their time to control as they wanted, and be in charge of their own lives, they soon discovered that a lot of this autonomy had been taken away from them. In high school they had been their own agents. In college they represented the program and were agents of the coach, the team, and the school. Being a

college athlete meant that they had to relinquish some part of themselves, that personal independence that they had taken as a given of
their social self.

It was not difficult for them to see what kind of adjustment this
required. The nature of the necessary attitude was very clearly delin-
eated for them by the peer subculture. All they had to do was accept
the subculture's pragmatic solutions. This entailed diminishing the
salience of their social role. No longer would they decide on their own
social schedules; they would follow the dictates of the coaches. No
longer would they project their own image; they would assume some
version of the collective team image. To some extent they allowed the
coaching staff to control their associates, their vacations, their friends,
their leisure time, their priorities, their goals, and their beliefs. Their
coaches were more than athletic leaders or instructors to them; they
became some fusion of parents and employers. For athletes, the hard
part involved accepting all this authority and domination, letting go of
their freedom and individualism.

They had to relinquish not only the quality of their social lives, but
also its quantity. They could not go out as much as they liked, could
not relax and hang out as much as they were used to, could not be as
actively involved in social worlds as ordinary students. It took them a
while to realize this. Many of them thought, in the beginning, that
they could have it all. Those athletes who embarked on too active a
social life soon found that they were falling far behind in academics,
and that this could seriously compromise their athletic careers. Ben
described how he had to make an adjustment:

> For a while I had a really good social life, but I saw it was not
> good, 'specially if you got athletics. It seems like every night I
> was doing something with my friends. One showed me you
> could party all you want, have your social life, and still do your
> academic, still graduate. But he didn't have the athletic demands
> on him that I have. That social life will kill you. I had to tone it
> down or I wouldn't still be here.

The degree to which athletes toned down their social lives varied.
As we noted in chapter 2, some groups subverted their recreational
time and activities, while others only did so moderately. These differences were more relative than absolute, however, in that none of the
groups could afford too much social activity. Members of the whiners

and the bad niggas did get out of the dorms more, and players with arts and sciences majors had more non-athlete friends. Yet all of them were fairly isolated by their lodging in the athletic dorm. Looking back on his college years, Marcus reflected sadly as he compared himself and his friends to Lionel, the walk-on player who had lived in the regular dorms:

> I think he had a better experience in college than we did. He enjoyed somethin' that we missed out on, I think. Interaction with the students. Student life. Social life. I feel like my time here has been really blocked away from student life. I mean, I never voted for class president, student association president. I never knew who the candidates were. An' you're always interested in all that stuff. You know, pictures in the yearbook, that type of stuff. Never, [quietly] never involved with that kind of stuff.

All athletes, then, had to diminish the salience of their social role. While it had started out in elementary or high school as an interlinked role, piggybacking onto their athletic prowess to gain them popularity, it became separated and subjected. For the large majority of athletes it retained a second place role, but lost position relative to the now overwhelmingly dominant athletic role. Only a few individuals held to their academic goals so strongly that they placed these close to or above their desire to have recreational time.[5]

Academic

The most marked transformation occurred within the academic role. This was the one least reinforced by the athletes' peer subculture and the one where they encountered the greatest feelings of inadequacy. Athletes' first shift involved externalizing the blame for their academic failures. These were caused not by their own shortcomings or lack of effort, but by boring professors, stupid courses, exhaustion, the coaches' demands, and/or injuries. Shifting the blame allowed them to accept the frequent signs of failure more easily and served as an important neutralizing mechanism for their highly competitive orientation.

More significantly, however, they made a series of downward *pragmatic adjustments* in their academic goals.[6] These were prompted by various events that weakened their commitment to academics. Factors precipitating these adjustments differed among individuals. During his junior year Darian attributed it to a suddenly overwhelming drive to succeed in basketball:

> I've always had that dream, but I think I used to keep it in perspective just a little bit more. But something happened to me over the summer. I feel like I'm average, but I want to be a better than average player. That will to excel just came up over me, and I've been really giving it everything I've got. I haven't been hitting the books this year like I used to.

Clyde credited it to a more gradual enticement into the athletic realm:

> I came in here to be a student, but I basically just lost track of my reason for being here. And my grades started slacking then. My commitment to school just got away from me, probably because of basketball and the boosters, and that whole scene, and I just started letting those things take over.

Jesse located the source of his academic demise in the social arena:

> I made some changes in my attitude toward academics. I think it was because I was stretched too thin, trying to get involved with too many things. Socially, I was dating a lot of different people, socializing with the boosters, and still trying to get in my time in the gym. So I wasn't able to put in the kind of time into academics any more that I wanted to at that point. And what happened, was that academics came last on my list.

After realizing that their commitment had waned, and recognizing limits on their time and energy for academics, most athletes progressively detached themselves from this role. This adjustment took several forms. The first involved changing their major. Of the individuals who began with pre-professional majors (47 percent), about one-fourth of them stayed with these all the way through college and graduated. Some coupled this with a shift of major from one pre-professional field to another, as Darian explained:

> It had always been my childhood dream of becoming a vet, but after the second semester I realized I couldn't be a science major because of the afternoon labs. So I spoke to [one of my profes-

sors] and he suggested to me that maybe I would like a pre-law major. I thought I could really get into being a sociology major, and plus I had a pretty good math and science background from my freshman and sophomore years. I wanted to stay in something hard where I could prepare myself to be a contributing member of society.

Nevertheless, they expended less effort and had less success than they initially anticipated. Although they graduated in an academic major, their scholastic performance was largely characterized by an attitude of getting by; in most cases they achieved only the minimum GPA and took the minimum number of hours required for eligibility. They ceased attending classes regularly, diminished their attempts to get to know professors, did not bother to get class notes or reading assignments until just before tests, and exerted a modicum of effort. James described Buck this way:

Buck does his work just when he has to. He sees to it that he keeps up a 2.3 or 2.4, but he doesn't bother to try any harder than that. He could do a lot better than that, but I guess he figures, why should he? No one else does. And compared to the rest of us, he's around at the top of the pack.

More commonly, athletes in pre-professional majors re-assessed their academic abilities and found that a more concrete adjustment was necessary. This second group (the remaining three-fourths of this original group) adjusted by both shifting their behavior and changing from their pre-professional program to a more manageable major. This shift signified that they had abandoned both their academic idealism and their earlier career goals. Clyde described how he drifted into this adjustment:

Well, you talk about my freshman year, I came in here as an accountant. That lasted 'till about a month or so after the first semester. Then I went to business for awhile. Then I bummed around for a semester and a half with no major. Then I decided on phys. ed. It seems like the more practicing I did, the more, the closer I got to phys. ed. Not that it's a sellout, I'm not trying to down-talk phys. ed., I think there are a lot of good benefits in phys. ed., but it's a curriculum that I can handle, with my physical obligations. And a lot of the things we'd discuss in class, I could relate to what I do for my scholarship, what I've done with my life.

Despite these players' adjustment, they still held to the goal of graduating. Here, the predominant attitude changed to getting a diploma, regardless of the major.[7] As Damon remarked, echoing Coach's rhetoric:

> When you apply for a job all that matters is if you have that piece of paper. They don't care what you majored in as long as you keep your nose clean and get that piece of paper. Look at Rob. He was a rec major, but now he's got a job in sales and he's got a nice place and a nice car.

Many of the athletes in this group managed to graduate or keep on a steady course toward graduation. Much like Merton's (1938) innovators, they retained the socially approved goal of graduating, but replaced their earlier means (getting an education) with a creative alternative (getting by).[8]

Athletes who had begun their college careers with lower initial academic aspirations, and who had majored in physical education or recreation from the start (45 percent), made corresponding adjustments. Approximately one-fifth of these athletes held on to their initial goal and graduated in one of these fields. But like the pre-professional majors, they did not perform as well as they had planned. The other four-fifths realized, usually relatively late, that their chances of graduating from college were slight. This genuinely distressed them, because getting a degree had become both a hope and an expectation. They shifted their orientation, then, toward maintaining their athletic eligibility (what Brede and Camp, 1987, have referred to as "majoring in eligibility"). Tyrone's remarks in his junior year illustrate how this shift affected his attitude toward academics:

> I used to think I was goin' to school, but now I know it's not for real. . . . I don't have no academic goals. A player a coach is counting on, that's all he think about is ball. That's what he signed to do. So what you gotta do is show up, show your smilin' face. Try as hard as you can. Don't just lay over in the room. That's all the coach can ask. Or else you may not find yourself playing the next year. Or even that year. But you've gotta go to class—it's a must.

The final group, those who had entered college with no aspirations of ever getting a degree (eight percent), played the eligibility game throughout their college careers. They did the minimum required to slide by and still qualify for basketball. These (and other) players were able to maintain their eligibility, even in the face of overwhelming athletic distractions, in several ways. First, they were required to pass only 24 credit hours (eight courses) in a 12 month period with a 2.0 grade point average or better. Any courses they could neither take, complete, or pass with a high enough grade could be taken or re-taken (up to a maximum of three courses) in the summer. This gave them considerable leeway to recover from courses they had dropped, done poorly in, or failed to take during the regular school year. And when they were in especially difficult courses the coaching staff tried to find them tutors. Second, they occasionally received preferential treatment from professors who were either friends of the program, or who were sympathetic to the plight of college athletes. Third, their course schedules were loaded with as many easy or athletic-related courses as the coaches thought necessary to somehow keep them eligible. Really tough eligibility cases were handled in a creative manner. For instance, Frank, an outstanding recruit who came in unable to read beyond the sixth grade level, was diagnosed as having learning disabilities, enrolled outside of school in a private reading program, and squeezed through his classes (by enormous effort on the coaches' part) under special consideration because of his learning disability. Slick summed up his overall attitude, common to those with little academic interest:

> From my senior year, where I missed 40 to 50 days because of recruiting visits, I never really took academics as serious as I should have. School was always easy to get grades in; I could get by halfway doing the assignment. Things came easy for me so I didn't have to work, and I got used to not working, not studying. I guess I was brought up the wrong way for being concerned about academics, or else it's me as a person—I'm really not interested. I manage to stay eligible here because of a little brain knowledge, passing the right number of courses. And I've been put in courses that were not that hard: HPER [health, physical education, and recreation].

By the time they reached their senior year, many of these athletes who had focused exclusively on maintaining their eligibility abandoned

the academic role entirely. They had met their final eligibility requirements and could no longer be withheld from play for failing to pass
the minimum number of credit hours. They anticipated being finished
with college shortly, and either playing professionally or getting a job.
In either case, as Lamont said in his senior year, wasting their time in
class no longer seemed necessary:

> I don't see no reason to go to classes no more, 'cause it's my last
> year. They got no more hold over me. Once the season's over, I
> be splittin'. So I haven't gone to a single class this whole semes-
> ter. I finally get to relax, hang out, go to movies, go out to
> bars.

In sum, the escalating encroachments of athletes' athletic role were
accommodated by diminishing their involvement in or detaching from
their academic role (cf. Lance 1987). Once this adjustment was made,
athletes managed to cope better with their multiple role demands.

For the most part, then, athletes entered college enthusiastic and
idealistic about their impending academic role. Their experiences at the
University made them increasingly cynical about and uninterested in
academics. As a result, they progressively detached themselves from
caring about or identifying themselves with this arena. Athletes thus
re-aligned, reduced, or eliminated the salience of their academic role
because of several interlinked conditions: (1) an overwhelmingly demanding athletic role and powerful role-set members; (2) a peer subculture that emphasized both athletics and recreation while devaluing
academics; (3) a series of frustrations and failures in the academic realm
caused by their poor academic training, their lack of proper study skills,
the perceived difficulty and/or irrelevance of their courses, and their
gradually diminishing effort, and (4) a paucity of role reinforcing
others in the academic sphere.

SUCCESS AND FAILURE

While college athletes' role conflict led them all to adopt resolutions
whereby they reduced the salience of their academic role, there were
some who, despite these obstacles, managed to graduate. By contrasting the individuals who graduated with those who did not, we can
gain some insight into the factors associated with athletes' academic
success and failure.

The most prominent variables correlated with success and failure were race and class. Although this sample is too small for statistically meaningful correlations, the graduation rates when examined by race and class cross-tabulated were as follows: roughly two-thirds (66 percent) of the white middle class players graduated, compared to all (100 percent) of the white working class players, four-fifths (80 percent) of the black middle class players, two-thirds (66 percent) of the black working class players, and none (0 percent) of the black lower class players. The overall graduation rate for the players we studied was 50 percent.[9] Examined by race and class separately, 76 percent of the white players graduated compared to 35 percent of the blacks, while 71 percent of the middle class players, 50 percent of the working class players, and none (0 percent) of the lower class players graduated.[10] This suggests that these factors are roughly comparable in importance, with a slight edge to race.[11]

Examining the underlying sociological contributors to these trends, black middle class players tended to be successful for three reasons: they attended high schools that prepared them more adequately for the academic rigors of college; they came from families that subscribed strongly to the social norms and values emphasizing the importance of education; and their parents could afford to pay their tuition for a fifth year of college. White middle class players had these same three advantages, but they were also encouraged to retain self-investment in academics by two other factors. First, there was a greater cultural expectation that they should graduate. Second, they had the most to gain, in terms of future job expectations, from graduating. If they graduated, they were more likely to be "connected" with a job through either their parents or the boosters in the community. This resource was not generally available to the black players.

Working class players had lower ratios of graduation than their middle class counterparts, yet these figures still place them above the national average. Upon examination, two sociological factors emerge that significantly helped several of these individuals overcome the barriers to success: those who graduated had either previously attended a junior college, had a steady girlfriend throughout most of their college years, or had both. The junior college experience offered these players two advantages. First, they were in an easier academic environment for two years where they got some positive reinforcement for their academic role by passing their classes. As Apollo commented:

Junior college wasn't too difficult, like a step above high school. I expected a very hard school, the books would be, phew! I expected people go to college because they're smart, but I found out that wasn't the case. You go to college to learn some things. And I learned a lot. A lot more than I ever thought I could.

Second, these junior college players were able to transfer two full years of college credits to the University (although that is not always the case), which gave them a significant advance toward graduating.

In addition, all of the working class players who graduated without the assistance of a junior college background had a steady (often middle class) girlfriend throughout most of their college careers who helped and/or pushed them academically. These women helped teach them the study skills they lacked, helped correct their grammatical and writing mistakes, helped them write their papers (and turn them in on time), helped them negotiate the administrative academic matters that their coaches were too busy to do for them, and helped to instill in them at least the semblance of an academic drive. These women were able to overcome players' academic deficits and counteract the anti-academic effect of the athletic subculture by serving as academic role-set members who influenced their boyfriends' role bargains and buoyed their academic identity.

Resolutions

In sum, athletes struggled to resolve the searing role conflicts they encountered that troubled them, often deeply. Their high school experiences had not prepared them for what they would encounter in the world of big-time college athletics. Wise in the ways of high school, they were naive to the complexities of college. Thrust into this new arena, their selves underwent transformation. While their identities in high school had been under their control, they found strong outside factors influencing them in college. As a result, their self-conceptions underwent reconstruction.

Most athletes entered college holding their athletic role as primary, their social role secondary, and their academic role tertiary. Their experience did little to change that order. The most profound effect of their role realignment lay in its increased separation between the roles.

While these roles had initially been clumped closer together, the college experience caused greater differentiation. In high school, these individuals had thought little about the distinction between their roles. They let them flow together, with their social status resting on their athletic prowess and their academic aspirations of going to college following the same route. Their identity as athletes combined the package into one. Yet once in college, they found enormous pressures to disengage these roles. While their social lives and academic experiences were still very much subject to the vicissitudes of their athletic role (in fact, even more so), at the same time these roles were wrenched apart by the extreme demands of the athletic role, leaving them few remaining resources. Athletes thus became more focused and specialized on this one dimension, diminishing or abandoning self-investment in the others.

8
Terminating the Role

ONCE THEY became seniors, the athletes had begun to sense their impending change of status. They were now treated differently by Coach and boosters. However, the pressures and excitements of the season provided a distraction, so they did not fully sense their impending "retirement" until after their final game, when their thoughts turned to their futures. Those who were trying to graduate focused again on their schoolwork. The others relaxed, but also thought about where to turn next.

From Exchange to Exploitation

As they neared the end of their senior year, their approaching "retirement" spurred many athletes to think about and review their college years. Their recent experiences of disenchantment with the boosters, and to a lesser extent, Coach, caused them to take a different attitude toward their entire career. They thus recast their perception of their relationship to the University from one of exchange to one of exploitation.

When they had first arrived they were awestruck and overwhelmed. They felt small and insignificant compared to the University and the people they encountered there, who appeared self-confident and impressive. At this point, they felt like they were receiving a lot and offering the school little in return. Everything seemed to be given to them, from their new uniforms to their new living quarters and new friends. They were getting the opportunity to play Division I basket-ball, on the same team as nationally known players; they were warmly embraced by a group of "millionaires," and they were getting a shot at their dream. They felt exceedingly fortunate. While this whole experi-ence seemed overwhelming, they sensed they were surrounded by people who cared about them and would protect them. Clyde voiced his feelings as an early freshman about Coach:

> I don't think I'm being taken advantage of at this school. At other schools it might be true. I think for us to be taken advan-tage of, first we'd have to have a crooked coach, or have a coach that would let something like that go on. I don't think Coach would let that kind of thing go on 'cause he's for the betterment of ourselves. Maybe he's trying to better himself through us but I think he'll sacrifice himself for our betterment, 'cause I'm sure he did already.

Once players got into the system and were caught up in the excite-ment of their celebrity roles, they entered a new phase in their exchange relationship with the University. Their conception of a reward struc-ture became entwined with their craving for attention and playing time. When queried as sophomores about their views on whether they were being exploited, they were likely to respond as James did:

> To a degree I think we are. But you play basketball because you love to play ball. When I was out for three months I couldn't even go to the gym because I'd have a cast on, but I'd get up to play still. You feel empty when you're not playing. When Daryl started bugging out and was missing all those games Coach asked me to give up my red-shirt and come back to help the team. I didn't hesitate for a minute, even though I knew I'd be getting only an end of a year with my bum leg instead of a whole 'nother year later where I could play for the full year and be healthy.

Players in their early to middle years, then, held a fairly satisfied conception of their relationship with the school. No longer were they overwhelmed by the novelty of the arena or the presence of its inhabi-tants. They were the status incumbents now. They were starting to make a contribution to the program, and not just standing on the receiving end. Their athletic performance had improved. They were contributing effort, time, energy, and sacrifices in their social and academic lives. Yet the intangible factors of glory, involvement, and importance, rewarded them to the point that they felt the exchange was equitable. They were happy in the present, and they were confident that their futures would be adequately ensured by those around them.

By their junior year, they were contributing even more to the program. They were starting to assume responsibility for the boosters, the media, the image of the program in the community, the play of the game, and socializing their younger teammates. They had also been around long enough to partially sense their contribution to the financial solvency of the University. While they had no exact figures, they knew vaguely that there was a lot of money coming in from boosters, gate receipts, media revenues, and post-season play. This heightened their awareness of how much the University was benefiting from their labor. Reconsidering their exchange with the University, they wondered if they were being adequately compensated for their efforts. While they did not describe their situation as exploitive, many began to express feelings that the exchange was not as equal (or favorable to them) as they had previously imagined. As Darian expressed in his junior year:

> The way I figure it, they're giving me a free scholarship, they're sending me through school, they're feeding me. If it wasn't for basketball I wouldn't be getting the little clothes here and there. I feel we use each other, but I feel, in the long run, they get the best end of the deal. Fifteen free scholarships is a small sacrifice. They're making money on you, they're making money on your game, they're making a killing, any way you look at it. But you get through school, you get your degree, most of the time you get you a nice job, you get enough pubs and you're good enough you can go on to bigger and higher places for the big money. I guess I was exploited to a certain degree but that's just the way it is—I don't feel I was a victim.

Tyrone added these thoughts as a junior as well:

> I feel like the school has used me and I has used the school. I feel I'm getting a fair exchange. It's not like that for all the players. It's not over yet for me, but when it's over, how can you answer that question? Did you git what you wanted to out of school?

Hell, no! They didn't give me nothing. I probably have a little wardrobe up there . . . I didn't get what I wanted to out of school because I expected next thing I was supposed to be buying my house. Only way I see I can buy my house is to make it to the NBA.

Players were thus influenced by the level and type of expectations they brought with them to the program. They also developed increased feelings of inequality in the exchange as their contribution to the team grew.

Players developed their strongest feelings of exploitation during their senior year. At this stage, they began to think more about what they would do after college. They were no longer content with being occupied by the moment and entrusting the responsibility for their futures to someone else. This led them to regard their present situation from an occupational framework and to wonder what future value they were getting out of their experience. They were doing a job, they reasoned, had been for years, and wanted some return. Their perception of the revenues generated by the athletic sphere influenced their conception of what a fair return should involve. As Marcus said during his senior year:

I think the truth needs to be told about it, that colleges and universities are makin' big money offa athaletics. You getcha education, true, but it's a money makin' thing. If we could make the money that we bring in, the revenue from the TVs, and the tournament, and tennis shoes, and the prices of admission, at least some of that money, it'd be alright. I mean, you do your job, you get paid for it. We do our job and we get a education.

For those athletes who remained academically motivated and who were on track for graduation, their degree represented some reward (although not, in their minds, an adequate one). Others, who had lost interest in academics as their chances of graduating diminished, or who had never really cared much about academics, regarded this as a paltry compensation. As a senior, Slick expressed:

The going to school part is almost like you're getting ripped off. 'Cause if you don't like it, you still got to do it. And then it's not a bonus to you, it's a chore. If you don't go to class they're goin' to get this report in that you ain't goin' to class, and then they be on your back. But you're mad because it seems like you ain't getting it and they're getting it all. "You owe it to the school," they say. I don't owe the school nothing. All's they cover is this room and board, and the living ain't the way I'm used to it.

Still others were unable to benefit from this kind of exchange, as Buck pointed out during his senior year:

But what about the kid that can't get his education, that can't pass his ACT test? The ones they keep here for four years and keep them eligible. Like Frank. They done used him. An they say that they care about him. Him gettin' his education. He still can't read at no more than a eighth grade level. They got him takin' all his exams orally. I don't think he's gettin' much of a education. An he sure ain't gonna graduate.

Seniors thus tended to look more toward the tangible instead of the experiential aspects of their exchange relationship. It was no longer adequate that they were part of an elite group, or that they were having fun, or feeling fulfilled. The future, which had always been abstract and assured, was near, and it did not hold the promised opportunities. Clyde expressed his disillusionment:

When I first got here people were tellin' me, "All you need to do is get your education and you're goin' ta have a job. The boosters'll see ta that. Play good basketball. Beat [the cross-town rivals], be in the top 20, that typa thing. Go to class everyday and you getta good job." I was just overwhelmed with the college atmosphere, being young, away from home, the responsibility. I was more overwhelmed with that and not really lookin' toward reality. Still had a dream of the NBA, and I wasn't really into a booster job, per se. But then when I seen guys like Darian, Brandon, and the guys that didn't get drafted in the pro's start working at burger spots, and you know, they got their education and everything, those good paying jobs that we all dream about, I knew right then and there, I shoulda woke up then, but I was still young, that it was all fantasy and it was all just what they thought they could do for us. They could provide that promise for us, and I shoulda known then that they couldn't really do it. It was just a big come on, just a fantasy. The snow job.

It was on this basis that athletes concluded they were getting exploited.[1] Suddenly they awoke to the fact that their playing years had
been characterized by *false consciousness,* by hopes and dreams that they
would never be able to realize. They then resented the University,
Coach, and the boosters for their unfulfilled promises.

Future Options

With the end of basketball season, senior athletes turned toward preparing for their futures. Some individuals recognized that their dream
of making the NBA, which had guided them throughout their college
careers, was an unrealistic goal; they simply hadn't played well enough.
This was a smaller group than one might expect, however, as most still
clung to some hope of a professional career. These individuals planned
to defer their thoughts about non-athletic futures until after they had
exhausted all possibilities of staying in basketball.

ATHLETIC

The first choice of all players was to get drafted by an NBA team. Only
this would mean the big money, the major status, and the opportunity
to play in the league with all the players about whom they had read
and watched. Throughout college, they never relinquished their focus
on training for this opportunity. As Slick explained:

> From the pro's perspective, college ball is a minor league. Ninety-
> five percent of professional players come from college, and when
> they're recruiting you they stress this a lot. But they don't men-
> tion it too much once you go to they school. Ninety percent of
> the schools just use you for their purposes in the four years, and
> when that's over they have no more use for you.

While all players hoped to make it into the NBA, some had a more
realistic chance of achieving this goal than others, particularly the
team's stars. Slick was especially riveted to this goal. He revealed the
character of his daily thoughts and the place of his dream among them:

> A lot of times around the dorms I'll be sitting around with the
> other guys and hanging out. We'll all be laughing, but under-

neath I'm not really laughing. I'm just waiting, getting up and going to sleep. Waiting for my shot at the NBA. It's in the back of my mind, and in the middle of my mind, and in the front.

Players who were contacted by agents became more optimistic about getting a good shot at a tryout. Numerous agents prowled around college players, and some actually spoke or wrote to them before their graduation. NCAA regulations prohibit players from signing with an agent before their eligibility expires, but this did not keep agents from trying to recruit clients. Although athletes were cognizant of the danger these agents posed, many of their hesitations about talking to agents were neutralized within the athletic subculture. One agent tried to sign a University ballplayer before the end of his eligibility by using one of his current clients, already a professional, to contact the college athlete. In his conversation, the NBA player couched the athlete-agent relationship in a positive light, pointing out how everyone in the professional leagues began this way, and suggested that there would be no way the NCAA could trace them. The athlete described this contact:

> He calls me on the phone, right in my room in the dorms. I don't know how he got the number, 'cause it's unlisted. I was really impressed to get a call from [a famous pro player] because he's a hot shot, plays in the League [the NBA]. I never even met him before, not at summer camps or nothing. But he tells me how he thinks I'm the type of calibre player that can make it in the NBA and how he'd like to help me. Says he'll stay in touch, and he might be able to be of some help to me in finding an agent. Sure enough, this agent calls me on the phone.

This player was somewhat confused by the attention, and unsure about whether he had done anything wrong. But the calls served to cement his athletic dreams more solidly. Another player contacted by an agent described the effect this attention had on him:

> The summer after my junior year I was really playing well. That's when I made my mind up that I was good and I'm gonna show all my talents. I had my mind made up senior year. Agents approached me too—I don't know if it was good or bad, but it gave me more drive.

Several players we studied were looked at by agents, but only one entered into some informal arrangement. This did not involve signing a contract, but merely talk and financial support. The player received $200 a month throughout his final year of college in the hopes that he would get drafted and sign a contract with his benefactor. While he was not legally bound, he felt morally obligated to this agent. Had he made it in the NBA, he would undoubtedly have found these sums treated as advances and withheld from his future earnings. The player described his feelings about his relationship with this agent:

> I have a little help from this one agent who's helping me, Sam Marshall. Last year when he called he gave me a lot of confidence about me being able to play in the league, which really helps me a lot—keeps me going. It's like having an extra person in my corner. He builds me up, tells me how I'm good and I'm gonna make it high in the draft. Coach doesn't tell me you can go ahead and make some money; I would be strictly unmotivated if it weren't for Sam. So when he offered me a little pocket money until I am really making it on my own, I said sure. That way I don't have to have my hands out to the boosters for a $10 here, a $20 there. I don't have to be kissing up to them all the time and I can be my own man. And Coach don't even know about it.

As soon as the season ended, agents began to recruit players more openly. They hung around the post-season tournaments and came to the coaching offices and dorms. They ferreted out players' private, unlisted phone numbers and called them. They came to campuses and made presentations. All the while, they were talking to the better players about how much they could do for them. Unsure of what it took to get drafted by an NBA team, most players listened to these agents avidly. Agents raised their hopes by telling them that a particular team was watching and considering them. Players regarded these agents as their most direct link to the NBA, since agents often told players they would put in a good word for them with teams where they had contacts. During his senior year, Danny, who would become a first-round draft pick, had just returned from a series of post-season All-Star games, when he observed the following:

> I couldn't believe it, all those guys there [at the tournament] have agents already. It seems like I'm the only one who's not hooked

up yet. And it's not that I'm not looking. I just want to find one that I feel comfortable with, that has handled other athletes. Coach, he be bringing somebody in to talk to me next week. I know I got to get one soon.

While Danny chose to move slowly and interview potential agents, his approach was not widespread. Most athletes relied on the recommendations of their coaches, friends, boosters, or other players.[2]

At last, in June, the day of the NBA draft arrived. With much anticipation, players gathered to watch it on television, hoping to see themselves, their friends, or their leaguemates selected. If there was a senior with a particularly good shot in the draft (one contacted by many agents, appointed to the All-American squad, invited to post-season All-Star games), he usually watched the draft on the television in the coaches' suite, where they all assembled and where he could be contacted immediately after his selection by the local and/or national news media. He could also expect to receive a call there from the club that had just announced him as its pick.

Players who were selected, either high up or further down in the proceedings, walked around on a cloud for days or weeks. It was then that the real courting by agents began. While any agent was free to contact a player at this point, Coach usually did some screening for favorite players, to help ensure that they signed with someone of integrity. He and the player met with agents and reviewed their offers. He made inquiries around the league to check on agents' reputations. He consulted with players' parents to offer them assistance and advice. He fielded the incessant stream of inquiries from boosters who wanted to get a vicarious thrill from being close to the whole process.

Less talented or well-known players passed over in the draft did not automatically abandon their NBA hopes. They could still pursue their dream with an invitation to an NBA team's mini-camp, held over the summer, where they could get a tryout. To get this far, they had to attract the team's attention. There were several ways of doing this. Playing in a prestigious summer league located in a major metropolitan area might bring the notice of professional scouts. Entry to such leagues usually required a connection to someone already playing in the league, however. An agent with the ear of a team might also recommend them for a tryout. Most of these options required connections and money (to travel to leagues or camps, and to pay for living expenses). At this point, many players gave up. They had neither the resources nor the energy to pursue their dream to this extent. Others continued to strive for their goal. For these players, a desperate search began. Instead of agents wooing them, they chased after agents, meeting them in summer leagues, through fellow athletes, and at mini-camps. Some of these players coaxed loans or planefare out of agents (which would come out of future commissions) in order to fly to training or tryout camps. Throughout this period they expended enormous effort and received a series of disappointments. Their intense desire helped them to persevere, pursuing their dream to the end. As Apollo said:

> I'm not gonna quit, I'm gonna keep on trying until I get my shot at the NBA. I'm not gonna give up until some NBA coach says right to my face that I'm not good enough to make it.

Unlike the more sedate courtship that occurred between agents and first-tier players, the relationship between agents and athletes on this secondary level was chaotic. Agents signed athletes and dropped them shortly afterward, they made promises that went unfulfilled, and they gave advice that turned out to be contrary to the players' best interests. Lamont, in the midst of scrambling for a job, explained how an agent misled him:

> I was guaranteed a try-out at the "Wildcats" mini-camp and I thought I had a shot because they needed a power forward. My agent suggested that I stop and try out at the "Redbirds" mini-camp which was two weeks earlier. I was worried, because I thought that might mess up my chance with the Wildcats, but he guaranteed me that this wouldn't happen. Well, I made a bunch of cuts with the Redbirds, but not the final one. So I showed up in [at the Wildcat's site] but they said they weren't interested in me any more because of the Redbirds camp.

The weak ties between athletes and agents, particularly for more marginal players, lessened agents' already low commitment to athletes' future careers. It was not uncommon, then, to see agents indiscriminately "shopping" their athletes from team to team, even though this might dilute their desirability in the eyes of the franchises.

If athletes failed to get a tryout, or got one and were not signed by the team (or were drafted in a later round and cut from the team during tryouts), their next best option was to negotiate a contract with one of the teams in Europe, South America, or some other part of the world. Tyrone discussed his feelings about playing in these leagues:

> If I don't make it on some NBA team then I want a career in basketball—four, five, or six years, if I have to go to Europe, make $45,000, $35,000 for four-five years and I don't make the NBA, then I'll say my dream was fulfilled.

While foreign teams were not as prevalent at one time, they expanded rapidly in number and popularity in the early 1980s. Although these teams were limited to two Americans each, they nevertheless served to absorb a number of the University's lesser stars.[3]

ATHLETIC-RELATED CAREERS

Players who could not get a job with any kind of professional team often turned their frustrated ambition toward an athletic-related career. Coaching was the most prestigious of these, and several players gave it thought. Apollo voiced his interest in this field, and reflected on the skills and qualifications necessary to be a good coach:

> I wouldn't mind coaching. I really like it, more and more every day. I think that's the type of man I am. I'm a teacher and I'm a leader. I know the game. I think I have a certain knack that a coach has to have—the way I can come across to another player and make him believe in me, make him believe what I tell him. I think I have a little charisma. More could come as I get older. I think I'd have to learn the administrative part of the game. The paper work, the money, how to talk in banquets.

Other players thought about coaching at the high school level. They preferred the idea of high school coaching because they liked working with youngsters. In addition, the play was not as competitive and pressured, and the jobs were easier to get. Both college and high school coaching jobs required a college degree, however, which prevented several players from realistically aspiring to them. One player left the University and returned to his former junior college to coach their team. Several players who wanted to coach at the college level, yet who did not have their degrees, tried to find some source of support to finish their education. They could then go on to graduate school in physical education and hope for a graduate assistantship on their college's team as an initial entry into the field. By his third year at the University, Coach had established a policy of sponsoring a final semester of tuition for players who had used up their eligibility and were within one semester of graduating. Yet few of the players who were most serious about wanting coaching careers took advantage of this opportunity; they had either graduated or gone on to play in one of the professional leagues.

Other athletic-related opportunities lay in the business arena. A few University players thought about going into the manufacturing, promotion, or selling of sporting goods. One University player got a job in a sporting goods store after school, where he utilized his love of sports and his knowledge of athletic play and equipment to sell products.

A final set of athletic-related jobs involved former athletes' using their brawn. One player got a job as a bouncer at a nightclub. Another began working for a moving company, lifting and packing heavy pieces of furniture onto moving trucks. A third got a job doing construction work. These represented menial or blue-collar labor, but they built on athletes' self-images as fit and strong.

ATHLETIC-CAPITALIZING

A third category many players considered were jobs capitalizing on their athletic experience and/or former star status. In this category fell the much-anticipated booster job. According to Coach, he discouraged players from expecting too much from the boosters:

> A lot of players feel that once they have played, that people owe them something. That's sad and that's a myth. It's too bad that players that come through here and once they get through playing they'll come back and say, "I done played Coach. I thought I was goin' get 'hooked up.'" That's not true. You can go out there and get it yourself. But no one's gonna say you done played here, made all-American, so now we're just giving you this because you were here. That's a myth.

Yet players disagreed. From their perspective, they had heard specific promises from the coaches while they were being recruited, from the older players in the early years, and from the boosters themselves.

A few years after graduating, Rob discussed these promises as a fairly prevalent pattern:

> Oh yeah, they really promise that type of stuff and it never comes through. And I think it's all over America. When I go home and I visit guys that go to smaller colleges, even the small college boosters would tell them that they would be in that type of position. This happened to some of my closest friends, they never came through, and then they're just really back where they started from. I remember when I was movin' outta the dorm. I didn't even know where I was gonna stay. And all these rich boosters, you know, said they was gonna hook me up with somethin.' They'd come through. But no way.

While many had grandiose presumptions, Clyde expressed a more modest level of expectation:

> I think the boosters will be of some help to me down the line. If they don't open the door for me, they'll let me put my foot in it. Just like I felt the obligation to speak to them, I think they have, they probably feel the same obligation too. As long as I'm not walking with my hand out, I'm not draining them.

Upon graduating, a few players were offered employment by boosters. These were often office jobs in industrial, service, or financial industries. Overwhelmingly, however, the players who received these offers were white. Only one black athlete that we observed (a law student) was offered a job by a booster (as a law clerk), and this lasted only for a few months. He perceived that he was being treated like an object or a token philanthropic gesture, and found the situation exceedingly uncomfortable:

> A lawyer that I work for right now, I don't really think she cares about ME. I think she cares about my image that I projected over the last four years. 'Cause she told me one time that she wants to get recognition for hirin' me 'cause I'm black, and she doesn't think she gets that recognition. That told me that she didn't care about me. Everywhere we go, "Well this is my law clerk, Darian Robinson. He a former University basketball player." That's how she introduces me.

The observation of a general trend toward racial discrimination was also made independently by members of the team. As Mark noted:

> Getting out afterwards and getting a nice job is a whole lot easier for the white guys. It's harder for white guys to get a sugar daddy while they're in school 'cause all the boosters want to help out the poor, black players. It makes them feel good. But then when it comes time to coughing up a job, they don't want to have anything to do with them, and they head straight toward the white guys.

Since the black players considerably outnumbered the whites on the team (and the local economy was undergoing recessionary times), there were few booster jobs forthcoming.

Other areas where athletes could capitalize on their sport-related experiences included jobs where they could use either their skills (as in public relations or broadcasting) or their knowledge of different types of people. As Apollo said:

> I think I had the opportunity to mingle with different types of people through basketball. I probably wouldn't have met these kinds of people otherwise. I learned how to be around white people, how to talk to them. For a black person in business, that is essential.

Another type of athletic-capitalizing job was one where the owner liked athletes. Many individuals favored hiring athletes because they believed sports participation bred a competitive and unyielding nature.[4] These employers were scattered around the country in various corporations, and often included former athletes.

Other ex-athletes found jobs where they could use their connections and reputation to get a start. This included sales jobs in fields such as real estate, insurance, and other miscellaneous products. One former player, now out on his own and selling industrial cleaning products, was frequently cited by Coach as a prime example of the type of opportunity he desired younger players to derive from their University athletic careers. While this player was not employed by a booster, he did business with people who were fans of the University's team. As Coach noted:

Take Rob Green for example. He gets a job in selling. He only got that job because he was Rob Green, player for the University. He's making his sales because he was a basketball player. Your average black guy who would have gotten Rob's job would be through working today. But Rob is making it because he is selling to the people who came and clapped their hands for him.

EDUCATION AND EDUCATION-CAPITALIZING

A group of athletes either stayed in school or went into fields where they took advantage of their education. Individuals who remained on campus to get their degrees included those who did not graduate, but whose families could afford to send them for another year. One or two were able to benefit from Coach's semester plan and stayed for that reason. Some students talked about staying at the University to attend one of its graduate programs, but only one ever did (Darian, the law student, who dropped out after his first year). The areas most often discussed by athletes as appealing to them included masters degrees in business administration (MBAs), social work or counseling and guidance, and communication, broadcasting, and public relations.

Several players who graduated (either in four years or after another one or two) did go into fields where they drew upon their academic interests and credentials. These included work in applied sociological areas such as criminal justice (probation and parole), social problems (juvenile delinquency, drug rehabilitation), and mental health (psychiatric hospitals and wards). Others went into the communications industry (a popular major) working for one of the local newspapers, radio, or television stations.

UNPLANNED

Some athletes made no plans. When their athletic eligibility expired, they suddenly had to find work. That many athletes found themselves in this situation is not surprising. Individuals forced to disengage from a role that has served as the linchpin of their core identity often have little idea of what they will do next. In fact, some lag or adjustment time may be common, where individuals have extreme difficulty re-engaging in another role for a period of time.

Individuals without plans were sometimes saved from having to make a decision by the offer of employment from friends or relatives. This often required moving back home. Such jobs ranged in character enormously, although they were often in sales. Individuals fortunate enough to be connected to jobs through family or friends were more likely, once again, to come from the ranks of the white and middle class players.

Those without connections (a sizable group) often ended up in what they called "shit jobs," menial work in undesirable, low paying, or insecure positions. In large part they did it because they had been so focused on their athletic-related futures that they gave no thought and made no provision for any other alternatives. As Slick said:

> If I don't make the NBA or some European team I'll just probably be working eight hours somewhere. Flipping hamburgers or something. Really, there's no telling what. Ironically, then, some of the best players left school with the least promising futures.

Others found themselves under-employed or unemployed because they had little occupational motivation outside of athletics. Tyrone described his aspirations:

> I never dreamed of building a big fancy home for myself and my mother. And I don't picture myself living here once I'm finished. I'm not a part of this community. Once you're out you're as good as gone, even if you stay. I just want to get a car and live my old mediocre life and just be one of those persons that's around.

Some players who worked hard, gave considerable thought to their futures, and who graduated still ended up working in menial jobs. This included individuals who made an attempt at graduate school but dropped out, individuals who held responsible jobs working for the University's athletic department in some coaching position, and those who had short-lived careers in some professional basketball capacity. What these players had in common was their race (black) and their engulfment in the basketball world. They were successful in athletics, but did not make it in another enterprise.

Losing the Role

As seniors, college athletes' basketball careers at the University were nearly over. Soon the pressures, the scrutiny and attention, and the conflicting multiple role demands would be gone. They would leave both the dorms and the relationships they had made with peers over the last four years. As the end of the year approached, athletes began to think about losing the role to which they were now fully socialized. As Marcus exclaimed:

> The worst thing about being here is having to leave when it's all over. That's true. It's been peaches and cream so far. At home it's sleep, go to school, play basketball. You go to college it's sleep, go to school, play basketball. After college there'll be no more basketball and you have to start worrying about work.

Some players, especially those from ghetto backgrounds, felt particularly acute anxiety about the future. Before coming to college they had been adjusted to their lives and home communities. They had lived like their "homeboys," and imagined this would always be the case. These were the individuals on whom Coach had made his strongest imprint, as he tried to resocialize them to his norms and values. In so doing, he changed them. Tyrone remarked on these changes:

> I used to know how to make money. He [Coach] didn't like the way I made money; I knew how to make it though. But he got rid of it just a slight. He phased this down, build this up, get him into a ballplayer and make the public like this guy. Now what I'm gonna do when I get out if I don't make the NBA?

Concluding their college careers thus posed a paradox to athletes: they were at the peak of their skills, strength, and knowledge, yet the very role for which they had spent the last four years training was ending. They could no longer continue in this life. Only a few would go on to work in basketball-related careers. The rest would have to find other spheres of life. As the end of the academic year approached, some of them grew increasingly depressed and anxious about this prospect.

ADJUSTMENT DIFFICULTIES

Despite their knowledge that their playing days were ending, the conclusion of the season and the loss of their athletic role came as a shock. They had been so focused on the present, so involved with the intensity of the immediate season, that they were unprepared for its end. They experienced their change-of-status rites with sadness: the final home game, which included special ceremonies for the seniors and the bestowal of awards after the game (for most popular player and other distinctions), and the post-season banquet. By this time they already felt invisible. The media, the boosters, and the coaches were turning away from them toward talk of the new prospects they were recruiting.

Why were athletes so existentially unprepared for the loss of their athletic role and identity? Merlin Olsen (quoted in Coakley 1986:205), former defensive lineman of the Los Angeles Rams and later an NBC commentator, offered this insight into the nature of the athletic subculture:

> The athlete doesn't have to grow up because the coach lives his life for him. . . . The sad thing is [that] it actually benefits the team to keep the player naive and dependent.

It was in the interest of the athletic program for Coach to keep the players focused on the immediate present. If players started anticipating their futures too much, they might expend less than their full energy, commitment, and effort toward the athletic role. Coach thus continued his manipulations, begun during freshman year, of keeping athletes poised between complete interest and overconfidence, extracting the most from them while discouraging them from letting their attention wander. Accustomed to being handled in this manner, players remained focused on the task at hand and did not anticipate their futures and the loss these would hold. As Jesse reflected:

> I guess I should have paid more attention to some of the things going on around me. Should have noticed what was happening to the seniors before me, what they were feeling like and the trouble they were having. But you get used to thinking of your life as being centered around a few very intense things and you don't pay as much attention as you should outside of that. And then again, you always say to yourself, it can't happen to me.

When the year ended the loss of the athletic role came upon athletes abruptly. Suddenly there were practical problems to face that they had never considered before, such as where they were going to live, how they were going to feed, clothe, and shelter themselves. More difficult, for many, were the existential problems inherent in the sudden loss of their core identity. They had to endure the abrupt shift in how people treated them, now that they were devoid of their celebrity. They were forced to grapple with the question of who they were now and who they would become. As Darian, in his second year out of college, explained:

> It used to be, people comin' up to you at shopping centers, (laugh) you know, ten, twenty kids around you. You signin' autographs. And you're just the center of attention. And then once that attention is gone after you graduate, you know, you *crash* down. And I think I did that. Now a few of them might recognize me. But when I was playing with the University it'd be the whole shopping center, you know, whisperin', pointin' and all that. And like on campus, after the game or at a party, you'd be the center of attention. I 'member I just went over to a party right when school let out. You know, I went in, and I knew nobody, and nobody knew me.

Crashing was a common feeling athletes reported upon disengaging from their athletic role. Another former player, Lamont, reported that his sense of loss was coupled with a newfound sense of freedom:

> I miss it sometimes, especially when they go in there and they're practicing. I miss talking to the media, miss everybody knowing you on campus. It's a lot different, to be honest with you. But if that wasn't all you wanted out of college life then I don't think it should bother you too much. Actually. I feel a little more comfortable, really, because the pressure is not as intense now. I can cool out more and not have to worry about walking across campus drinking a beer. I'm my own person, I'm not part of the University, I'm not part of Coach.

ROLE EXIT

The concept of role exit, at one time overlooked, has come under more frequent examination by sociologists since the 1970s. Instead of being solely interested in the entry aspect of role change, or socialization, recent research has focused on the characteristics of exiting a variety of groups or statuses.[5] Ebaugh, who first studied nuns abandoning their vows (Ebaugh 1977), and later role exit more generally (Ebaugh 1988) has focused on the process by which individuals disengag ious roles and re-engage in new ones. She has suggested that role exit most often involves a gradual process of withdrawing commitment (ties) and attachment (emotional involvement) from a role. She characterizes the most common form of role exit as having four stages: developing first doubts; seeking and weighing role alternatives; encountering a turning point, and establishing an ex-role identity.

Our findings differ in some ways from Ebaugh's model and resemble it in others. First, while Ebaugh's role exiters made a conscious choice to abandon a role that remained available to them, college athletes had no such choice. Although eight players left the team because they could not meet the calibre of play or had personal conflicts with the coach, university, or community, most remained in the program for as long as they were permitted. They thus underwent an institutionalized role exit, complete with a senior year rite of passage marking the end of their college playing careers. This form of exit is characterized by a *lack of control* over the decision to conclude the role, leaving athletes to experience the usual feelings of powerlessness and, often, frustration. Second, unlike most of Ebaugh's role exiters, college athletes *collectively* arrived at the termination of their role. Having role partners in the same situation, experiencing similar confusion and stress, served to help them. They could share their thoughts and feelings with each other (to the extent that such behavior was enabled within the athletic subculture), talk to each other about future plans, and anticipate their own role exits by watching the behavior of older players (to the extent that they were able to unplug themselves from the immediacy of their present-riveted situation). Third, for most athletes, their exit from the college athlete role was *irreversible*. While some managed to extend their involvement with it by going on to play professional ball or to coach, most college athletes came to the end of their elite-level playing careers at the end of four years of eligibility. Finally, college athletes' role exit was profoundly affected by the *centrality of the role* to their sense of core self. Exiting such an engulfing role required athletes to undergo a radical self-reformulation, for which they were fundamentally unprepared and, often, unsuccessful. This had serious implications for their ability to adjust and adapt to their life after basketball.

DETACHMENT DIFFICULTIES

Just as some players felt the loss of the athletic role more poignantly than others, some had more difficulty detaching emotionally from this role and its associated dream. No matter how long they had been out, many still longed for their college days and regarded them as the apex of their lives. Merely leaving school and ceasing to play basketball did not ensure role disengagement. Once they were out and it was all over, they had to accept the loss of the role and create a new life and identity for themselves. Giving up their role involvement was complex and problematic, as Darian remarked:

What I'm goin' through right now is tryin' to detach from the dream. Because it's haaarrdd. I thought it would be easy to detach from all the publicity. The center of attention. It's not. I've been out a year and a half now, goin' on two, an' I still haven't. I dream about runnin' up an' down the court. Wishin' that I had maybe a chance to be a junior again this year. With the knowledge that I've already gained for the four years and going back with that knowledge an' just bein' a junior. I would take that.

Marcus, discussing his father, shed some insight into the long-term difficulty athletes face in detaching themselves from the elite athletic role and its dreams:

It's hard to get it offa your mind. I don't think my father never did. He played basketball, and he only finished two years of college. I know he wanted all his heart for me to get drafted and go pro. All through college he was living that dream with me. He had his college player, he came down for all the games, and he was proud of that. I almost think he enjoyed it more than I did. But I think, if you don't get rid of that dream and wake up to reality, then it hurts you. I think it's hurt me, and I need to start to get rid of it. But, you know, I'm only 22. And I still think I can play. But my father, he never did grab onto something else because he was always hopin' he would get called back to college, or would play in the pros or something.

Because of their difficulty in relinquishing the role, a few players went through phases where they oscillated into and out of sport (cf. Adler and Adler 1983). They made lives for themselves that they would give up to re-enter sport, only to find that they couldn't hold on in sport any longer. Rob Green, the player Coach held up as a role model for making it in the business community by utilizing his fan connections, is a good example. From the start, he had trouble adjusting to his loss of the athletic role. He spent every weekend hanging around the gym. He joined the college players in their summer pick-up games. He organized a team in the church leagues with a couple of his former teammates. He spent so much time in the gym that Coach started using him to help with the new arrivals in the fall, teaching them the offense and getting the practices organized. Soon he became a volunteer assistant coach in addition to his regular sales job. And when Coach was offered a job at another university, he accepted Coach's offer to be the part-time, and later full-time, assistant coach on the team, giving up his local job for an opportunity that, at first, paid less than a graduate assistantship. Two players discussed his situation:

DARIAN: It's just like not making it in other ways, like graduating and not getting a job, or having talent and not using it, or having the brains and not gettin' the degree. Never being able to detach from the dream. You know. Look at Rob Green.
MARCUS: Okay, yeah.
DARIAN: He, he had finally got himself that job . . .
MARCUS: Job, yeah.
DARIAN: Selling.
MARCUS: He had a good job.
DARIAN: And then he gave it all up.
MARCUS: Gave it up.
DARIAN: He could'a been a success, but he's a failure, because he can't detach.

Rob's case is ironic because he swung from being an exemplar to its reverse; once he relapsed into the athletic realm players labeled him a failure rather than a success. He represented an especially acute failure to them, in fact, because he gave up his successful life to return to the dream. He could not stay away from the gym. There are thus multiple dimensions and challenges in the role exit phase that can potentially result in failure: letting the dream and role go (getting away); making a new life after basketball (creating an ex-role); and holding oneself back from relapsing (staying away).

What becomes apparent here is the fact that conflicting messages are embodied in the culture shared by these athletes and ex-athletes. They are told throughout their playing careers that athletics is *the* thing. They are exhorted to and rewarded for placing this role before all others (cf. Weistart 1989). Recalling athletes' preferences in considering their future options, nearly all wanted to retain, in some way, involvement with the athletic role. Yet once they were out, success was suddenly evaluated by a different measure. Success became defined in terms of how well individuals cast off the role they were once rewarded for elevating above all. After their forced role exit, former athletes were judged by a new standard: how well they disengaged from the role. If they were not able to set it aside, they were viewed by former peers (and society) as failures. The case of Rob Green is particularly interesting because in dropping his "real world" success story and revivingthe athletic role he was following the priorities of the athletic realm.

POST-DISENGAGEMENT

A number of studies have examined the disengagement of athletes from elite-level sport, positing a variety of hypotheses as most appropriate to depicting the character of their role exit. By far the most commonly depicted pattern suggests serious difficulties (such as depression, lack of adjustment, occupational failure, etc.) for retired athletes who can no longer maintain the participation, competition, camaraderie, excitement, and identity associated with the athletic role.[6]

A second hypothesis is that elite athletes do not make an abrupt cutoff from their sport upon terminating their participation at the elite level. Rather, they continue their involvement, modifying it in two ways: they decrease the amount of time spent playing sports, and they diminish their level of competition.[7] They may even switch to another sport that they can pursue in a more recreational manner. This "buffering" to their disengagement serves to reduce the negative effects of a more abrupt termination.[8]

Alternately, Coakley (1983) has posited a "rebirth" hypothesis, suggesting that upon being freed from the extreme demands of participation in elite-level sport, former athletes blossom by becoming involved in alternate pursuits they find equally rewarding. Instead of suffering, they feel released from the heavy burden of their training schedules and the attention, expectations, and demands of others. Role termination is thus theoretically as likely to produce a positive effect as a traumatic one.

Finally, Curtis and Ennis (1988) have offered a view of sport disengagement as characterized by role acquisition. Elite-level sport, they have argued, should be viewed as a short-term (or what Gallmeier 1987, in writing about professional hockey players, has called a "compressed") career, such that when it ends athletes move on gracefully. They point to the existence of other short-term careers and the way participants find new pursuits after their involvement in these comes to an end. Terminating an elite sport role may be sad, but it is no more traumatic and negative in its consequences than leaving any other short-term career. Individuals adjust, and they carry the positive remnants of their former elite sport participation and identity with them throughout their lives.

Involvement. The athletes we observed followed a variety of paths to exiting the college athlete role. The first was to avoid exit by remaining immersed in athletics. Several former athletes had such a high degree of role commitment that they thrust aside all other considerations and held tightly to the athletic realm. Those with the most talent ascended to a higher plane by making it in one of the professional leagues. Others, who had the tenacity and ability to graduate from college, could also remain within the athletic arena by continuing in some high school or collegiate athletic program. For as long as individuals could continue to play or work toward a coaching position, they deferred the loss of their athletic role and status.

Vestigial Involvement. Those who exited elite sport had to decide whether or not there would be a place for athletics in their lives and what that place would be. Many chose to maintain vestigial involvement with it by continuing to play basketball recreationally. This was partly affected by whether or not they remained in town. Those who stayed in the local area were more likely to continue playing basketball, as they were surrounded by former teammates who they could recruit or who would recruit them to play in recreational games and leagues. One former player discussed his involvement in such a league:

> We have a pretty good time, and the games are pretty competitive too. There's about four teams in the league that have former University athletes playing on them. Tonight we're playing the "Snake's" team. He's got Lamont on it, but we've got me, Foss, and Robinson. There's also Green's team, and he's got Oliver, Morrison, and Rand. We play all summer long, about two nights a week.

The majority of athletes continued their involvement with sport on this reduced level.

No Involvement. Still others chose to fashion their post-college lives without any further involvement in basketball. They made this decision for several reasons. Several individuals said they were sick of the sport:

> They had me playing this game for so long now, when I want to and when I don't want to, I'm fed up with it. In high school I never got tired of playing, but in college you have to get out there whether you want to or not. You have to drag your ass through practice when you're tired, when you're hurting, when you're sick of seeing another goddammed basketball. And it stops being fun. When this is all over, I don't want to see another basketball.

Some cut themselves off from playing basketball because they found themselves unable to adjust to playing or attending games at a lesser level. As Darian explained:

> I just can't do it, Doc. It hurts too much. To go to the games, to see all those phoney boosters who used to fall all over me, and now they just ignore me, to watch the guys play and I'm not one of them. I don't feel like I belong there anymore. I'd like to go to support the friends I still have on the team, but I hardly do. I can't hardly play anymore, for the same reason.

Buck also remarked:

> I guess it's a combination of I injured myself so much playing those four years that I don't want to take on all that hassle of getting myself taped up and worrying I might pull something or pop it out of place, and my job is so demanding now I really don't have time for basketball. But, uh, I guess if I really wanted

to those reasons wouldn't stop me. I just don't have the heart for it anymore. Playing is not the same as it was and I don't like to play this way. I guess I can't adjust to the change.

Our findings thus show that no exclusive pattern of adaptation emerged, as individual team members followed a variety of these three patterns. Many athletes were saddened to leave their college days behind, setting aside forever the rhythm of the seasons, the collegiality, the intense competition, and the celebrity. Others left with a sense of relief, of freedom and loss of oppressive responsibility. Some managed to remain in sport, not wanting to leave this intoxicating arena. Of those who left, some adapted better to their transition into a new life than others, either by buffering themselves with vestigial involvement in sport, or by cutting it out completely.

Once their careers as college athletes were over, athletes returned to the status of civilians. For four years they had learned to adjust to the cyclical rhythm of the basketball life: calm in the summer; weary but filled with anticipation during the pre-game practice season; overwhelmed during the playing season, lonely but peaceful once the season was over. Like the seasons, they had come to interpret each one in relation to the one just past and in anticipation of the upcoming one. But now the cycle was broken; there would be no new season to look forward to, no new season of hectic intensity that would make the summer a welcome relief in comparison. The end of each year had always come abruptly, going from the frenzied havoc of post-season tournament play to an empty void. But this time it was worse. In May, school was out and they were on their own.

9
The Engulfed Self

WE HAVE focused on the experiences of athletes during their years of playing eligibility at an NCAA Division I university. Our aim has been to describe their world as structured, complex, and richly textured. Now, we move beyond empirical knowledge to explore ways of expanding our insights about basic issues relevant to social psychological knowledge of the self, society, and social change. We also analyze the self-processes and self-outcomes we have described to generate a greater understanding of the self and its surrounding social conditions. We begin by considering the implications of these data for theories of the self, and then analyze the relationship between the engulfed self and features of contemporary American society.

Self and Identity

Most incoming freshmen athletes entered college with an already established sense of their athletic abilities and identity, nurtured during their elementary and high school years by family, friends, coaches, and members of the community. However, this did not preclude development of other dimensions of their self-identity. In high school, they had led active social lives in which they were often accorded high status because of their athletic ability. They had also managed to complete their academic requirements with varying degrees of success, and some had developed a broader range of academic goals for college than those defined by athletics alone. From these experiences and the descriptions of college life given to them by athletic recruiters, they expected that college would be, in many ways, an extension of high school. They believed they would continue to perform satisfactorily in the social, academic, and athletic arenas and that they would continue to be independent persons, moving only to a higher plane of performance. There were several basic differences that they did expect, however: an improvement in their social lives as they moved from the smaller pond of high school to the exciting atmosphere of a college campus; a move to the "big-time" athletic realm of big gymnasiums, supportive boosters, fancier uniforms, and more extensive media coverage; and courses that would "educate" them either for business and/or professional careers or, if not so helpful, at least be manageable within their athletic regimen. In general, they supposed that life would continue as before, but be better.

Their expectations were soon dashed. As they learned from their experiences, became socialized to this new arena, and met the people who would be associated with their new lives, they saw that their expectations differed from reality. No longer were they merely playing a game; college athletics involved "big money" and was a very serious business. This was work. They were not expected to have fun on the court. In fact, they were disciplined and drilled until the enjoyable aspects of playing had all but disappeared and a new way not only of playing but also of thinking about the game was instilled. Moreover, the demands placed on them were far more serious than they had anticipated.

Their athletic role also encroached on other facets of their lives. Not only were they athletes on the court, they were also expected to be athletes in the classroom and during their recreational time. They had to spend time socializing with people about whom they cared little , all the while acting to disguise their true feelings. They had to relinquish their privacy and interact with people through the medium of public images that were often quite different from their own. As ambassadors for the basketball program they were expected to curtail their youthful exuberance and refrain from the kinds of pranks and carefree living enjoyed by other college students. Any conduct that would cast aspersions upon their teammates, their coach, their program, or their university was prohibited.

This pattern of encroachment applied to their academic experiences as well. They discovered that they had limited autonomy over academic decision-making. Coaches selected their courses and mediated between them and their professors. For some, required afternoon practices restricted their choice of majors, especially when basic courses were given at the same time period. Their "greedy" athletic roles consumed their time and absorbed their emotional focus, leaving them with little energy or capacity to concentrate on their schoolwork. They came to see that their athletic role carried with it a burdensome responsibility that diminished its enjoyment and expanded its tentacled reach into other spheres of their lives. It conflicted and competed with other roles and activities for access to athletes' time, effort, and self-identification.

Yet at the same time, their experiences in the athletic role bedazzled them. Once the season began, they were treated with glamour, celebrity, excitement, and adulation. Cheered wildly by thousands of screaming fans, worshipped by kids in malls and hailed by fans on the streets, their selves were elevated and transformed by glory. Sought after by rich and important people, they were, in effect, reborn, larger-than-life. Such experiences bred feelings of dizzying euphoria, gratifying their egos and riveting them to this role in which their euphoria could be continued. Once committed to this identity, they encountered conflicts between their athletic and other roles; these were resolved, almost always, in favor of the former. For the most part, they acquiesced to the coaches' demands on their social lives, going to public relations functions and dinners, and observing proper decorum in public. Yet they did not give up those friends or girlfriends that the coaches found objectionable, nor did they abandon their partying altogether. Instead, they reserved this form of moral autonomy and personal integrity as a haven for privacy and refuge from the pressures and expectations inherent in their particular situation. With regard to their academic role, they made a series of pragmatic adjustments to their academic goals, abandoning more ambitious dreams by changing their majors from the more highly academic subjects to those in physical education or recreation that were less challenging. They changed their orientation toward their education from one that might have prepared them for a career to one that would lead to their getting a degree and/or staying eligible. These attitudinal and behavioral modifications resulted from athletes' burgeoning, and ultimately complete, engulfment in the athletic role.

IDENTITY SALIENCE AND ENGULFMENT

Such tangible shifts in attitudes and behavior signified a realignment of athletes' roles and their relative salience, increasing their attachment (Goffman 1961b) to the athletic role. Several variables from identity theory bear on this process. First, Stryker (1968) has proposed that a correlation exists between role salience and role commitment, positing that those roles harder to relinquish have a greater possibility of being invoked in any given situation. To this, Turner (1978) and Hoelter (1983) have added the variable of role evaluation, suggesting that the degree to which individuals are positively or negatively evaluated by others in a role affects the salience of that role to their overall self-definition. Our research supports these authors' findings and suggests the relevance of three additional variables. These bear on engulfment as they influence the ascendance and subversion of all other roles by the athletic role.

Athletes' resolutions of their perceived role conflicts suggest a reaffirmation of the relationship between *role evaluation* and role salience. Many of the college athletes in our sample received poor or marginal grades and had to relinquish or adjust the academic goals they had held upon entering college. This awakened them to the contradiction between their expectations that college would be very much like high school, and their realization that the academic demands at the University were greater than they could meet. Their emphasis on competition and winning, derived from sport, made the evaluative stigma of failure especially difficult to accept. When faced with an extreme version of this role conflict, individuals doing poorly in their classes engaged in a variety of practices that distanced them from their student identity (Ball 1975). In effect, they diminished the importance of academic success to their self-identity. Individuals from stronger academic backgrounds fared slightly better, however, and did not reduce their academic identity as greatly. Thus, it would appear that as individuals assess their relative strengths and weaknesses within given roles, they accord higher salience to those in which they excel and are evaluated positively and ascribe lower salience to those in which they do poorly and are negatively assessed. A related dimension of athletes' role evaluation is associated with their relative *role reinforcement*. Generally, college athletes lacked significant others within the academic realm. As a result, they received little positive reinforcement for their own academic accomplishments. On the other hand, their membership in an athletic role-set yielded significant reinforcement for their athletic achievements, but little acknowledgment for even moderate academic success. According to van de Vliert's (1981) "choice behavior hypothesis," individuals experiencing role conflict where role A (the athletic role) is legitimate and sanctioned, while role B (the academic role) is legitimate but sanctionless, will usually choose to follow the prescriptions of role A. A lack of reinforcement for their academic role influenced these athletes to diminish their efforts and reduce their identity salience in this area. Only when athletes received significant academic reinforcement from social role-set members, their girlfriends and families, or from employers promising them jobs upon graduation, were they able to overcome the predominant tendency toward devaluing their academic role. Without positive reinforcement (or sanctions) it is unlikely that individuals will invest much of their self-identity in a particular role. Athletes' willingness to sacrifice the salience of their academic role, under situations of conflict and stress, may also be related to that role's weak prior reinforcement, where they invested dreams but not much self-identity in it.

Third, our data lend support to the thesis that *role commitment* is a significant factor in role salience. Most athletes' initial commitment to the academic role was induced by general cultural expectations and by the encouragement of specific others, but it was not firmly embedded in their self-conceptions. A few came to college with a keen desire to use their education to pursue a career in a professional field or to seek learning for its own sake, but these individuals were in the minority. Once in college, their commitment to work hard academically was easily dislodged by their first experiences of adversity and by the peer culture's devaluation of academics. That significant others (coaches, professors, students) had limited academic expectations of them made it easier to abandon their role commitment. Their athletic scholarship (a side-bet, see Becker 1960) merely required that they maintain eligibility. In contrast, their commitment to the athletic role was more deeply entrenched, since this was where their idealized self-images had been lodged since childhood. No matter how little playing time they were granted or how much Coach criticized them, they clung to this primary source of gratifying self-identification. As their commitment to the academic role and to the possibility of a future career based on academic pursuits declined, so too did their academic role salience. Hence, we may suggest that the more committed individuals are to a given role, the more they take that role to heart (Erikson 1957) or feel bound to it by institutional obligations (Goffman 1961b),[1] the more they are likely to accord that role high identity salience. Roles to which they are less deeply attached are not considered as central to their self-conceptions.

Role identification is another variable associated with role commitment, identity salience, and engulfment. As college athletes learned the nature of their new status, they came to see that they were identified as basketball players by nearly everyone they encountered; their athletic identity superimposed itself over other roles in almost every situation. They found this in their academic and social lives both on and off campus. This designation grew even more pervasive as they progressed through their playing careers and advanced to more prominent and visible positions on the team. Their label as athletes was influential in their accepting this as their "master status" (Hughes 1945). Having adopted this status, college athletes acted as athletes in non-athletic situations, thereby reducing the visible display of behaviors associated with their academic role. We conclude that when people are identified in one role to the near total exclusion of all others, they become increasingly committed to that role; moreover, it is likely to take precedence in influencing their self-conceptions.

Finally, we note a correlation between role salience and a related dimension of role commitment: *role power*. As college athletes' preconceptions were shattered by the role conflict they encountered, they began to perceive a power structure operating among their various roles and role-set members. Athletes' position at the University can be characterized as "institutionalized powerlessness" (Edwards 1973), because their coaches controlled nearly all aspects of their lives. By influencing how they spent their personal time, the courses on their academic schedules, and their playing on the team, coaches dominated not only their athletic, but their social and academic roles as well. Regardless of their own goals, expectations, or desires, then, college athletes had to take into consideration the wishes and demands of the coaches. Players also believed, albeit in a vague and unspecified way, that their coaches had some power or influence over their professors. This was revealed in their feeling that Coach could ultimately keep them eligible to play if he wanted to, even if they got into academic difficulty. The supposed omnipotence of their athletic over their academic role influenced them to shift greater identity salience to the former. Roles characterized by more powerful role-set members, then, are more likely to command greater role commitment and identity salience.

The role conflict resolutions of college athletes were highly influenced by their acculturation within an athletic subculture that stratified the importance of their various roles. This resocialization process and its resultant academic outcomes were set forth by the peer subculture, reinforced by the coach, and fueled, ultimately, by the structural demands of college athletics. Yet college athletes were not simply pulled from their academic and social spheres by the demands of their athletic identities and their fellow athletes and coaches; they actively chose to invest their time, effort, and selves in this arena. They volunteered to join their interests with those of their coaches and to immerse themselves in the athletic role.

While identity theorists have focused on the effects of the role-salience hierarchy on individuals' performance in various statuses or roles, this work augments that literature by suggesting the dynamics leading to the shift between those roles and on the consequences of that shift for self-engulfment.

ENGULFMENT AND THE MASTER STATUS

In introducing the concept of master status, Hughes (1945) referred to an individual's position in society as it is influenced by the most salient role in his or her repertoire. As such, the master status influences individuals' interaction with others by affecting the way both they and significant others perceive, interpret, and define them and their behavior. The master status, then, is critical to individuals' lodging within society. It locates them within their social group, institution, and community, providing them with a structured set of ties, duties, and relationships. As the position most central to their lives, the master status also internally influences or determines individuals' other roles or identities within their role repertoire. It is germane to the structure and position of these various roles or identities that comprise the totality of the self. Over the course of individuals' lifespans, shift occurs among these identities, leading them to ascend or fade in salience, and causing circulation of the master status. Yet in Hughes' discussion, he offered no explanation of the dynamics underlying the shift among roles leading to one's assuming a master position.

Our research discloses the process by which a master status arises.

One role, whether new or already existent, ascends from its former stature to a heightened position of prominence or "psychological centrality" (Rosenberg 1979) in an individual's constellation of identities. In the case of the basketball players we studied, the athletic role rose to dominance through a combination of both internal push and external pull. Internally are the athletic role's promise to fulfill players' dreams, its ability to make them feel important and famous, and its larger-than-life media stature; externally are the demands of their athletic scholarship, its reinforcement by athletic role-set members, and its status as the primary identity cast onto them by others. As the athletic role rose to prominence, it captivated their self-involvement. Actions that athletes took within this role increased their level of commitment to it, making them less available for alternative lines of action. Moreover if, as Kornhauser (1962:322) has suggested, "the strength of a commitment can be measured by the number of social spheres for which it enforces lines of action," the dominance of their athletic role over their social and academic spheres contributed to their growing commitment to this role and its ascent to a master status. The other dimensions of their identity were thus relegated to secondary, or what Hughes called subordinate, statuses. Not only did players receive less gratification from these other roles, but they distanced themselves from them and lost much of their desire and ability to see the world through them. Once established, the longer their gloried, athletic self served as their master status, the harder it became for them to conceive of any other identity for themselves. This master status spilled over into and infused other facets of their selves, a point Turner (1978) has discussed in his concept of "role-self merger." It became the generative category from which all others took their meaning.

Schur (1971) has discussed the process of "role engulfment," whereby individuals engaged in deviant activities become increasingly centered around their deviant role through the effects of labeling, leading to changes in self-concept and to activities of secondary deviance. Supports to a legitimate self-identity are withdrawn, leaving the individual with only the deviant role. Schur's study highlights the effect of external forces on individuals' engulfment in a role, but it is incomplete; he neglects to consider internal pressures moving deviants further within their roles. Athletes' engulfment by the athletic role was fueled both from within and without. They developed gloried selves within the athletic role as new, more powerful and alluring identities were set before them. They then actively chose to diminish the salience of other self-dimensions in order to seek fulfillment from the new, intoxicating one. In so doing, they shunted aside significant others associated with their former identities and sought the company of those who would reinforce their gloried self. Thus, as labeling theory implies but never clearly states, a preoccupation with one role can lead to the neglect of other roles; moreover, the labeling can be done by the person himself or herself.

As the athletes we studied merged their person with their athletic role they developed engulfed selves: selves guided by a single, rather than multiple set of interests and foci. Their behavior, lives, and identities were consumed by their one dominating status. Concomitant with this unfolding role domination, athletes experienced a process of role abandonment. The athletic role's aggrandizement brought with it a constriction and/or transformation of their other roles and identities. These were all subordinated to the engulfing role, becoming tempered and modified through it. As they diminished in salience, ceasing to motivate athletes or define their sense of self as they had previously, they became neglected or relatively abandoned, left powerless and distant. Developing an engulfed self is thus a two-pronged process: while one role ascends to master status, others experience role abandonment or role neglect.

An engulfed self thus represents a more powerful centralization of identity than a master status. The latter signifies a primary identity through which individuals are perceived by themselves and significant others, yet does not preclude the existence or import of other roles and identities, some of which may be relatively unrelated to the master status. An engulfed self, in contrast, denotes a constellation of roles all organized around and through one central identity. The engulfing role, in the position of power and predominance, influences and mediates all other roles. Thus, in contrast to a self where one status stands as the most noticeable among several potential contenders, an engulfed self has only one potential master status. When a single role comes to dominate not only the individual, but all the other roles as well, the self becomes unifocused. No other identity exists that can possibly vie for dominance or even reasonably alternate with the master role. It is this concentration, this absence of breadth, that characterizes both the internal social psychological composition and the outward demeanor of the engulfed individual. The engulfed self, then, is one typified by a large degree of self-involvement, centrality of identity, focused concentration, and a blinded narrowness to one set of expectations above all others. The engulfed self thus stands in sharp contrast to that of the classic "renaissance man," i.e., one who is broadly rounded in a wide range of knowledge and interests; it is highly specialized, and converged around a single domain.

As such, the engulfed self stands in direct relation to central features of contemporary Western society. These athletes do not symbolize an aberration created out of a unique or even unusual set of cultural or structural circumstances. Rather, they stand as metaphors for many groups in modern times. Elite college athletes, like medical students (Becker et al. 1961; Haas and Shaffir 1987), seminarians (Kleinman 1984), and a variety of professionals have become subject to the trend, first described by Durkheim, toward increasing specialization. We are witness now to the extremely high division of labor Durkheim forecast nearly a century ago, exaggerated and exacerbated by technologization. Specialized knowledge and skills are required to perform important jobs in society, with an ascending level of credentials, in the way of higher educational degrees or experience, required to compete for them (Collins 1979). Like individuals pursuing other specialized careers in society, college athletes have had to become increasingly focused to develop the skills necessary to successfully compete in both their current NCAA league and to acquire an opportunity for entry into the professional leagues. These attributes of society may make the features that characterize the engulfed self more common as we continue moving in current directions.

The Engulfed Self and Social Change

The self is surrounded and framed by both distal and proximate conditions. In this work we have described and analyzed the proximate conditions college athletes encountered, from the institution to the interactions, focusing on their socializing effects on the self. Yet college athletics is lodged within a larger social and historical context. These distal conditions also surrounded basketball players, influencing the character and form of their socialization. Just as the engulfed self reflects the structural characteristics of its arena, so too does it embody social and historical trends in contemporary American society.

In recent years we have witnessed the evolution of several modernist trends begun during the nineteenth century (Lash 1987). Our culture embodies a constriction of concerns and values, a self-interested individualism, and the conservative orientation of occupational specialization and conformity (Bellah et al. 1985). Bureaucracies have flourished, bringing massification into occupational and other arenas. Technology has continued to advance, requiring higher levels of education, more sophisticated and massive equipment, and introducing pervasive media effects into both the character of interpersonal relations and the structure of large institutions. The trend toward increasing specialization has also spiraled, thrusting people into evermore narrowly focused and defined work roles. Referred to by Bellah et al. (1985) as the "culture of separation," we live in a society that has become fragmented into a host of specialized and diffused niches. To succeed requires narrowing one's scope to some highly focused arena and burrowing deep within it. The contemporary self is "privatized" (Moffatt 1989), inwardly directed to encapsulate itself against the complex, bureaucratized world of impersonal institutions.

The countercultural movement of the late 1960s and early 1970s has receded to a mere blip on the temporal landscape. In its place the current ethos has spawned a rationalistic career-orientation, unconcerned with the creative autonomy fought for by its predecessors. To assure entry into a comfortable, materialist lifestyle, it has cast off the "process" theme of unfocused self-realization and reinstituted a "product"-conception (Wood and Zurcher 1988), complete with its associated control, structure, and socially driven tangible goals. Diminished also is the "impulse" orientation, directing people toward spontaneity, viscerality, and the search for inner nature in its stead is the goal-oriented, regulated, "institutional" approach, with its reliance on rigorous external standards (Turner 1976).[2] It represents a return to the age of institutionalization, specialization, and rationalization.

These athletes fit squarely into this world, reflecting the institutional, rational, and normative both within the culture and within their selves. They willingly subordinate themselves to the domination of their coach, program, and university. These are individuals living and working within a highly institutionalized structure, striving for upward mobility and success as conventional society measures it, along the legitimately prescribed means. They are goal-oriented individuals who seek to conform to high behavioral standards through polished, error-free performance. They voluntarily accept constraints on their behavior in consideration of institutional demands. Spurred by their institutional goals, they embody the single-mindedness and unidirectionality of their nonathletic student peers. Enticed by the intoxicating appeal of glory, they have abandoned their broader range of interests and invested their selves in building structured athletic futures.

The engulfed self thus complements the trends fundamental to today's society. In its generic form, it is specialized, narrow, and singular in its focus. Centralized in its identity, it is focused in a single role and comparatively blinded to all others. It is self-involved and goal-oriented, well framed within the individualism of the era. These traits both reflect and adapt well within the careerist orientation and institutional character of contemporary American society.

Postscript

Despite its structural fit within the trends current in American society, the engulfment of college athletes raises questions and conflicts that cannot be easily answered. On the one hand, these young men are spending formative years sacrificing themselves to entertain and enrich others, lured by the hope of a future that is elusive at best. For other students, this kind of narrowing and intense focus may lead to a prosperous career in such fields as medicine, law, education, or business. For college athletes, however, their specialization, dedication, and abandonment of alternatives leads to their becoming finally proficient at a role that, for most, will end immediately following the conclusion of their college eligibility. For those fortunate enough to achieve a professional career, the end comes only slightly later.

It is ironic that these athletes are thus partly socialized to failure; although some sustained the athletic role temporarily, they were released by the system at the end of four years engulfed in a role destined to become an "ex" (Ebaugh 1988). College athletes entered the university thinking that they would expand their horizons and opportunities in a variety of ways. They ended up narrowing their selves enough that their more grandiose expectations were not met.

Yet their college years were not without value. For most, these remained the most memorable times of their lives. They were touched by fame in a way few experience. Like many college students, they acquired considerable "social learning" about adulthood and society from the exposure to the "real world" that they obtained in school (Moffatt 1989). This was especially valuable for the many individuals from poor backgrounds who broadened their horizons beyond what they might otherwise have been able to encounter. They were exploited by the school and the institution of college athletics in many ways, but they also managed, like many regular students, to muddle through, meet people, learn some things from their courses, and have a measure of sex, fun, misery, success, and failure. From the data we have gathered, it would be premature to offer a definitive assessment about athletes' ability to achieve social mobility as a result of their involvement in sport. In the absence of longitudinal data, we cannot make any prediction about the ultimate meaning of their victimization as student-athletes. Like other members of American society, they have learned the necessity for specialization, focus, and deferred gratification. Perhaps some will be able to use their "credentials" to carve out future careers, while others will not.

Notes

1. In our previous studies we have also pursued our belief in researching within the yard, conducting studies while traveling in our car (Adler and Adler 1984), socializing with our next door neighbors (Adler 1985; Adler and Adler 1978), and exercising at our recreation center (Adler and Adler 1982). This time we made it all the way to school.

2. For a more thorough discussion of current thinking on this epistemological issue see Adler and Adler 1987; Corsino 1987; Douglas 1976; Ellis 1990; Hayano 1979; Johnson 1975; Krieger 1985; Peshkin 1985; Reinharz 1979.

1. OVERVIEW

1. Academically, attention has focused predominantly on several subjects: racism and sexism (American Institute for Research 1987–88; Chu 1989; Edwards 1985; Kiger and Lorentzen 1986; Lapchick 1990; Leonard 1986b); the academic performance of college athletes (American Institute for Research 1987–88; Baumann and Henschen 1986; Brede and Camp 1987; Chu 1989; Eitzen and Purdy 1986; Figler 1987; Henschen and Frey 1984; Hochfield 1987; Kiger and Lorentzen 1986; Purdy, Eitzen, and Hufnagel 1982; 1985; Raney, Knapp, and Small 1983; Shapiro 1984; Underwood 1984); the political economy of collegiate sport (Chu 1989; Frey 1982b; Hart-Nibbrig and Cottingham 1986; Porto 1985; Sack 1985), and policy analysis/recommendations, many of which arose in response to journalistic exposes denouncing the problems, hypocrisy, and exploitation inherent in college athletics (Edwards 1984; Gerdy 1987; Hammel 1980; Hanford 1979; Lapchick and Malekoff 1987; Lapchick and Slaughter 1990; Odenkirk 1981; Porto 1984; Sack 1984; Sage 1987).

2. The dearth of ethnographic research on this topic is especially surprising

for two reasons. First, given the attention focused on the problems of college athletics, in-depth research is the best way to investigate both its deviant and multi-faceted character and solutions (Ball 1975; Jonassohn, Turowetz, and Gruneau 1981). Second, as much academic research is carried out on college students, one might expect a captive population, such as athletes, to be overstudied. One possible explanation for this ethnographic void lies in the anti-sport bias held by many academicians; sport is somehow viewed as anti-intellectual (Snyder and Spreitzer 1989), the "toy department of life" (Novak 1976). Gathering participant-observation data on this subject requires a longitudinal research commitment, one that could incur stigma for the researcher(s) (Kirby and Corzine 1981). While these negative factors cannot be overlooked, the advantages outweigh the cost.

3. These range from those focusing on drawing attention to the immediate crisis (Axthelm 1980; Golenbock 1989; Kennedy 1974; Marcin 1983; Shaw 1972; Telander 1989; Underwood 1969; 1980a; 1980b), to the travelogue mode (Feinstein 1988), to the more detailed and ethnographically textured day-in-the-life genre (Feinstein 1986).

4. See Gallmeier (1989) for an insightful elaboration of the differences between sport journalism and sport ethnography.

5. While our findings have implications for such dimensions as race, community, deviance, social control, and culture, these issues require complex treatment and fall outside of our primary concern. We will address them tangentially as they are indicated by our data, while focusing predominantly on the socialization of college athletes.

6. In this way we add to other theories bridging these two perspectives, such as structural symbolic interactionism or identity theory (Handel 1979; Heiss 1981; Stokes and Hewitt 1976; Stryker 1964, 1968, 1980) and processual role theory or role-identity theory (McCall and Simmons 1978; Turner 1962; Zurcher 1977).

7. Stryker (1968, 1980) used the term "salient," while McCall and Simmons (1978) spoke of certain roles being more "prominent" for an individual's self. The phrase "real self" is Turner's (1978).

8. At the height of its success, the University's recruiting budget swelled to around $80,000.

9. Yet the program's comparability to those at other, more average schools is evidenced by the fact that as soon as the charismatic and successful coach moved on to a more prestigious position, the University's basketball team once again lapsed into mediocrity.

10. Our estimates of team members' class backgrounds are rough, based on their parents' occupation, the neighborhoods from which they came, and their cultural upbringing.

11. The identifiers we have selected for these four typologies of players are drawn from their own terms for each other. While they are slightly pejorative

in nature, this negativity is characteristic of the athletes' peer subculture, which was often sardonic in tone, and is not meant to reflect our assessments of the groups. Throughout the book, however, we draw extensively on direct quotations obtained from players and coaches during interviews and casual conversations. In transcribing these we have tried to preserve the flavor and character of the members' "argot" with as much integrity as possible. For this purpose we have created phonetically based spellings to reproduce common features of their pronunciation and left their grammar intact. This is done to pay homage to the speaking patterns we learned and appreciated during the course of this research. For an excellent discussion of this technique and its rationale, see Blauner (1989).

12. These clique names were not used at all times by all players and coaches in referring to the various groups. Team members generally regarded players as clumped into informal friendship groups whose membership was easily discernible. Occasionally these groups were identified by people according to a leading member of the clique, such as "Brandon and them," or "Marcus and those boys." At other times, however, descriptor names, such as the ones we present, were used. Because team personnel did not rigidly divide up the players into cliques or use the clique divisions on organized occasions such as in practices, there were no formal names for the groups. Instead, members of these groups were informally typologized by these monikers in several ways: by the coaches in discussing issues relating to social control (how much trouble various groups of players were going to get into), academics (who was going to class and getting decent grades), and playing ability or dependability on the court (who had heart); and by players in contrasting their friends with members of other social groups with regard to specific behavior such as hanging out (who they were hanging with and what they were going to do), people's willingness to get into a fight (who had heart), academics (who was showing them up), and gossiping about interpersonal team behavior (who was snitching on whom, who was behaving disreputably). Clique monikers were thus drawn from the most common players' and coaches' composite usage, and were usually used in complaining about or making fun of other groups, a practice common to all team personnel.

13. Fine's (1987) study of Little League also showed the importance accorded to toughness, competitiveness, effort, heart, and tolerance of pain in this youthful sport culture.

14. As Rudman (1986) has noted, this attitude is characteristic of ghetto blacks due to a combination of racial and social structural influences.

2. ROLE EXPECTATIONS

1. Messner (1990) particularly noted the motivational influence of *family* members on early athletic participation and identification among white boys

from higher status backgrounds. This contrasts with the black boys from lower status backgrounds he interviewed who reported that most of their early encouragement came from their broader *communities*.

2. Of all the athletes we observed, in fact, the individual who went on to have the most successful NBA career (Danny) was completely overlooked in high school by Division I recruiters. He began his college playing career at a junior college and was signed by the University after he graduated in his second year.

3. The phenomenon of clustering large numbers of athletes in less academically rigorous majors, such as general studies, recreation, and hotel/restaurant management, is designed to enhance their likelihood of graduation.

4. This figure includes a small number of athletes who decided, usually during their sophomore or junior years, not to aim for a career of playing professionally, but to go into an athletically related occupation, such as coaching.

5. During the third and fourth years of our research, Peter was responsible for this as well. He worked both with Coach Mickey and on his own, advising players academically and setting up their schedules. While he consulted players about their preferences in selecting courses and tried to ensure that they stayed on track toward graduation, he also felt constrained by the need to put them in courses they had a likelihood of passing.

3. THE ATHLETIC ROLE

1. Yet, ironically, those athletes from the local area, who did not leave their fans and supporters behind, had the toughest time adjusting to their identity transition. Local players felt the greatest pressure to sustain their previous high school star status without the benefit of a grace period wherein they could adjust to the new team and build themselves a role within it. In the setting we studied, both of the local players who were recruited to play at the University left after their first year.

2. According to Blau and Scott's (1962) "theory of office," bureaucratic organizations seek to break down the individuality or uniqueness of people entering the system and mold them into predetermined categories because they are more easily and efficiently processed when they fit established roles.

3. For example, athletes were segregated from other students while eating and traveling, during class time, and in their living quarters. The athletic arena encompassed the dominant portion of their lives; it imposed on them a common body of rules and scheduling, devised by authorities without consulting players; and these rules were designed for the explicit benefit of the coaching staff and educational institution rather than for the athletes themselves.

4. The businesslike nature of the relationship between athletes and univer-

sities has caused several experts to call for a greater solidification of the employer-employee relationship. In particular, scholars have suggested that athletes receive some financial compensation for the work they do for universities and that they become eligible for workers' compensation should they become injured during the course of their athletic participation (cf. Meggyesy 1990; Porto 1985; Sack 1985; Yasser 1984).

5. See Coakley (1986), Gaski and Etzel (1987), McKillop (1989), and Weisstart (1989) for a discussion of how athletics are thought to influence the academic sphere and general welfare of a university.

4. THE SOCIAL ROLE

1. Jesse expressed Coach's moralistic bias in discussing his admonitions about players' social lives:
Daryl—Coach'll always look on him as a weedsmoker, though he has other good qualities. But he won't see these. Always try to get me not to hang around with him. You make your bed—hard or soft—and you're goin' have to lay in it.

2. Faunce (1984) has suggested that individuals' self-concepts are anchored in social relationships. As their most significant others, athletes' peers had the strongest influence on their self-identity and self-esteem.

3. While this was accepted to a degree, especially among those whites who were close friends with black team members, white players had to be careful to show respect and not act too black.

5. THE ACADEMIC ROLE

1. This was not a favorite duty, however, and after the first part of the year the enforcement and attendance became lax.

2. This, in fact, was the very role that Peter filled for the 1982–83 season (with both the basketball and football teams) when he held his official position with the University's athletic program.

3. This was exacerbated by the changes the University was undergoing at the time, as it attempted to upgrade itself academically, institute a demanding new curriculum, and cut away the "gut" courses.

. 4. Moffatt (1989) has noted that the average college student at Rutgers was typically behind in his or her academic work. Workaholics were derided, like this athlete, for being rate-busters.

6. THE GLORIED SELF

1. This dualism has some parallels to Laing's (1960) and Sennett and Cobb's (1972) conceptions of the "divided" self.

7. RESOLVING THE ROLE CONFLICT

1. The abundant energy approach (Marks 1977) takes human energy as variable and suggests that it expands, or increases, with the demands placed upon it. Individuals feel energized and inspired by the challenges of different roles to which they are committed, and discover abundant reservoirs of energy. Multiple roles would not conflict, then, but would complement each other, leading to "role accumulation" (Sieber 1974). The scarcity approach (Marks 1977) takes the opposing perspective, positing that humans have a finite amount of energy that can be divided only in a limited manner. Multiple roles, then, could drain the energetic potential of the person and leave him/her exhausted and spent. They would compete against each other for scarce energy resources, leading to role strain, role conflict, and/or role overload (Goode 1960; Merton 1957).

2. Goode (1960) has suggested that such role bargains function to hold the larger social structure in place.

3. These findings serve as an interesting point of comparison to the general pool of high school students surveyed by Coleman (1961) and Eitzen (1975). In Coleman's study, he found that traits perceived as necessary to membership in the leading crowd fell into the social, athletic, and academic dimensions, respectively. Replicating Coleman's study, Eitzen found that high school students wished to be remembered, first, as athletic stars (44 percent), second as brilliant students (31 percent) and only last as popular students (25 percent). In recalling their high school experiences, the athletes we studied, in contrast, generated a different image of these roles and their relationships. As athletes in high school, their social status had rested upon, and been highly intertwined with, their physical prowess. Their academic role had been more independent, with some athletes holding serious academic interests and goals while others regarded school as a necessary avenue into the professional leagues. Our subjects, then, saw these dimensions, especially the social, as "piggybacked" onto other, more noticeable ones.

4. Many studies have shown a strong correlation between interscholastic athletic participation and high academic performance and/or aspirations (cf. Buhrmann 1972; Coakley 1986; Eitzen and Sage 1986; Hauser and Lueptow

1978; Loy et al. 1978; Phillips and Schafer 1971; Rehberg and Schafer 1968; Spreitzer and Pugh 1973).

5. One distinction should be specified involving the correspondence, or lack thereof, between the stratifications along the social and academic dimensions. It would be simple to assume an association between the continuum of cliques from those who partied the most to those who partied the least (bad niggas/ whiners/candy-asses/L-7s) and academic performance as figured by grade point averages, majors, or graduation rates. This would be a mistake, however. There was no clear relation between social groupings or activity and academic goals or performance. Athletes who did well in school (compared to each other), who had academic majors, and/or who graduated came from among the ranks of all cliques. In addition, each clique had roughly the same number of individual members on academic probation at any one time.

6. Moffatt (1989) has noted that downward academic adjustments were also a common practice among the college students he studied, with freshmen often shifting majors to something less difficult.

7. This corresponds to Becker, Geer, and Hughes' (1968) finding that students tended to focus on "making the grade" at the expense of substantial intellectual understanding of the material they were learning.

8. In discussing structural causes of deviance, Merton (1938) hypothesized that some individuals who encountered blocked opportunities in using legitimate means to achieve their goals would seek out, create, or otherwise "innovate" alternative means of illegitimately or non-normatively attaining those goals.

9. Compared to other figures on the graduation rates of college athletes, these rates fall somewhere in the middle. Several studies have suggested that athletes have a greater likelihood of graduating than their non-athletic peers. Stecklein and Dameron (1965) indicated that at a major university, the graduation rates for male athletes was higher than for male non-athletes (although the dropout rate was higher). Billick (1973) found that 93 percent of the 1963 University of Pittsburgh football players graduated. Pilapil et al. (1970) cited a graduation rate for the 1967 class of University of Minnesota's athletes of 50 percent (compared to 41 percent for non-athletes). Michener (1976) has reported that 88 percent of male athletes in the sports of baseball, basketball, football, swimming, and track graduated from Stanford during the year 1969–70 (compared to 82.5 percent of the general student body).

More prevalent, however, are the studies that show a negative correlation between collegiate athletic participation and graduation. Webb's (1968) five-year study of Michigan State University athletes found that only 49 percent of team sport athletes (and only 38 percent of black athletes) graduated. Harrison (1976) tracked football players who entered North Texas State University between the years of 1966–71 and found that less than 20 percent graduated from that University. A study conducted by the University of New Mexico (1980) showed that only 21 percent of its football players had graduated since 1970, compared to 24 percent for track, 24 percent for wrestling, and 28 percent for basketball. Madigan (1976) reported the following graduation rates for football players in 1975–76: University of Nebraska 69 percent; University of Oklahoma 56 percent; University of Colorado 39 percent; Oklahoma State University 32 percent; Colorado State University 29 percent; Arizona State University 28 percent, and Brigham Young University 25 percent. Similar results have been found in studies of the Southeast and Southwest Conferences (Benagh 1976). Purdy, Eitzen, and Hufnagel's (1982) research on athletes at Colorado State University from 1970 to 1980 showed a graduation rate of 34 percent (compared to 47 percent for the general student population). And Henschen and Fry's (1984) investigation of male athletes at the University of Utah between 1973 and 1982 reveals that graduation rates ranged between the low of basketball (34 percent) and the high of football (58 percent), with an overall total for all team sports averaging 49 percent. Finally, a sampling of Division I basketball programs, conducted by the General Accounting Office of Congress, compared the graduation rates of basketball players with the overall student body. Basing their calculations on the percentage of individuals graduating in five years, only 30 percent of the programs graduated more than 40 percent of their basketball players, compared to 72 percent who graduated at least 40 percent of their general student body. Further, as many as 36 percent of the programs graduated fewer than 20 percent of their basketball players, compared with only 4 percent of the programs whose general student body graduated at such a poor rate (Bagley-Foote and Cox 1989).

The conflicting reports of these studies offer little clear empirical support for a positive relationship between athletic participation and graduation. Their optimism may be further undercut by well-publicized reports of grade forging, recruiting violations, transcript alterations, and the placement of athletes in gut courses (see Underwood 1980b).

10. These figures were compiled by tracking basketball players who entered or were already at the University between 1980 and 1985. Like Stecklein and Dameron (1965) we found a high dropout or transfer rate among athletes. Many left because they were disenchanted with the basketball program, the coach, the community, their role on the team, or because they got injured. In assembling these graduation rates we included those players who spent their entire careers at the University (even those remaining after we left), who dropped out of college altogether, or who transferred and we were able to follow. We excluded those who transferred and we were unable to track.

11. In a study of the relative effects of gender, race, and sport (revenue versus non-revenue) on the academic performance of college athletes, Kiger and Lorentzen (1986) also found race the most significant variable. Eitzen and

Purdy's (1986) study, comparing the academic performance and graduation rates of white and black students, found that 35 percent of the former and 21 percent of the latter matriculated (compared to 47 percent of the general student body).

8. TERMINATING THE ROLE

1. For further analysis of the exploitative nature of college athletics see Lapchick 1984; Leonard 1986a; Sack 1977.

2. In fact, the belief that college athletes need agents has become so taken for granted that some colleges are offering mini-courses on how to select the best agent.

3. Out of the 39 players we followed, 12 were selected in the NBA draft. Being chosen guaranteed them a tryout at the beginning of the next season with the team that drafted them. An additional four were invited to these NBA camps to try out on a free agent basis. Of these all, two were offered contracts and played in the NBA. One of them, Marcus, played for two and one-half years, while Danny has been playing for nine years as of this writing. This is typical of NBA careers, because although the average career length is five to seven years, people who play for only one to two years far outnumber those who last more than the average length of time (Coakley 1986). Seven other players spent some time playing professionally, four in the domestic minor league, the Continental Basketball Association (CBA), and three on foreign teams (although some of those who eventually made it to foreign teams had played for a year in the CBA). The four who made it no further than the CBA (Ben, Daryl, Slick, and Derrick) lasted there only one to two years. Although players considered this league desirable because it was in the United States, and hence both close to home and visible to the NBA (so that they might be called up), the CBA paid extremely poorly (not a living wage). Players had to work hard for the rest of the year just to be able to afford the financially losing proposition of hanging on for a shot at the real pros. The four who went abroad (Apollo, Tyrone, Damon, and Lew) played in such diverse places as South America, Europe, and the Middle East. Their careers lasted from one year to eight and still playing. While foreign leagues paid well, they involved the difficulties of living in an alien culture and negotiating a foreign language. This brought to a total of ten (25 percent), then, the number of University players who had some post-collegiate professional basketball careers. Yet although this is a good percentage, most of these careers were short-lived.

4. Several studies of athletics, mostly directed toward the interscholastic level, have suggested a crossover effect, where the type of experiences athletics

offers inculcates individuals with drive, character, determination, and a competitive spirit (Coakley 1986).

5. Some of the topics in which role exit has been examined and analyzed include marriage (Goode 1956; Vaughn 1986), cult religious groups (Barker 1984; Beckford 1985; Jacobs 1984; Richardson 1978; Richardson et al., 1986; Wright 1984), and deviant careers (Adler and Adler 1983; Brown 1988; Erikson et al. 1973; Ray 1964; Shover 1985; Wheeler 1961).

6. Myriad forms of stress and its associated consequences have been associated with forced role-exit from athletics (Curtis and Ennis 1988), ranging from decreased life satisfaction, depression, loss of self-esteem, greater probability of marital breakdown, inability to succeed in a second career, and even pathological behavior such as suicide, crime, and substance abuse (cf. Bouton 1970; Brandmeyer and Alexander 1982; Haerle 1975; Hill and Lowe 1974; Kramer 1969; Lerch 1981, 1984; McPherson 1980; Mihovilovic 1968; Rosenberg 1981, 1984; Rozin 1979). At the most extreme end, some writers have posited that role termination from elite-level sport creates serious enough consequences to warrant applying the concept of "social death" (see especially Lerch 1984, and Rosenberg 1984) to its incumbents.

7. This concept has been adapted from gerontological theory, where the retired individual is conceived as shifting his or her energy and interest from the lifetime occupational role into some new pursuit or hobby.

8. For a fuller discussion of this more positive view of athletic role exit, see Curtis and White (1984), Greendorfer and Blinde (1985), McPherson (1980), and Snyder and Baber (1979).

9. THE ENGULFED SELF

1. This version of commitment resembles Goffman's (1961b) notion of attachment.

2. Turner has noted that this diametric opposition is ideal typical, noting that, "few people are strictly institutional or strictly impulsive" (Turner and Schutte 1981:15).

References

Adler, Patricia A. 1985. *Wheeling and Dealing*. New York: Columbia University Press.

Adler, Patricia A. and Peter Adler. 1978. "Tinydopers: A Case Study of Deviant Socialization." *Symbolic Interaction* 1:96–105.

——1982. "Championing Leisure: The Professionalization of Racquetball." *Journal of Sport and Social Issues* 6:31–41.

——1983. "Shifts and Oscillations in Deviant Careers: The Case of Upper-Level Drug Dealers and Smugglers." *Social Problems* 31:195–207.

——1984. "The Carpool: A Socializing Adjunct to the Educational Experience." *Sociology of Education* 57:200–210.

——1987. *Membership Roles in Field Research*. Newbury Park, Calif.: Sage.

Adler, Peter and Patricia A. Adler. 1978. "The Role of Momentum in Sport." *Urban Life* 7:153–76.

Altheide, David L. 1984. "The Media Self." In J. A. Kotarba and A. Fontana, eds., *The Existential Self in Society*, pp. 177–95. Chicago: University of Chicago Press.

Altheide, David L. and Robert Snow. 1979. *Media Logic*. Beverly Hills, Calif.: Sage.

American Institute for Research. 1987–88. "Studies of Intercollegiate Athletics." Reports sponsored by the President's Commission of the NCAA.

Axthelm, Pete. 1980. "The Shame of College Sports." *Newsweek*, September 22:54–59.

Ball, Donald W. 1975. "A Note on Method in the Sociology of Sport." In D. W. Ball and J. W. Loy, eds., *Sport and Social Order*, pp. 35–50. Reading, Mass.: Addison-Wesley.

——1976. "Failure in Sport." *American Sociological Review* 41:726–39.

Bagley-Foote, Angela and Staci Cox. 1989. "Athletes' Grad Rates Could Go Public." *U.: The National College Newspaper* (December),3:18,23.

Bandura, Albert. 1971. *Social Learning Theory*. Morristown, N.J.: General Learning Press.

Barker, Eileen. 1984. *The Making of a Moonie*. London: Basil Blackwell.

Baumann, Steven and Keith Henschen. 1986. "A Cross-Validation Study of Selected Performance Measures in Predicting Academic Success Among Collegiate Athletes." *Sociology of Sport Journal* 3:366–71.

Becker, Howard. 1960. "Notes on the Concept of Commitment." *American Journal of Sociology* 66:32–40.

Becker, Howard, Blanche Geer, and Everett Hughes. 1968. *Making the Grade*. New York: Wiley.

Becker, Howard, Blanche Geer, Everett Hughes, and Anselm Strauss. 1961. *Boys in White*. Chicago: University of Chicago Press.

Beckford, James A. 1985. *Cult Controversies*. London: Tavistock.

Bellah, Robert N., Richard Madsen, William M. Sullivan, Ann Swidler, and Steven M. Tipton. 1985. *Habits of the Heart*. Berkeley: University of California Press.

Bem, Daryl J. 1972. "Self-Perception Theory." In L. Berkowitz, ed., *Advances in Experimental Social Psychology* 6:1–62. New York: Academic.

Benagh, Jim. 1976. *Making It to Number 1*. New York: Dodd, Mead.

Bensman, Joseph and Robert Lilienfeld. 1979. *Between Public and Private*. New York: Free Press.

Berger, Peter and Thomas Luckmann. 1966. *The Social Construction of Reality*. New York: Doubleday.

Bernstein, Stanley. 1978. "Getting It Done: Notes on Student Fritters." In J. Lofland, ed., *Interaction in Everyday Life*, pp. 17–23. Beverly Hills, Calif.: Sage.

Billick, Dean. 1973. "Still Winners." *National Collegiate Sports Services Bulletin*.

Blau, Peter M. and W. Richard Scott. 1962. *Formal Organizations*. San Francisco: Chandler.

Blauner, Bob. 1989. *Black Lives, White Lives*. Berkeley: University of California Press.

Blumer, Herbert. 1969. *Symbolic Interactionism*. Englewood Cliffs, N.J.: Prentice-Hall.

Bogardus, Emory. 1959. "Race Reactions by Sexes." *Sociology and Social Research* 43:439–41.

Bouton, Jim. 1970. *Ball Four*. New York: Dell.

Brandmeyer, Gerard and Luella Alexander. 1982. "Dealing with Tempered Dreams: Reflections of Aging Ballplayers on Careers that Used to Be." In A. Ingham and E. Broom, eds., *Proceedings of the Conference on Career Patterns and Career Contingencies in Sport*, pp. 454–61. Vancouver: University of British Columbia.

Brede, Richard M. and Henry J. Camp. 1987. "The Education of College Student-Athletes." *Sociology of Sport Journal* 4:245–57.

Brown, J. David. 1988. "Towards a Revision of Labeling Theory: The Deviant Career of Alcoholics from Patient to Healer." Masters thesis, University of Denver.

Buhrmann, Hans C. 1972. "Scholarship and Athletics in Junior High School." *International Review of Sport Sociology* 7:119–28.

Burger, Jerry M. 1985. "Temporal Effects on Attributions for Academic Performances and Reflected-Glory Basking." *Social Psychology Quarterly* 48:330–36.

Case, Bob, H. Scott Greer, and James Brown. 1987. "Academic Clustering in Athletics: Myth or Reality?" *ARENA Review* 11:48–56.

Chu, Donald. 1989. *The Character of American Higher Education and Intercollegiate Sport*. Albany: State University of New York Press.

Cialdini, Robert B., Richard J. Borden, Averill Thorne, Marcus Randall Walker, Steven Freeman, and Lloyd Reynolds Sloan. 1976. "Basking in Reflected Glory: Three (Football) Field Studies." *Journal of Personality and Social Psychology* 34:366–75.

Clifford, James. 1989. "Traveling Selves, Traveling Others." Talk delivered at the University of Colorado, October 20.

Coakley, Jay J. 1983. "Leaving Competitive Sport: Retirement or Rebirth?" *Quest* 35:1–11.

——1986. *Sport in Society*. Third Edition. St. Louis: Mosby. [Second edition, 1982.]

Coleman, James S. 1961. *The Adolescent Society*. New York: Free Press.

Collins, Randall. 1979. *The Credential Society*. New York: Academic.

Cooley, Charles H. 1902. *Human Nature and Social Order*. New York: Scribners.

——1962. *Social Organization*. New York: Scribners.

Corsino, Louis. 1987. "Fieldworker Blues: Emotional Stress and Research Underinvolvement in Fieldwork Settings." *Social Science Journal* 24:275–85.

Coser, Lewis. 1974. *Greedy Institutions*. New York: Free Press.

Cross, Harry M. 1973. "The College Athlete and the Institution." *Law and Contemporary Problems* 38:151–71.

Curtis, James and Richard Ennis. 1988. "Negative Consequences of Leaving Competitive Sport? Comparative Findings for Former Elite-Level Hockey Players." *Sociology of Sport Journal* 5:87–106.

Curtis, James and P. White. 1984. "Age and Sport Participation: Declining Participation with Age or Increased Specialization with Age." In N. Theberge and P. Donnelly, eds., *Sport and the Sociological Imagination*, pp. 273–93. Fort Worth: Texas Christian University Press.

Cusick, Phillip. 1973. *Inside High School*. New York: Holt, Rinehart, and Winston.

Denzin, Norman K. 1970. *The Research Act*. Chicago: Aldine.

Douglas, Jack D. 1976. *Investigative Social Research*. Beverly Hills, Calif.: Sage.

——1985. *Creative Interviewing*. Beverly Hills, Calif.: Sage.

Ebaugh, Helen R. 1977. *Out of the Cloister*. Austin: University of Texas Press.

——1988. *Becoming an Ex*. Chicago: University of Chicago Press.

Edwards, Harry. 1973. *Sociology of Sport*. Homewood, Ill.: Dorsey.

——1984. "The Collegiate Athletic Arms Race: Origins and Implications of the 'Rule 48' Controversy." *Journal of Sport and Social Issues* 8:4–22.

——1985. "Beyond Symptoms: Unethical Behavior in American Collegiate Sport and the Problem of the Color Line." *Journal of Sport and Social Issues* 9:3–11.

Eitzen, D. Stanley. 1975. "Athletics in the Status System of Male Adolescents: A Replication of Coleman's 'The Adolescent Society.' " *Adolescence* 10:268–76.

——1979. "Sport and Deviance." In D. S. Eitzen, ed., *Sport in Contemporary Society*, pp. 73–89. New York: St. Martin's.

Eitzen, D. Stanley and Dean A. Purdy. 1986. "The Academic Preparation and Achievement of Black and White Collegiate Athletes." *Journal of Sport and Social Issues* 10:15–29.

Eitzen, D. Stanley and George H. Sage. 1986. *Sociology of North American Sport*. Third Edition. Dubuque, Iowa: William C. Brown.

Elliot, Gregory C. 1986. "Self-Esteem and Self-Consistency: A Theoretical and Empirical Link Between Two Primary Motivations." *Social Psychology Quarterly* 49:207–18.

Ellis, Carolyn. 1990. "Sociological Introspection and Emotional Experience." *Symbolic Interaction* 13.

Erikson, Kai T. 1957. "Patient Role and Social Uncertainty—A Dilemma of the Mentally Ill." *Psychiatry* 20:263–74.

Erikson, Rosemary J., Wayman J. Crow, Louis A. Zurcher, and Archie V. Connett. 1973. *Paroled But Not Free*. New York: Behavior Publications.

Faunce, William A. 1984. "School Achievement, Social Status and Self-Esteem." *Social Psychology Quarterly* 47:3–14.

Feinstein, John. 1986. *A Season on the Brink*. New York: MacMillan.

——1988. *A Season Inside*. New York: Villard.

Felson, Richard B. 1981. "Self and Reflected Appraisal Among Football Players: A Test of the Meadian Hypothesis." *Social Psychology Quarterly* 44:116–26.

Felson, Richard B. and Mark D. Reed. 1986. "Reference Groups and Self-Appraisals of Academic Ability and Performance." *Social Psychology Quarterly* 49:103–109.

Fenigstein, Allan, Michael F. Scheier, and Arnold H. Buss. 1975. "Public and Private Self-Consciousness: Assessment and Theory." *Journal of Consulting and Clinical Psychology* 43:522–27.

Festinger, Leon. 1954. "A Theory of Social Comparison Processes." *Human Relations* 7:117–40.

Figler, Stephen K. 1987. "The Academic Performance of Collegiate Athletes: Of Playpens and Backyards." *ARENA Review* 11:35–40.

Fine, Gary A. 1987. *With the Boys.* Chicago: University of Chicago Press.

Frey, James H. 1982a. "Boosterism, Scarce Resources and Institutional Control: The Future of American Intercollegiate Athletics." *International Review of Sport Sociology* 17:53–70.

—— (ed.). 1982b. *The Governance of Intercollegiate Athletics.* West Point, N.Y.: Leisure Press.

Gallmeier, Charles P. 1987. "Dinosaurs and Prospects: Toward a Sociology of the Compressed Career." In K. M. Mahmoudi, B. W. Parlin, and M. E. Zusman, eds., *Sociological Inquiry: A Humanistic Perspective,* Fourth Edition, pp. 95–103. Dubuque, Iowa: Kendall-Hunt.

——1989. "Toward an Emergent Ethnography of Sport." *ARENA Review* 13:1–8.

Gaski, John F. and Michael J. Etzel. 1987. "Collegiate Athletic Success and Alumni Generosity: Dispelling the Myth." In A. Yiannakis, T. D. McIntyre, M. J. Melnick, and D. P. Hart, eds., *Sport Sociology,* Third Edition, pp. 166–72. Dubuque, Iowa: Kendall-Hunt.

Gerdy, John R. 1987. "No More 'Dumb Jocks.' " *The College Review Board* 143:2–3, 40–41.

Glaser, Barney and Anselm Strauss. 1967. *The Discovery of Grounded Theory.* Chicago: Aldine.

Goffman, Erving. 1959. *The Presentation of Self in Society.* New York: Anchor Doubleday.

——1961a. *Asylums.* New York: Anchor.

——1961b. *Encounters.* Indianapolis: Bobbs-Merrill.

——1963. *Behavior in Public Places.* New York: Free Press.

——1967. *Interaction Ritual.* New York: Anchor.

Goldsmith, Barbara. 1983. "The Meaning of Celebrity." *New York Times Sunday Magazine* December 4:75–82; 120.

Golenbock, Peter. 1989. *Personal Fouls.* New York: Carroll and Graf.

Goode, William J. 1956. *After Divorce.* New York: Free Press.

——1960. "A Theory of Role Strain." *American Sociological Review* 25:483–96.

Greendorfer, Susan L. and Elaine M. Blinde. 1985. " 'Retirement' from Intercollegiate Sport: Theoretical and Empirical Considerations." *Sociology of Sport Journal* 2:101–10.

Gross, Edward and Gregory Stone. 1964. "Embarrassment and the Analysis of Role Requirements." *American Journal of Sociology* 60:1–15.

Haas, Jack and William Shaffir. 1987. *Becoming Doctors: The Professionalization of Medical Students.* Greenwich, Conn.: JAI.

Haerle, Rudolph. 1975. "Career Patterns and Career Contingencies of Professional Baseball Players: An Occupational Analysis." In D. Ball and

J. Loy, eds., *Sport and Social Order,* pp. 461–519. Reading, Mass.: Addison-Wesley.

Hammel, Bob. 1980. "Student Athletes: Tackling the Problem." *Phi Delta Kappan* 62:7–13.

Handel, Warren. 1979. "Normative Expectations and the Emergence of Meaning as Solutions to Problems: Convergence of Structural and Interactionist Views." *American Journal of Sociology* 84:855–81.

Hanford, George H. 1979. "Controversies in College Sports." *Annals* 445:66–79.

Harris, Donald S. and D. Stanley Eitzen. 1978. "The Consequences of Failure in Sport." *Urban Life* 7:177–88.

Harrison, James H. 1976. "Intercollegiate Football Participation and Academic Achievement." Paper presented at the annual meeting of the Southwestern Sociological Association, Dallas.

Hart-Nibbrig, Nand and Clement Cottingham. 1986. *The Political Economy of College Sports.* Lexington, Mass.: D.C. Heath.

Hauser, William J. and Lloyd B. Lueptow. 1978. "Participation in Athletics and Academic Achievement: A Replication and Extension." *Sociological Quarterly* 19:304–309.

Hayano, David M. 1979. "Auto-ethnography: Paradigms, Problems, and Prospects." *Human Organization* 38:99–104.

Heiss, Jerold. 1981. "Social Roles." In M. Rosenberg and R. Turner, eds., *Social Psychology,* pp. 94–129. New York: Basic.

Henschen, Keith and David Fry. 1984. "An Archival Study of the Relationship of Intercollegiate Athletic Participation and Graduation." *Sociology of Sport Journal* 1:52–56.

Hill, P. and B. Lowe. 1974. "The Inevitable Metathesis of the Retiring Athlete." *International Review of Sport Sociology* 9:5–29.

Hoch, Paul. 1972. *Rip Off the Big Game.* New York: Doubleday.

Hochfield, George. 1987. "The Incompatibility of Athletics and Academic Excellence." *Academe* 73:39–43.

Hochschild, Arlie. 1983. *The Managed Heart.* Berkeley: University of California Press.

Hodge, Robert W., Paul M. Siegel, and Peter H. Rossi. 1964. "Occupational Prestige in the U.S., 1925–1963." *American Journal of Sociology* 70:286–302.

Hoelter, Jon W. 1983. "The Effects of Role Evaluation and Commitment in Identity Salience." *Social Psychology Quarterly* 30:140–47.

Hughes, Everett C. 1945. "Dilemmas and Contradictions in Status." *American Journal of Sociology* 50:353–59.

Ingham, Alan G. 1975. "Occupational Subcultures in the Work World of Sport." In D. W. Ball and J. W. Loy, eds., *Sport and Social Order,* pp. 337–89. Reading, Mass.: Addison-Wesley.

Jacobs, Janet. 1984. "The Economy of Love in Religious Commitment: The Deconversion of Women from Non-Traditional Religious Movements." *Journal for the Scientific Study of Religion* 23:155–71.

Johnson, John M. 1975. *Doing Field Research*. New York: Free Press.

Jonassohn, Kurt, Allan Turowetz, and Richard Gruneau. 1981. "Research Methods in the Sociology of Sport." *Qualitative Sociology* 4:179–97.

Jones, E.E. and R.E. Nisbet. 1972. "The Actor and the Observer: Divergent Perceptions of the Causes of Behavior." In E. E. Jones et al., eds., *Attribution: Perceiving the Causes of Behavior*, pp. 79–94. Morristown, N.J.: General Learning Press.

Kelley, Harold H. 1952. "Two Functions of Reference Groups." In G. E. Swanson, M. Newcomb, and E. L. Maccoby, eds., *Readings in Social Psychology*, pp. 410–14. New York: Henry Holt.

———1967. "Attribution Theory in Social Psychology." In D. Levine, ed., *Nebraska Symposium on Motivation* 15:192–238. Lincoln: University of Nebraska Press.

Kennedy, Ray. 1974. "427: A Case in Point." *Sports Illustrated*, June 10:87– 100; June 17:24–30.

Kiger, Gary and Deanna Lorentzen. 1986. "The Relative Effects of Gender, Race, and Sport on University Academic Performance." *Sociology of Sport Journal* 3:160–67.

Kirby, Richard and Jay Corzine. 1981. "The Contagion of Stigma." *Qualitative Sociology* 4:3–20.

Kleinman, Sherryl. 1984. *Equals Before God*. Chicago: University of Chicago Press.

Kornhauser, William. 1962. "Social Bases of Political Commitment: A Study of Liberals and Radicals." In A. M. Rose, ed., *Human Behavior and Social Processes*, pp. 321–39. Boston: Houghton-Mifflin.

Kramer, Jerry. 1969. *Farewell to Football*. New York: World.

Krieger, Susan. 1985. "Beyond 'Subjectivity': The Use of the Self in Social Science." *Qualitative Sociology* 8:309–324.

Laing, R.D. 1960. *The Divided Self*. London: Tavistock.

Lance, Larry M. 1987. "Conceptualization of Role Relationships and Role Conflict Among Student Athletes." *ARENA Review* 11:12–18.

———1989. "Exploration of Perceived Role Conflict Among University Student-Athletes: A Description of Gender and Revenue/Non-Revenue Differences." Paper presented at the annual meeting of the Southern Sociological Society, Norfolk, VA.

Lapchick, Richard E. 1984. *Broken Promises*. New York: St. Martin's.

———1990. "Racial Discrimination in College Sport." In R. E. Lapchick and J. B. Slaughter, eds., *The Rules of the Game: Ethics in College Sports*. New York: MacMillan.

Lapchick, Richard E. and Robert Malekoff. 1987. *On the Mark: Putting the Student Back in Student Athlete.* Lexington, Mass.: D.C. Heath.

Lapchick, Richard E. and John B. Slaughter, eds. 1990. *The Rules of the Game: Ethics in College Sports.* New York: MacMillan.

Lash, Scott. 1987. "Modernity or Modernism? Weber and Contemporary Social Theory." In S. Lash and S. Whimster, eds., *Max Weber, Rationality and Modernity,* pp. 355–77. London: Allen and Unwin.

Leonard, Wilbert M. 1986a. "Exploitation in Collegiate Sport: The Views of Basketball Players in NCAA Divisions I, II, and III." *Journal of Sport Behavior* 9:11–30.

——1986b. "The Sports Experience of the Black College Athlete: Exploitation in the Academy." *International Review for the Sociology of Sport* 21:35–49.

——1988. *A Sociological Perspective of Sport.* Third Edition. New York: MacMillan.

Leonard, Wilbert M. and Jonathan E. Reyman. 1988. "The Odds of Attaining Professional Athlete Status: Refining the Computations." *Sociology of Sport Journal* 5:162–69.

Lerch, Stephen. 1981. "The Adjustment to Retirement of Professional Baseball Players." In S. Greendorfer and A. Yiannakis, eds., *Sociology of Sport,* pp. 138–48. West Point, N.Y.: Leisure Press.

——1984. "Athletic Retirement as Social Death: The Applicability of Two Thanatological Models." In N. Theberge and P. Donnelly, eds., *Sport and the Sociological Imagination,* pp. 259–72. Fort Worth: Texas Christian University Press.

Loy, John, Barry McPherson, and George Kenyon. 1978. *Sport and Social Systems.* Reading, Mass.: Addison-Wesley.

Madigan, Mike. 1976. "Graduation Academic to College Gridders." *Rocky Mountain News,* December 26:96.

Marcin, Joe. 1983. "College Football Notebook." *The Sporting News,* October 24:48.

Marks, Stephen R. 1977. "Multiple Roles and Role Strain: Some Notes on Human Energy, Time, and Commitment." *American Sociological Review* 42:921–36.

McCall, George J. and Jerry L. Simmons. 1978. *Identities and Interaction.* New York: Free Press.

McKillop, Peter. 1989. "Seton Hall on the Map." *Newsweek,* April 17:63.

McPherson, Barry D. 1980. "Retirement from Professional Sport: The Process and Problems of Occupational and Psychological Adjustment." *Sociological Symposium* 30:126–43.

Mead, George H. 1934. *Mind, Self and Society.* Chicago: University of Chicago Press.

Meggysey, David. 1990. "Still Out of Their League: Who is Speaking for the Athlete?" In R. E. Lapchick and J. B. Slaughter, eds., *The Rules of the Game: Ethics in College Sports,* pp. 113–220. New York: MacMillan.

Merton, Robert K. 1957. "The Role-Set: Problems in Sociological Theory."
   British Journal of Sociology 8:106–20.
——1938. "Social Structure and Anomie." *American Sociological Review* 3:672–
   682.
Messner, Michael. 1989. "Masculinities and Athletic Careers." *Gender and Society* 3:71–88.
——1990. "Boyhood, Organized Sports, and the Construction of Masculinities." *Journal of Contemporary Ethnography* 18:416–44.
Michener, James A. 1976. *Sports in America.* New York: Random House.
Mihovilovic, M. 1968. "The Status of Former Sportsmen." *International Review of Sport Sociology* 3:73–96.
Miller, Walter B. 1958. "Lower Class Culture as a Generating Milieu of Gang
   Delinquency." *Journal of Social Issues* 14:5–19.
Moffatt, Michael. 1989. *Coming of Age in New Jersey.* New Brunswick, N.J.:
   Rutgers University Press.
Novak, Michael. 1976. *The Joy of Sports.* New York: Basic.
Nyquist, Ewald B. 1979. "Wine, Women and Money: College Athletics Today
   and Tomorrow." *Educational Review* 60:376–93.
Odenkirk, James E. 1981. "Intercollegiate Athletics: Big Business or Sport?"
   Academe 67:62–66.
Peshkin, Alan. 1985. "Virtuous Subjectivity: In the Participant-Observer's I's."
   In D. N. Berg and K. K. Smith, eds., *Exploring Clinical Methods for Social
   Research,* pp. 267–81. Newbury Park, Calif.: Sage.
Phillips, John C. and Walter E. Schafer. 1971. "Consequences of Participation
   in Interscholastic Sports: A Review and Prospectus." *Pacific Sociological
   Review* 14:328–38.
Pilapil, B., J.E. Stecklein, and H. Liu. 1970. "Intercollegiate Athletics and
   Academic Progress: A Comparison of Academic Characteristics of Athletes
   and Non-Athletes at the University of Minnesota." Bureau of Institutional
   Research, University of Minnesota.
Porto, Brian L. 1984. "College Athletics on Trial: The Mark Hall Decision and
   Its Implications for the Future." *Journal of Sport and Social Issues* 8:23–34.
——1985. "Athletic Scholarships as Contracts of Employment: The Rensing
   Decisions and the Future of College Sports." *Journal of Sport and Social
   Issues* 9:20–36.
Purdy, Dean A., D. Stanley Eitzen, and Rick Hufnagel. 1982. "Are Athletes
   Also Students? The Educational Attainment of College Athletes." *Social
   Problems* 29:439–448.
——1985. "The Educational Achievement of College Athletes by Gender."
   Studies in the Social Sciences 24:19–32.
Raney, Joseph, Terry Knapp, and Mark Small. 1983. "Pass One for the Gipper:
   Student Athletes and University Coursework." *ARENA Review* 7:53–59.
Ray, Marsh V. 1964. "The Cycle of Abstinence and Relapse Among Heroin

Addicts." In H. Becker, ed., *The Other Side,* pp. 163–77. New York: Free Press.

Rehberg, Richard A. and Walter E. Schafer. 1968. "Participation in Interscholastic Athletics and College Expectations." *American Journal of Sociology* 73:732–40.

Reinharz, Shulamit. 1979. *On Becoming a Social Scientist.* San Francisco: Jossey-Bass.

Richardson, James T. 1978. *Conversion Careers.* Beverly Hills, Calif.: Sage.

Richardson, James T., Jan van de Lans, and Frans Derks. 1986. "Leaving and Labeling: Voluntary and Coerced Disaffiliation from Religious Social Movements." In K. Lang, ed., *Research in Social Movements, Conflicts and Change* 9:97–126. Greenwich, Conn.: JAI.

Riemer, Jeffrey. 1977. "Varieties of Opportunistic Research." *Urban Life* 5:467–77.

Rooney, John F. Jr. 1980. *The Recruiting Game.* Lincoln: University of Nebraska Press.

Rosenberg, Edwin. 1981. "Gerontological Theory and Athletic Retirement." In S. Greendorfer and A. Yiannakis, eds., *Sociology of Sport,* pp. 118–26. West Point, N.Y.: Leisure Press.

——1984. "Athletic Retirement as Social Death: Concepts and Perspectives." In N. Theberge and P. Donnelly, eds., *Sport and the Sociological Imagination,* pp. 245–58. Fort Worth: Texas Christian University Press.

Rosenberg, Morris. 1979. *Conceiving the Self.* New York: Basic.

Rozin, S. 1979. *One Step from Glory.* New York: Simon and Schuster.

Rudman, William J. 1986. "The Sport Mystique in Black Culture." *Sociology of Sport Journal* 3:305–19.

Sabo, Donald. 1985. "Sport, Patriarchy, and Male Identity: New Questions about Men and Sport." *ARENA Review* 9:1–30.

Sack, Allan L. 1977. "Big Time College Football: Whose Free Ride?" *Quest* 27:87–97.

——1984. "Proposition 48: A Masterpiece in Public Relations." *Journal of Sport and Social Issues* 8:1–3.

——1985. "Workers' Compensation for College Athletes?" *Journal of Sport and Social Issues* 9:2–3.

Sack, Allen L. and Robert Thiel. 1979. "College Football and Social Mobility: A Case Study of Notre Dame Football Players." *Sociology of Education* 52:60–66.

——1985. "College Basketball and Role Conflict." *Sociology of Sport Journal* 2:195–209.

Sage, George H. 1987. "Blaming the Victim: NCAA Responses to Calls for Reform in Major College Sports." *ARENA Review* 11:1–11

Schein, Edgar H. 1987. *The Clinical Perspective in Fieldwork.* Newbury Park, Calif.: Sage.

Schur, Edwin M. 1971. *Labeling Deviant Behavior*. New York: Harper and Row.

Semyonov, Moshe and Ephraim Yuchtman-Yaar. 1981. "Professional Sports as an Alternative Channel of Social Mobility." *Sociological Inquiry* 1:47–53.

Sennett, Richard and Jonathan Cobb. 1972. *The Hidden Injuries of Class*. New York: Vintage.

Shapiro, Beth. 1984. "Intercollegiate Athletic Participation and Academic Achievement: A Case Study of Michigan State University Student-Athletes, 1950–1980." *Sociology of Sport Journal* 1:46–51.

Shaw, Gary. 1972. *Meat on the Hoof*. New York: Dell.

Shover, Neal. 1985. *Aging Criminals*. Beverly Hills, Calif.: Sage.

Sieber, Sam D. 1974. "Toward a Theory of Role Accumulation." *American Sociological Review* 39:567–78.

Sigelman, Lee. 1986. "Basking in Reflected Glory: An Attempt at Replication." *Social Psychology Quarterly* 49:90–92.

Simmel, Georg. 1950. *The Sociology of Georg Simmel* (K.H. Wolff, ed. and trans.). New York: Free Press.

Snow, David A. 1980. "The Disengagement Process: A Neglected Problem in Participant Observation Research." *Qualitative Sociology* 3:100–22.

Snyder, Eldon E. and L.L. Baber. 1979. "A Profile of Former Collegiate Athletes and Non-Athletes: Leisure Activities, Attitudes Toward Work, and Aspects of Satisfaction with Life." *Journal of Sport Behavior* 2:211–19.

Snyder, Eldon E. and Elmer A. Spreitzer. 1989. *Social Aspects of Sport*. Third Edition. Englewood Cliffs, N.J.: Prentice-Hall.

Spady, William G. 1970. "Lament for the Letterman: Effects of Peer Status and Extra-Curricular Activities on Goals and Achievement." *American Journal of Sociology* 75:680–702.

Spivey, Donald and Thomas A. Jones. 1975. "Intercollegiate Athletic Servitude." *Social Science Quarterly* 55:939–47.

Spreitzer, Elmer and Meredith Pugh. 1973. "Interscholastic Athletics and Educational Expectations." *Sociology of Education* 46:171–82.

Stecklein, J.E. and L.D. Dameron. 1965. "Intercollegiate Athletics and Academic Progress: A Comparison of Academic Characteristics of Athletes and Non-Athletes at the University of Minnesota." Reprint Series #3, Bureau of Institutional Research, University of Minnesota.

Stokes, Randall and John P. Hewitt. 1976. "Aligning Actions." *American Sociological Review* 41:838–49.

Strauss, Anselm. 1978. *Negotiations*. San Francisco: Jossey-Bass.

Stryker, Sheldon. 1964. "The Interactional and Situational Approaches." In H. Christensen, ed., *Handbook on Marriage and the Family*, pp. 124–70. Chicago: Rand McNally.

——1968. "Identity Salience and Role Performance." *Journal of Marriage and the Family* 30:558–64.

Stryker, Sheldon. 1980. *Symbolic Interactionism.* Menlo Park, Calif.: Benjamin/ Cummings.

Sullivan, Harry S. 1953. *The Interpersonal Theory of Psychiatry.* New York: Norton.

Sykes, Gresham and David Matza. 1957. "Techniques of Neutralization." *American Sociological Review* 22:664–70.

Tannenbaum, P. M. and J. E. Noah. 1959. "Sportuguese: A Study of Sports Page Communication." *Journalism Quarterly* 36:163–70.

Taylor, S. E. and J. Koivumaki. 1976. "The Perception of Self and Others: Acquaintanceship, Affect, and Actor-Observer Differences." *Journal of Personality and Social Psychology* 33:403–408.

Telander, Rick. 1989. *The Hundred Yard Lie.* New York: Simon and Schuster.

Turner, Ralph H. 1962. "Role Taking: Process versus Conformity." In A. M. Rose, ed., *Human Behavior and Social Processes,* pp. 20–40. Boston: Houghton-Mifflin.

——1976. "The Real Self: From Institution to Impulse." *American Journal of Sociology* 81:989–1016.

——1978. "The Role and the Person." *American Journal of Sociology* 84:1–23.

Turner, Ralph H. and Jerald Schutte. 1981. "The True Self Method for Studying the Self-Conception." *Symbolic Interaction* 4:1–20.

Underwood, Clarence. 1984. *The Student Athlete: Eligibility and Academic Integrity.* East Lansing: Michigan State University Press.

Underwood, John. 1969. "The Desperate Coach." *Sports Illustrated,* August 26, September 1, September 8.

——1980a. "The Writing is on the Wall." *Sports Illustrated,* May 19:36–72.

——1980b. "Student-Athletes: The Sham, the Shame." *Sports Illustrated* 52(21): 36–72.

University of New Mexico. 1980. *1970–1979 Graduation Experience of University of New Mexico Student Athletes.* Report commissioned by the President and Faculty Athletic Council, University of New Mexico.

van de Vliert, Evert. 1981. "A Three-Step Theory of Role Conflict Resolution." *Journal of Social Psychology* 113:77–83.

Vaughn, Diana. 1986. *Uncoupling.* New York: Oxford University Press.

Vaught, Charles and David L. Smith. 1980. "Incorporation and Mechanical Solidarity in an Underground Coal Mine." *Sociology of Work and Occupations* 7:159–87.

Vaz, Edward. 1982. *The Professionalization of Young Hockey Players.* Lincoln: University of Nebraska Press.

Wax, Rosalie. 1952. "Reciprocity as a Field Technique." *Human Organization* 11:34–47.

Webb, Harry. 1968. "Social Backgrounds of College Athletes." Paper presented at the annual meeting of the American Alliance for Health, Physical Education, and Recreation, St. Louis.

Weistart, John C. 1989. "College Sports Reform: Where are the Faculty?" In
D. S. Eitzen, ed., *Sport in Contemporary Society,* Third Edition, pp. 174–82.
New York: St. Martin's.

Wheeler, Stanton. 1961. "Socialization in Correctional Communities." *American Sociological Review* 26:697–719.

Wiseman, Jacqueline P. 1970. *Stations of the Lost.* Englewood Cliffs, N.J.:
Prentice-Hall.

Wood, Michael R. and Louis A. Zurcher. 1988. *The Development of a Postmodern
Self.* Westport, Conn.: Greenwood.

Wright, Stuart A. 1984. "Post-Involvement Attitudes of Voluntary Defectors
from Controversial New Religious Movements." *Journal for the Scientific
Study of Religion* 23:172–82.

Yasser, Raymond. 1984. "Are Scholarship Athletes at Big-Time Programs Really
University Employees? — You Bet They Are!" *Black Law Journal* 9:65–78.

Zurcher, Louis A. 1977. *The Mutable Self.* Beverly Hills, Calif.: Sage.

Index